Understanding Chinese Families

Understanding Chinese Families

A Comparative Study of Taiwan and Southeast China

C. Y. Cyrus Chu and Ruoh-Rong Yu

OXFORD
UNIVERSITY PRESS

OXFORD
UNIVERSITY PRESS

Great Clarendon Street, Oxford OX2 6DP

Oxford University Press is a department of the University of Oxford.
It furthers the University's objective of excellence in research, scholarship,
and education by publishing worldwide in

Oxford New York

Auckland Cape Town Dar es Salaam Hong Kong Karachi
Kuala Lumpur Madrid Melbourne Mexico City Nairobi
New Delhi Shanghai Taipei Toronto

With offices in

Argentina Austria Brazil Chile Czech Republic France Greece
Guatemala Hungary Italy Japan Poland Portugal Singapore
South Korea Switzerland Thailand Turkey Ukraine Vietnam

Oxford is a registered trade mark of Oxford University Press
in the UK and in certain other countries

Published in the United States
by Oxford University Press Inc., New York

British Library Cataloguing in Publication Data
Data available

Library of Congress Cataloging in Publication Data
Data available

Typeset by SPI Publisher Services, Pondicherry, India
Printed in Great Britain
on acid-free paper by
the MPG Books Group, Bodmin and King's Lynn

ISBN 978-0-19-957809-2

1 3 5 7 9 10 8 6 4 2

Foreword

This book uses unique longitudinal data to analyze the contemporary Chinese family in Taiwan and southeast China. The two regions have common cultural roots. In the past fifty years, they have experienced very different political and economic systems. The authors place the Chinese family in the context of Western families and contrast Mainland Chinese families with families in Taiwan. From their analysis it is possible, for the first time, to begin to understand some enduring features of the Chinese family and the features that have been changed by divergent social and economic forces in the two regions of China. The data gathered in the Panel Study of Family Dynamics project allow the authors to examine differences in behavior across cohorts, including differences across linked generations.

The authors review conventional economic and demographic models of the family developed for Western families. Using the research tools of contemporary demography and economics, they delineate areas of agreement and divergence of Chinese family practices with those in Western societies. While the book is not primarily about methodology, it sheds valuable new light on conventional models of the family. It challenges their generality and demonstrates certain culture-bound features of the conventional theory as well as some features that have claim to universality.

The authors document the dislocations in traditional Chinese family life brought about by policies in Mainland China including the one-child policy and public policy emphasis on gender equality. Despite vastly different economic and social policy environments, there are important similarities in many aspects of household behavior in Taiwan and southeast China. Gross reproduction rates are similar, as are average ages of married females, sex ratios at birth, and many other features of fertility and marriage.

Their research demonstrates the persistence of parental influences in determining the marriages of their children in both China and Taiwan. Although the role of the parents in choosing marriage partners is greater than in the West, patterns of marital sorting in southeast China and in

Taiwan are similar to those in the West. The mechanisms of search for mates may be different but the outcomes are similar. Their analysis suggests common optimizing behavior in Taiwan and southeast China, and in China and the West.

Traditionally, Chinese families have been large. This is so for two reasons. The first is a larger number of children. The second arises from co-residence across generations. The one-child policy on the mainland reduces family size there by reducing the number of children. Yet co-residence across generations is more common there than in Taiwan, contributing to larger family size. The authors theorize that a better market for babysitters, and a wealth elasticity for privacy, explain the divergence between the mainland and Taiwan.

Their analysis of fertility patterns in southeast China and Taiwan challenges the conventional "quantity—quality" model of Becker and Lewis (1973). There is no relationship between sibship size and the educational attainment of children. The authors' analysis of the division of labor in the family suggests, in accord with conventional economic theory, that the wife's opportunity costs outside of the family and the resources she commands are major determinants of household work by wives within the family.

Interviews using subjective questionnaires indicate that a significant fraction of Chinese in the mainland and in Taiwan maintain traditional views towards women. The traditional view of women is held more strongly in Taiwan. In both regions, bequests and *inter-vivos* transfers favor boys. A similar pattern appears in educational attainment decisions. The standard Western patterns of effects of sibship and child spacing on child educational attainment that are neutral across genders are not neutral in Chinese societies. However, the authors find that in recent cohorts in Taiwan, gender bias is waning. The more educated the parents, the weaker the gender bias. This suggests that Chinese society is undergoing a quiet revolution that will gradually end the practice of son preference.

The Cultural Revolution plays a large role in explaining differences in intergenerational mobility in educational status between Taiwan and the mainland. The Cultural Revolution promoted downward mobility of the educated classes on the mainland. Apart from this exceptional feature, educational mobility is greater in Taiwan, which has a pattern close to that of the USA. Rural Mainlanders exhibit particularly low mobility and their fate is largely determined by the accident of birth.

The analysis of family insurance markets presented in this book shows the folly of applying conventional Western models to Chinese contexts. Their analysis of family transfers to the elderly suggests that standard models of risk pooling have to be modified for the Chinese context. Reciprocity of transfers for acts rendered—*quid pro quos* for child care or subsidies previously given—plays an important role in Chinese families that has not been documented in Western societies. More than the simple risk sharing featured in the models of Wilson (1968) or Townsend (1994) appears to be at work in explaining family insurance mechanisms.

The analysis of transfers *by* parents to children also challenges conventional models. Chinese parents in Taiwan rely on kinship networks and cultural values inculcated by the parents to police behavior by children. Parents trust their children and fully transfer assets in advance of their death. Relying on induced child preferences, Chinese parents do *not* rely on the mechanism postulated by Bernheim, Shleifer, and Summers (1985) under which parents buy services from their children in the form of *inter-vivos* transfers. The evidence from Mainland China suggests such effects are much weaker there. Traditional Chinese values have been disturbed there.

This study of aspects of the Chinese family in two very different economic and institutional settings is a gold mine of new knowledge. The findings reported in this book challenge and enrich the economics of the family.

James Heckman,
Henry Schultz Distinguished Service Professor at the
University of Chicago, Professor of Science and Society,
University College Dublin, and Senior Research Fellow of the
American Bar Foundation.

Preface

This book pulls together various topics concerning Chinese families. As we consider the topics to be covered in this monograph, we have in mind two kinds of connections and one possible elaboration. On the one hand, we try to explore the connection between the special features of Chinese families and the existing theories mostly based on observations of Western societies, as well as the connection between two Chinese societies with different economic structures, that is, the two areas across the Taiwan Strait. On the other hand, we try to see whether the special features in Chinese families can broaden the scope of family analysis in general. Other than the chapters of introduction, conclusion, and a preview of social background, this book consists of ten subjects, including co-residence, marriage, fertility, education, mobility, gender preferences, family supports, filial feedbacks, housework allocation, and the dynamics of family norm changes. Our coverage is certainly not comprehensive, but hopefully it provides readers some help in understanding Chinese families.

Most of our analyses in this book are empirical ones. For that purpose, a series of panel surveys were conducted in various areas across the Taiwan Strait, and the resulting data sets provide abundant family-related information for our empirical analysis. The geographic qualification of our title specifies the areas of our surveys: Taiwan, two coastal provinces, and a centrally administered city of southeastern China. These areas are geographically close, ethnically homogeneous, and all open to the modern market economy; these features make them appropriate choices of area research. Except in the very rare case when China's one-child policy has limited our respondents' choice of fertility and hence the variability of related data, we have always provided a parallel analysis of southeastern coastal China and Taiwan. More often than not, this comparison gives us some insights into how families are similar/different in various dimensions, and how these similarities/differences are formed.

Our research has benefited from the help of many people. The Panel Study of Family Dynamics (PSFD) project team has worked together to design, revise, and finalize various questionnaires. They have also implemented the pretests, the data cleaning, and field supervising as the surveys were executed. We are heavily indebted to them, for without such detailed administrative support, the PSFD data could never have been successfully compiled, and our research relies so heavily on these data sets. The counterpart survey team affiliated with the Institute of Population and Labor Economics of the Chinese Academy of Social Sciences also provided much help. We are also indebted to various scholars who have helped our research projects over the years, including Yin-hua Chang, Kamhon Kan, Hui-wen Koo, Ronald Lee, George Tiao, Ruey Tsay, Wen-jen Tsay, Yu Xie, and Junsen Zhang. Professor Gary Becker of Chicago provided useful suggestions for our questionnaires in early stages of our survey. We are especially grateful to James Heckman and three anonymous referees of the Press, who provided many useful comments and suggestions at an early stage of the preparation of this monograph. This book has certainly been greatly improved as a result of the help of the above.

We conclude by emphasizing, as we shall do again at several points in the text, that we consider this book a beginning rather than a completed line of enquiry. It is intended as a dialogue with the work of others who pursue Chinese family research. Writing and revising a book like this may be a time-consuming and strenuous effort. Hopefully our effort will be rewarded in the form of the pleasure of readers who feel inspired to pursue their own research on Chinese families.

C. Y. Cyrus Chu
Ruoh-Rong Yu

Contents

Contents

List of Figures

List of Tables

Abbreviations

BIC	Bayesian Information Criterion
CCK	Chiang Ching-kuo
CEPD	Commission for Economic Planning and Development
DGBAS	Directorate General of Budget, Accounting, and Statistics
GDP	gross domestic product
GRR	gross reproduction rates
HES	"helpful elder sister"
IUD	intrauterine device
IV	instrumental variable
JEE	joint entrance examination
KAP	Knowledge, Attitudes, and Practice
KMT	Kuomintang
MLE	maximum likelihood estimation
MRS	marginal rate of substitution
NRR	net reproduction rates
NSFH	National Survey of Families and Households
NTD	new Taiwan dollar
OLS	ordinary least squares
PSFD	Panel Study of Family Dynamics
PSID	Panel Study of Income Dynamics
RMB	renminbi
SRDA	Survey Research Data Archive

1

Introduction to Chinese Families

A common perception among social scientists who have at least some vague idea about China is that Chinese families and those in the West are quite "different," although the differences may be difficult to specify. Many Confucian philosophers described the family as the basic unit of Chinese society, and also attached to it an idea very distinct from the concept in the West. As Baker (1979: 26) described,

in the West we see the family as an institution which exists in large part to provide an environment in which the individual can be conveniently raised and trained ... but the emphasis in the traditional Chinese situation was reversed—it was not the family which existed in order to support the individual, but rather the individual who existed in order to continue the family.

Indeed, to traditional Chinese, the continuation of the family line seemed to be a very important objective (Chu 1991: 80). An individual living at any instant was simply a contemporary and instantaneous representation of his ascending line of parentage and descending line of offspring. Put differently, in a traditional Chinese family, individuals were a means rather than an end. In Chu (1991), members of traditional Chinese families were actually described as trying to pursue the objective of *lineage proliferation.*[1]

The above-mentioned difference in the notion of the family is just an abstract description, which can be elaborated into more phenomenal differences in reality. We do not argue that lineage preservation is *the* key to explain all aspects of Chinese family differences, but it certainly helps the understanding of Chinese families by listing various phenomena along a coherent line. For instance, given that lineage preservation is a main objective of many Chinese family members, it is not difficult to imagine the practice of ancestral worship as a necessary ritual to express gratitude to the progenitor, and filial piety as an essential custom to show respect to the lineage guardian immediately before. In addition, given the objective of lineage prosperity, it is also understandable that the traditional Chinese would manifest the desirability of large families (Freedman 1970). Furthermore, if an individual at any point of time has a limited role in the long history of his lineage, one's marriage is just a means of procreation. Therefore, it is customary to accept marriages arranged by parents or senior relatives, who presumably know better whether a man or a woman in the neighborhood or network may be a good marriage partner, and hence offers a better prospect for lineage proliferation. Because the lineage is characterized by the family surname, to which only the male line is entitled, the lineage-continuation objective naturally fosters the practice of sex discrimination against females, both in resource allocation, and in the types of marriage such as polygamy, concubines, and uxorilocals (Saso 1999).

The above-mentioned cultural differences are in fact first-tier ones; many second-tier customs can also be explained by the core concept of lineage preservation. For instance, in order to exercise filial piety, Chinese adults, especially the male ones, have to provide resources to their elderly parents or grandparents. The most common circumstances are the co-residence of the married children with their elderly parents, and the upward monetary transfer from the children to their parents. These resource arrangements again are different from what are generally observed in the West, where co-residence is less prevalent and transfers are mainly downward, from parents to their children. For another instance, because marriages are often arranged by seniors, the match is more likely to be accomplished between families with compatible economic backgrounds. As such, the basic unit of marriage assortment is the family, not the individual. The dowry and brideprice provided by a couple's respective parents, therefore, may be used to reveal the relative status of the couple in the new family (Zhang and Chan 1999). Again, these side payments along with marriages are not common in the West.

The purpose of this book is to provide theoretical and empirical analyses concerning the various features of the Chinese families, including but not restricted to the above-mentioned ones. This chapter starts with some background introduction, content layout, and methodology description. We shall explain further why the study of Chinese families is important, how the survey data for our empirical analysis are collected, and then how we shall exercise the analysis. Toward the end of this chapter we will briefly introduce the topics to be covered. Before proceeding, we shall first identify the difference between this monograph on Chinese families and the previous ones.

1.1. Previous Monographs

In the literature of economics and sociology, there have been numerous papers, journals, and books focusing on the content and structure of families, and even a handful of monographs on families, using the economics approach. It is impossible for us to survey all papers and publications, but we can certainly provide a brief review of the work contained in previous monographs. The classic treatise by Becker (1991) covers the broadest topics, ranging from marriage to divorce, from static child investment to dynamic income mobility, and from unilateral family decisions to complicated interactions between family members. Cigno's (1991) research puts more focus on household formation and fertility, and is mainly a theoretical discussion, with little emphasis on empirical analysis. The book by Razin and Sadka (1995) places more emphasis on the theoretical relationship between family fertility, population size or growth, and economic efficiency. The major topics covered by their work include social security, economic growth, and international migration. Cabrillo (1999) used neoclassical maximization and game theory to analyze family marriage, fertility, and inheritance, and his analysis is also mainly theoretical. The most recent monograph by Ermisch (2003) studies in detail the microeconomic foundation of various family resource allocation decisions. It has a balanced coverage of theoretical and empirical work, although much of the latter focuses on the practice of the UK.

We stated above that the purpose of this book is to study Chinese families; but we should stress that our endeavor is more than a pure application of the orthodox (Western) family theories to Chinese society. Becker (1991) made in his treatise roughly a dozen references to China, Taiwan, or Chinese families, and pointed out many special features of Chinese families, including some points we just mentioned. These features, in general, need different or at least modified social-science theories to characterize. Such revised theories then may give rise to distinct empirical implications to be estimated and tested. Conceptually, therefore, our effort in this book is better treated as a new ball game rather than an overtime extension after the regular period. We believe that there is much social-sciences theory and modeling to explore as we study the family-related phenomena in the Chinese social context.

Looking at the family research from an interdisciplinary angle, we found that generally anthropologists, sociologists, and demographers paid more attention to Chinese families than economists. Freedman (1970) wrote a well-received book on *marriage* in the Chinese family in Singapore; Saso

(1999) wrote on Chinese family *types* in China and Taiwan; Davis and Harrell (1993) emphasized the family *patterns* and changes in the post-Mao era; Hsieh and Chuang (1985) studied the *ritual* behavior of Chinese families across the Strait; and Thornton and Lin (1994) focused entirely on Taiwan, with special attention to the behavior of *fertility* and the *household size*. The approaches of the above-mentioned books are mainly anthropological and demographical; they provide us with rich field-study evidence and statistical descriptions. However, they do not match well with the methodology of empirical social sciences, by which we mean the emphasis of a theoretical argument behind the interaction of family decisions and social background, and the corresponding behavioral hypotheses ready for empirical scrutiny. The focus of this book is thus on the social-sciences-related aspects of Chinese families There are also books and papers on Chinese history, religion, and culture; but of course they are not highly relevant to the social-science aspects we are interested in, and hence we shall refrain from commenting on those aspects.

1.2. Why Study Chinese Families?

Scientific research in general does not have to *justify* itself by explaining its uses or functions; studying Chinese family patterns using social science methods certainly has its own merits. What is to be elaborated here concerns the following question: why is Chinese family research a particularly important topic to study? We believe that some explanation along this line can enlarge the readership of related research in general, and of our monograph in particular.

Population Size: The first reason we can provide is the size of the Chinese population. According to the statistics on The World Factbook website,[2] in July 2008 there were about 6.67 billion people worldwide, and the combined population of China, Taiwan, Hong Kong, Macau, and Singapore (the greater Chinese area) was about 1.36 billion. Of course, not all people in Hong Kong and Singapore are Chinese. But if one takes into account the immigrants and students around the world from the greater China area, who are still under the influence of Chinese culture, it should be safe to say that at least 20 per cent of the world's families are culturally Chinese. It would certainly seem odd to leave out the family behavior of the largest percentage of the world population in the study of the general family theory.

New Dimensions of Interest: As we mentioned in Section 1.1, Chinese families tend to put more emphasis on lineage extension, which in turn facilitates the appearance of various new decision dimensions that may help such an objective. For instance, if the cost-saving from household public goods is important to the prosperity of the family line, then the Chinese tend to tolerate more the cost of losing privacy in a large family, which in turn facilitates the expansion of the household size. Thus, whenever economic capacity allows, we tend to observe a larger average household size in various areas and historical periods of China. This has been much discussed by Freedman (1970), Baker (1979), and Wolf (1985). Thus, household formation is a particularly important decision for Chinese families.

For another instance, there was evidence (Chu 1991) showing that *inter vivos* transfers within Chinese families were prevalent in ancient time, not only between parents and children, but sometimes between siblings and clan members, as long as such transfers were believed to be potentially helpful to the lineage's future. Thus, commanded by the common idea of extending the lineage, Chinese family members are usually more tightly connected, and therefore interactions and transfers among them are more abundant, both in quantity and in variety. We believe that such connections enrich the behavioral dimensions to be observed, and also complicate the constraints and the decision context of the family in question. Elaborations and ramifications like these, though having originated in Chinese societies, broaden the Western theories of the family in general.

Richer Intrafamily Interactions: Complicated interactions among family members affect not only the theoretical setup, but also the empirical implications and variations. The classical family decision model, which treats the family as if it has a unitary objective function, has been recognized to be too simplified to provide empirical predictions. In reality, family members have common as well as conflicting objectives, and such conflicts may be between parents and children (Becker 1974, Bergstrom 1989), siblings (Bergstrom 1995), the wife and parents-in-law (Lillard and Willis 1997), and the husband and the wife (Becker 1985). Intuitively, when family members have tighter mutual attachment, their objectives, tolerance, and cost of conflicts are also different. Moreover, the tighter connection may also play the role of disciplining defiant behavior of family members. This in turn strengthens the family tie and further influences the behavior of members. As such, interactions between members of an enlarged family network broaden the scope of empirical analysis, which is the third reason for which we intend to analyze Chinese families.

Contrast in Social Background: The fourth factor contributing to the richness of Chinese family research is the rapidly changing social background in several Chinese societies. Goode (1982) predicted that along with the demographic transition and economic development, most "traditional" family features would gradually retreat. Related predictions include the diminishing influence of kin groups, the reduced prevalence of brideprice and dowry, the rise of the divorce rate, the improvement of women's human rights and social roles, the increase of marriage age, and the diminished parental control over married children. To see whether Goode's predictions are correct in some societies, it is better to have a contrasting social environment as the background of observation. If it takes more than one hundred years for the environment as well as the behavior to change, social scientists may not be able to find much evidence for the following reasons. On the one hand, few data sets trace such a long period of time; and on the other hand, the slow pace of behavioral and environmental changes may not reveal a sharp contrast, so that theoretical implications may not be easily estimated and tested. In some areas of Chinese societies, fortunately, we are able to observe a rapidly changing background and environment.

As is well known, demographic transitions are triggered by advances in hygiene, sanitation, and medical technology, which in Western countries may have taken more than one hundred years to accomplish. However, in Taiwan, Singapore, and many other East Asian areas under the influence of Chinese culture, people were able to adopt wholesale the hygiene and medical knowledge already developed by the West. This has dramatically quickened the pace of their demographic transition. In Taiwan for instance, it has taken less than fifty years to finish the demographic transition (Chu and Lee 2000). This rapid transition has created behavioral changes that vary across rural and urban areas, and across people of distinct ethnic backgrounds. Thus, from observations in such societies, we are able to disentangle the objective background factors from the subjective mindset and perceptions. Against this fast-changing environment and slowly changing family values, the factors influencing individual decisions can be identified relatively easily. In short, Chinese families in some areas provide us with a laboratory well suited for the observation of behavioral changes in response to changes in the social environment.

1.3. Obstacles in Chinese Family Research

We mentioned in the last section that the fast-changing environment often provides us with a contrasting background for observing behavioral relationships; we should also enter the caveat that this is not always true. Perhaps out of fundamentalist socialist zeal, Mao Zedong was bluntly eager to abolish the traditional Chinese clan system, and to remove gender and class inequalities. In 1950, two years after the Communists' victory over the ruling Kuomintang (KMT) in Mainland China, the People's Republic of China promulgated the Marriage Law, which abolished bigamy, concubinage, child betrothal, and interference with the remarriage of widows, and banned the extraction of money and gifts in connection with marriages.[3] This sudden disappearance of the practice of demanding or receiving brideprices or dowries means there is not much transitional behavior to be analyzed. In general, in a totalitarian society, sometimes the decisions of individuals are severely restricted, and hence the behavioral data one observes carry little information other than a change of government policy.

Another instance is the family planning program and the well-known one-child policy of China. Except in ethnic minority areas and in areas where the government regulation could not be implemented successfully, the fertility rate in China dropped significantly in response to the state's family planning policies. The total fertility rate (number of births per woman) in 1970 was 5.8, whereas it dropped to 2.7 in 1978. According to Davis and Harrell (1993: 14), this is a phenomenon unobservable in any peaceful time in human history. China in 1978 had a total fertility rate as low as Canada, but an economic development level roughly the same as Mexico or Brazil. Because the change was so abrupt in China, any comparison with other countries would be difficult. Moreover, since fertility is reduced almost uniformly in China, we are unable to observe any age-specific fertility change, not to mention changes across families and different social backgrounds. The experience may be unique, but at the same time there may be little corresponding cross-sectional or time series data variation for meaningful statistical analysis.

As Saso (1999: 75) pointed out, the heavy-handed regulations on traditional family practices and the turmoil during and following the Great Leap Forward (1958–60) and the Cultural Revolution (1966–76) in Mainland China have made Taiwan the only place to preserve traditional Chinese family features. Davis and Harrell (1993: 21) also said that Taiwan was able to preserve the "mosaic form" of families and behavior available for scientific research. This is perhaps why most previous statistical analyses on the Chinese family, such as the work by Thornton and Lin (1994), focused only on Chinese communities in Taiwan. Most social analyses on China before 1990, on the other hand, are qualitative field studies; sophisticated statistical analysis was rare.

The heavy-handed regulations in China lasted for several decades after 1950, and the Great Leap Forward and the Cultural Revolution left an especially large impact. However, it turns out that revolution is perhaps more effective in overthrowing a political regime than in changing culture. As Davis and Harrell (1993: ch. 1) demonstrated, despite the attempt of the Communist Party to change the traditional perceptions of the roles of marriage, fertility, and clans, family ties might actually have become *stronger* in China in the past fifty years. On the one hand, with improved hygiene and sanitation and with starvation brought under control, the death rate has been reduced. This contributes to the stable formation of family units. On the other hand, migration was much regulated, thereby intensifying intra-family interactions and transfers.

Davis and Harrell found that after Mao's death there was a revival of the practice of brideprice and dowry, indicating that much of the marriage custom or culture was not at all eliminated by government regulations. Unger (1993) also found that, during the post-Mao period when regulations on families were loosened, many married adults moved in with their parents, leading to an increasing proportion of stem families. Such evidence shows that the traditional Chinese family culture is still ingrained in the minds of many Chinese. Whenever the economic environment allows and the social background enables individual choices, we are able to observe rich behavior varieties. Such behavioral varieties originating from individual choices are indeed what social scientists try to analyze. At the beginning of the twenty-first century, we believe that it is a good time to start collecting data on Chinese families, and we also expect that in the near future fruitful research can be accomplished using such a collection of data.

The analysis in Davis and Harrell represents one view of the changing family dynamics in China. Whyte (2003) summarized several hypotheses (economic development, cultural diffusion, and state social engineering) that may dominate the change of families; the momentum created by the Marriage Law and the Cultural Revolution in China was a typical example of state engineering, which suggests that the family structure may be changed by the engineering endeavor of the government. It is difficult to say whether the Cultural Revolution in China was "successful" in changing the traditional family dynamics, since it (fortunately) lasted only for eleven years. However, Whyte did a brief comparative analysis between Baoding (a prefecture-level city in Hebei Province) and urban areas of Taiwan, and the references therein deserve more detailed reading by researchers interested in this topic.

1.4. Area of Interest, Data Sets, and Methodology

1.4.1. *Why Taiwan and Southeast China?*

As noted by Davis and Harrell (1993), Thornton and Lin (1994), and many other researchers, before 1990 Taiwan was perhaps the only place appropriate for in-depth Chinese family research. Starting from 1950, Taiwan has experienced a stable economic growth and a fast demographic transition, and has become a relatively free society allowing a diversity of familial decisions. These features make it easy for researchers to compare Taiwanese families with those in the West, or those in other progressing societies. Only through comparison can we tell whether there is any uniqueness associated with the Chinese families in Taiwan. Starting from 1978, China has begun to open up its market, and has gradually developed greater economic capacity, which is a key factor in family decision-making. A natural elaboration of the Taiwan analysis is to find a possible counterpart in Mainland China for comparative analysis. This is particularly urgent, since Taiwan, although typical, is too small to be representative of Chinese societies in general. In what follows we explain where the appropriate counterparts are.

Due to geographic constraints, China's economic development started from its southeastern coastal areas and spread inland. The typical southeastern coastal areas include Fujian, Guangdong, Zhejiang, and further north up to cities such as Shanghai. Thus, families in these areas of China have enjoyed more latitude in making household economic decisions in recent years. Other than such economic concerns, cultural factors are also important control variables in the comparative analysis. The population of Taiwan is mainly composed of four ethnic groups, which are the Fukienese, Hakka, Mainlanders, and aborigines, accounting for 73 per cent, 12 per cent, 13 per cent, and 2 per cent of the population respectively (Scott and Tiun 2007). Among these ethic groups, the Mainlanders immigrated from Mainland China during the Chinese Civil War (1945–9), and the Fukienese and Hakka were early immigrants from the Fujian and Guangdong provinces of China. Hence, in terms of ethnic and cultural background, the Taiwanese are also closely related to residents of the southeast coast of Mainland China. In summary, Taiwan and the southeast coastal provinces of China together form a group of regions which share Chinese culture, and greater opportunities of economic modernization. This is why we choose these areas to be the target of our analysis.

1.4.2. *The PSFD Survey Project*

To facilitate an empirical analysis of Chinese families which involve extensive interactions and distinct behavior patterns, we certainly have an urgent demand for high-quality data. For instance, because of the norm of
filial piety, the proportion of adult children co-residing with their parent(s)
is very high (23 per cent in Taiwan and 17 per cent in China, according to
our survey). In order to understand and to predict the behavioral pattern
of co-residence, it is necessary to obtain abundant information about the
parents, the adult children (who share the common burden of taking care
of their parents), and other family-related details. High-quality survey data,
therefore, are indeed indispensable.

For general macro patterns, of course, we resort to various published
statistics for analysis. For a rigorous empirical analysis in this monograph,
we mainly rely on the data sets from the project of Panel Study of Family
Dynamics (PSFD), implemented respectively in Taiwan and Mainland
China. The PSFD project was a panel survey started in 1999. In its first
five years, the PSFD project was conducted with the support of the Chiang
Ching-kuo (CCK) Foundation, the National Science Council of Taiwan, and
Academia Sinica. Starting from 2003, Academia Sinica established the
Research Center for Humanities and Social Sciences and formally included
PSFD as one of its long-term projects, so that this panel survey has been
supported by Sinica's hard budget ever since. The PSFD surveys were conducted using questionnaires in Chinese, but a parallel English version of all
questionnaires and codebooks has been made available. The project benefited from the guidance of internationally established scholars, including
Gary Becker, James Heckman, Angus Deaton, and many others.[4] The data
set is open to worldwide academic communities free of charge, and the data
release has no time delay after a standardized procedure of data cleaning.

The PSFD surveys collect panel data for both Taiwan and some southeast
areas of China, and are carried out annually or biennially, depending on the
type of questionnaires, by the Center for Survey Research of Academia
Sinica. In the first-wave survey conducted in 1999, some pilot respondents
were randomly sampled from 131 townships in Taiwan, covering males and
females in an approximately even manner. The cohorts of the 1999 interviewees were born in the period between 1953 and 1964, or aged from
35 to 46 in the survey year. And in years 2000 and 2003, individuals
born between 1935 and 1954 (aged 46–65 in year 2000) and 1964
and 1976 (aged 27–39 in year 2003) were respectively added to establish
the comprehensiveness of samples. The numbers of respondents first

interviewed in years 1999, 2000, and 2003 were 994, 1,959, and 1,152, respectively, roughly 1,000 observations for each ten-year cohort range. These samples were traced and interviewed annually; and up to year 2006, the cumulative attrition rates for the original respondents (the three-sample cohorts mentioned above) were about 31–3 per cent, which was similar to the attrition rate of the PSID (Panel Study of Income Dynamics) of the USA when that project proceeded to the comparable wave (Zabel 1998). The PSFD questionnaires were basically designed to study Chinese families, and hence contained many questions on intragenerational and intergenerational relationships, which could be used to construct extremely important variables for analyzing family behaviors. This to a large extent lessens the problem of measurement errors and omitted variables, which may result in biased or inconsistent results.

As the progress of the survey in Taiwan became stable, the PSFD team of investigators began in 2003 to establish collaboration with the Institute of Population and Labor Economics of the Chinese Academy of Social Sciences, for the purpose of launching a counterpart PSFD survey in Mainland China. The collaboration is multifaceted, and includes questionnaire and sampling design, survey implementation, and data cleaning. The first-wave survey was conducted in 2004, with the sample covering two provinces and one city, namely Fujian, Zhejiang, and Shanghai, all in the coastal area of southeast China. As we explained, these places were much exposed to China's economic reform after 1978, exhibit more behavioral varieties given their better economic conditions, and have features more suitable for analysis based on comparison with families in Taiwan and Western societies.

The surveyed respondents in China were sampled from individuals aged between 25 and 68 in 2003, and the sample size was 4,684. The first follow-up survey was conducted in 2006, and the respondents would be traced biennially in the future. In our later analysis, we shall use both the Taiwan and China data sets when possible. However, as we will explain later, on a few occasions when specific empirical models are applied, we may have to rely more on the Taiwanese data.

In 2000, the Taiwan project started extending its interviews to the main respondents' children aged 16–22. This is similar to the PSID project of the USA, and tries to collect the relevant information on the children of our adult respondents. To lessen the burden on the interviewers, the follow-up surveys are conducted every two years. When the child samples reach age 25, they will be interviewed with the same questionnaire as their parents, and henceforth traced annually. Prior to that specific age, they have their own questionnaires. We expect to collect rich information from these connected child samples in the near future. A brief introduction to PSFD is provided in Appendix 1.1, and details of the PSFD project can be found on the website http://psfd.sinica.edu.tw.

1.4.3. *Interdisciplinary Methodology*

As is well known, family research involves multidisciplinary foci. In the related literature, scholars from economics, sociology, anthropology, demography, and other areas of social sciences all provided important contributions. However, there are obvious discrepancies in the focus and methodology of research in such fields. For instance, in the analysis of parental investment on child education, economists have emphasized the quantity–quality tradeoff of parental decisions. To study such a tradeoff, economists have often explored the effect of sibship size on adulthood achievement. The foci of sociologists and psychologists, however, have been more diverse. Other than the negative impact of sibship size, they have often interested themselves in the effect of birth order, sibling density, sex composition, and sibling seniority on child achievement.[5] Since some of these factors (such as birth order) are not much of a decision for parents, the lack of interest by economists, many of whom study individual rational decision-making, is of course understandable. As we study Chinese families in this monograph, we tend not to be limited to economics, although it is our basic training, but adapt ourselves, to the extent possible, to a wider spectrum of literature from various disciplines of social sciences.

In fact, in family-related research, the difference between scholars of various disciplines is revealed not only in interest or focus, but also in methodology. Again, we take the study of child education as an example. For decades, economists were on the one hand intrigued by the theory of quantity–quality tradeoff, and on the other by the empirical technique of disentangling the casual effects between these two factors. Becker's (1991) analysis told us that the quantity and quality of children were determined *simultaneously* by their parents and therefore empirically it was necessary to solve this simultaneity problem in order to obtain a consistent statistical estimation of this tradeoff. Thus, much research effort in the past few decades was focused on the statistical technique along this line.

While sociologists and psychologists also appreciated the influence of sibship size on child achievement, which was called the resource-dilution effect, they were also interested in the effect of sibling *structure* and parental background on child education. To analyze the impact of sibling structure, for instance, they have often studied the possible influence of learning confluence, and demonstration effect among siblings possessing various traits. Thus, sociologists and psychologists began to divide the siblings into subsets based on more refined criteria than a single-dimensional sibship size. Given such different foci, the attention on sibship size has been shifted to several sibling variables refined by gender-order-seniority, and due to the complexity of the sibship variables, the concern for the simultaneity problem is largely ignored along this line of research. As such, the research focus and the methodology are very much interrelated.

In this monograph, we choose our focus and methodology following a very simple logic: If most of the related literature comes from a certain discipline, we adopt the common methodology of that discipline. The advantage of this strategy is that our analysis will be more coherent with the prevalent literature. After all, this is not a book on research methodology, and we do not plan to digress too much on research methods, given that the family content is what we really pay attention to. Since most of the topics we study come from literature in the fields of economics, demography, and sociology, we concentrate our literature review in these two areas.

Much of the analysis in Davis and Harrell (1993) and Thornton and Lin (1994) contains tables and figures of descriptive statistics, which help to give the reader a general picture of the society. Other than such descriptive analysis, in each chapter we shall also introduce some interesting hypotheses and tests, which are compatible with the existing literature in the West. Our choice of empirical hypotheses is to some extent idiosyncratic; but our hope is to use these conventional hypotheses to help the reader see the possible differences and similarities between Chinese and Western families.

1.5. Topics Covered

It is of course impossible and impractical to try to include all research topics concerning Chinese families in one monograph; what we have chosen to cover in this book is certainly idiosyncratic. As economists, we do not touch much on issues such as Chinese family rituals, religions, psychological perceptions, and attitude; these are either not within the boundary of economics, or on the fringes between economics and other disciplines.

Although this is a book on Chinese family behavior, we try our best to connect the unique observations we find in Chinese societies with the (orthodox) family hypotheses mostly established and tested in the Western world. This connection is important for the following reasons. First, the difference between Chinese and Western families sometimes is just a matter of degree; perhaps few social scientists would think that Chinese families need to be understood from a completely different angle. Indeed, if the modernization hypothesis of Goode (1982) is correct, then Chinese families will be more like those in the West when they are more open to the outside. Second, the established Western theories on families give us a very good reference point, from which we can easily see where the differences and common features between the East and the West lie. Third, the possible behavioral difference we observe from Chinese and Western families may originate from other aspects of the societies; a contrasting view may help us understand the background distinctions that may cause such behavioral discrepancies.

Chapter 2 on Background: In Chapter 2 we provide a background introduction to China and Taiwan in the past few decades. The foci of this chapter include general economic environment, education, and fertility. China is well known for its abrupt adoptions and changes of policies, which were usually very effective due to authoritarian control. The changes of educational regimes in the 1950s and during and after the Cultural Revolution have all significantly altered the education environment, in which individuals strive to move up the educational ladder. Likewise, China is also known for its strict one-child policy, which has limited the choice of most parents, at least in the urban areas. This also affects parents' decisions on child education. As we shall see, the abrupt changes in education regimes and fertility policies have made the empirical economic analysis of several topics in China more difficult. In contrast, the institutional changes in Taiwan are mostly smooth and gradual, more like what we observe in Western societies. We provide a brief introduction to the background in these two societies, and try to provide the readers with some basic knowledge to help them understand the analysis to be presented in later chapters.

Chapter 3 on Co-residence: For anthropologists or sociologists who did field research in some Chinese societies, the most commonly observed and studied phenomenon different from the West is the large household size, in particular the prevalent co-residence of married sons with their parents, and sometimes their siblings. The terms *nuclear family, stem family, extended family,* and *joint family* indeed were created to describe the family type ramifications observed in Chinese societies. Wolf (1985) found that the traditional large Chinese families are related to economic capabilities; people tended to form extended families when the environment allowed.

But when Western-style individualism gradually makes inroads in the Chinese society, economic capacity becomes a factor facilitating the children's moving out and forming their own household, as suggested by Becker's (1991: ch. 2) privacy-cost argument. Chapter 3 studies how the co-residence practice (and hence household size) changes through time. Following the literature, we use a modified statistical model to predict when an adult child will choose to co-reside with his or her parents, and what factors determine such a co-residence decision. We shall investigate whether Wolf's hypothesis is correct in contemporary Taiwan and China. In particular, we analyze which line of parents (one's own or in-laws) an adult child usually chooses to co-reside with or to avoid.

Chapter 4 on Fertility: Chapter 4 studies the family fertility practices across the Taiwan Strait. Our analysis is divided into three parts. The first part presents a tabular statistical analysis of family fertility across mothers' cohorts, geographic regions, and parental education, for both China and Taiwan. A comparison of sibship size and child education can give us a picture of the quantity–quality tradeoffs in Chinese societies. The second part is devoted to the empirical analysis of quantity–quality tradeoff in both Taiwan and China. We shall use the instrumental variable approach to identify the possible causal relationship between quantity and quality. The third part of this chapter analyzes the interaction between co-residence with senior parents and the fertility duration of the young couples, a special feature of the Chinese extended family. We study how wives adjust their fertility decisions in response to the presence of co-residing parents in the fast-changing society of Taiwan. Because China's family planning programs and one-child policy might have disturbed the fertility decisions of the respondents of our survey, we are careful not to apply this third-part analysis to China.

Chapter 5 on Marriage: The fifth chapter analyzes the marriage pattern in China and Taiwan. In the descriptive parts, we present the changing pattern concerning the age of marriage, and the decision entity of marriage (the couple, or their parents, or jointly). In the part on empirical analysis, we follow the literature to treat the marriage match as an equilibrium outcome of assignment games or dynamic search, and run regressions to analyze the pattern of assortative mating, for both China and Taiwan. The assortment we study concerns education, age, and ethnicity. The empirical analysis follows the most recent and comprehensive work of Choo and Siow (2006b).

Chapter 6 on Housework: In terms of economics, marriage is the equilibrium *outcome* of a searching and matching process, but it is also the *beginning* of various interactions between the husband and wife. Chapter 6 studies various family interactions, including some family decisions and the division of labor within a household. Other than the usual decisions such as in expenditures and durable good consumption, we pay special attention to the housework allocation between the husband and the wife. The classic analysis by Becker (1991: ch. 2) mainly focused on the efficiency of a division of labor between the couple, showing that even if the spouses possess equal endowment and capacity, a family division of labor may still be efficient. If in addition there is some minor comparative advantage between the couple, the compounding effect of capital accumulation may even push the division of labor to the extreme (specialization), perhaps making the husband specialize in market work and the wife in household chores. Many sociologists after Becker have put in much effort trying to disentangle the subjective gender perception and the objective factors, in particular the resources controlled by the couple, that favor an unequal division of labor. Chinese societies are known for their subjective male-dominance gender ideology, and their rapidly changing objective environment. We believe that it is particularly interesting to analyze Chinese household decisions and the division of labor against this changing background. The reader will be able to see some major differences between what is done in Chinese societies and the Western practices, with which most social scientists are familiar.

Chapter 7 on Son Preferences: Starting from Chapter 7 we move to the discussion of parents' resource allocation decisions toward their children. We start with an effort to identify the degree of parental gender preferences for boys, and against girls. The PSFD data set contains siblings' education achievement as well as their status in terms of whether they receive bequests from their parents. Taking advantage of the fact that some Chinese families leave unequal bequests to their children, we can derive implications from the parental behavior of an altruistic parent. The empirical data are then used to test whether son preferences exist and how serious they are, both for China and for Taiwan. We also provide some empirical evidence concerning whether parents transfer their assets in a compensating or a reinforcing way.

Chapter 8 on Child Education: We have shown in the previous discussion that gender inequality in a Chinese society exists between the spouses and among the siblings. For such an ideology to persist in a society, there must be a channel of transmission across generations. The most typical, and also best-studied one, is through the human capital investment among children of different genders. The earlier attention on sibling education difference was on the effect of birth orders (e.g. Zajonc 1976), but later the focus shifts to gender-differential treatment (e.g. Parish and Willis 1993). In Chapter 8 we study the parental allocation of education resources within a family. We try to establish the general pattern of allocation in a Chinese family: boys receive a more favorable treatment than girls; juniors are better treated than seniors; and for seniors, having a junior sibling aged far apart is more detrimental than having one with a close age difference. These observations are quite different from the findings in the West, where siblings' gender composition does not matter (Hauser and Kuo 1998), and close-by siblings suggest more resource competition than far-apart ones (Powell and Steelman 1990). We explain why the case is different in Chinese society.

Chapter 9 on Mobility: Chapter 9 studies the intergenerational mobility between parents and children. The usual measures of mobility include the correlation coefficient of education across generations, the regression co-efficient of child's education on parental education, and indices calculated from the intergenerational mobility matrix. We estimate such measures for both Taiwan and China, across family members of different genders, and compare our results with available evidence of other countries in previous literature. We explain how a Communist society in China performs in terms of mobility, compared with a capitalist counterpart in Taiwan.

Chapter 10 on Filial Feedbacks: In Chapter 10, we study the mechanism of family support and two-way transfers among Chinese family members. Our PSFD data show that the mainstream transfer pattern in Chinese families is upward, from adult children to their senior parents; this is different from the prevalent downward transfers we observe in the West. Moreover, we also note that a large proportion of Chinese adults have received parental subsidies in their early adulthood, either in the form of housing support, or as business loans. This means that the current upward transfers and the previous downward subsidies have to be considered jointly in order to have a comprehensive understanding of family transfers. Furthermore, the co-existence of parental earlier support when children need it and children's later feedback when parents need it shows that there is an implicit insurance and feedback scheme within the family. We use the PSFD data to investigate the content of this family support scheme.

Chapter 11 on Transfers: Chapter 11 concerns the practices of intergenerational transfers in Chinese families. In modern Western economies, elderly people often have pensions, stocks, bonds, and other kinds of savings for their remaining years, whereas the young have to devote a large part of their resources to human capital accumulation. Because the human capital market is often imperfect, the young have to rely on their parents for financing.

Therefore, the within-family financial transfers mostly discussed in the mainstream literature are usually downward, from parents to children. What the parents expect from their children in return is their "service," characterized by the children's visits and phone calls. If parents are altruistic toward their children and children are selfish, Becker's (1991) rotten kid theorem says that the latter will still "voluntarily" provide the service desired by the former. Or, when some regularity conditions fail (Bergstrom 1989), the parents may use their transfer capacity to lure their children's service (Bernheim et al. 1985, the strategic bequest hypothesis). In Chinese societies, however, since the custom of filial piety prevails, neither the rotten kid theorem nor the hypothesis of strategic bequest applies. The social norm of filial duty is so strong that the children's negligence in visitation and service to their parents is unacceptable. Moreover, the male-dominance concept dictates most of the parent–child transfer practice. In this situation, the family transfer relation is quite different from the practice in the West, which is what we shall study in Chapter 11. We explain why Chinese parents do not worry about the alienation of children after the transfer of all parental assets, and how the role of kinship network affects the child's decision on visiting parents.

Chapter 12 on Transition: Goode (1982) predicted that most traditional family norms will gradually go away along with economic development, and in particular, a gender-specific preferential treatment in child education by parents is expected to weaken for younger cohorts. This weakening process, however, is unlikely to be uniform across all families. In a transitional economy, parents from different social backgrounds have different attitudes toward their children. In Chapter 12 we analyze how parental backgrounds affect the education resource allocation among children. This helps us understand how and how fast the traditional gender ideology disappears.

The last chapter (Chapter 13) summarizes our findings, identifies research areas that deserve further investigations, and points out directions in which we shall be able to achieve more results when further data are collected. When we started to write this monograph, there were only three to seven waves of data sets available for the adult interviewees of Taiwan, and the China survey had just started. We expect that more interesting topics can be explored when the survey project proceeds to its later waves. In the concluding chapter, we will hopefully set the ball rolling for a fruitful future research agenda on Chinese families.

APPENDIX 1.1 INTRODUCTION TO PANEL STUDY OF FAMILY DYNAMICS

We have explained in Section 1.4.1 why our sample of interest covers Taiwan and the southeast coastal areas of China. The following is a brief account of the PSFD surveys conducted in these two areas.

Taiwan

The main respondents of the Taiwan PSFD survey are composed of three birth cohorts, including: (1) cohort born during 1953–64, (2) cohort born during 1935–54, and (3) cohort born during 1964–76.[6] These respondents were drawn by a stratified three-stage random sampling procedure. The 131 townships of Taiwan were first stratified according to their urbanization levels. In each stratum, townships were randomly selected. In the second stage, smaller administrative districts (villages, or equivalent districts in urban area, called "lis" in Taiwan) were randomly selected. And in the third stage, individuals were randomly drawn from the chosen districts.

The three groups of respondents mentioned above were first interviewed in 1999, 2000, and 2003 respectively, and then the follow-up surveys were conducted annually. By 2007, we had conducted eight waves of follow-up for the main respondents of the 1953–64 cohort, seven waves of follow-up for the main respondents of the 1935–54 cohort, and four waves of follow-up for the main respondents of the 1964–76 cohort. The sample size and attrition rates for these three groups of sample are presented in Table 1.1.

Starting from year 2000, all children (aged between 16 and 22) of our main respondents were interviewed, with the follow-up surveys conducted every two years. When these children reached the age of 25, they were interviewed using the same questionnaire as the main respondents, and have been re-interviewed yearly ever since. All these surveys, including the ones for main respondents and their children, were conducted by face-to-face interviews.

For the questionnaires of the main respondents and the children, some questions were repeated year after year. These core questions include health condition, work information, marital status, spousal information, living arrangement, housing, income and expenditure, intergenerational contacts and transfers, and childbearing and -rearing. Other topics that appeared in selected surveys include information on parents and siblings, life history, family value, household decisions, risk attitude, job training, smoking habit, religious belief, social trust, family norms, etc. The fieldwork and data cleaning were jointly accomplished by the project coordinator

Table 1.1. Sample size and attrition rates for main respondents, Taiwan

Cohorts/ waves	Year of survey	Completed sample size	Accumulated attrition rate (%)
1953–64 cohort			
1	1999	994	—
2	2000	802	19.32
3	2001	726	26.97
4	2002	782	21.34
5	2003	751	24.46
6	2004	706	28.97
7	2005	677	31.89
8	2006	663	33.30
1935–54 cohort			
1	2000	1,959	—
2	2001	1,730	11.69
3	2002	1,642	16.18
4	2003	1,566	20.06
5	2004	1,489	23.99
6	2005	1,396	28.74
7	2006	1,341	31.55
8	2006	663	33.30
1964–76 cohort			
1	2003	1,152	—
2	2004	832	27.78
3	2005	808	29.86
4	2006	768	33.34

and the Center for Survey Research of Academia Sinica. As soon as the data sets were cleaned, they were released to the public by the Survey Research Data Archive (SRDA) of Academia Sinica. The average time duration from the end of the fieldwork to the release of data sets is about eighteen months. The files released contain data files (in SAS, SPSS, and STATA format), questionnaires, and codebooks, available in Chinese and English versions. Related files can be downloaded from the SRDA website (http://srda.sinica.edu.tw/) free of charge.

China Survey

The first wave of the China survey was conducted in 2004 under the cooperation of Taiwan's PSFD project and the Institute of Population and Labor Economics of the Chinese Academy of Social Sciences. Individuals aged 25–68 were randomly sampled from two provinces, Fujian and Zhejiang, and one city, Shanghai. For each area, a stratified four-stage random sampling procedure was adopted to select qualified respondents. The sampling units of the four stages were "xian" (administrative division under province or city), township, village, and household, respectively, and the Kish method was used to sample individuals from selected households. As in Taiwan, the survey was conducted by face-to-face interviews. The numbers of interviewees in 2004 for Fujian, Zhejiang, and Shanghai were 903, 1,856, and 1,925 respectively. Due to budget constraints, these respondents are re-interviewed biennially, with the first follow-up conducted in 2006.

The questionnaire of the 2004 China survey is basically the same as the one adopted in the first-wave survey of Taiwan, with only some slight modifications. First, the wording of the questionnaire is adapted to usage in China. Secondly, a few questions were added to help understand the socio-economic background of the respondents under a Communist society, which included *social class*, attendance at a *key-point* school, etc. The data set for the 2004 China survey has been released on the SRDA website.

Notes

1. If we adopt the hypothesis of selfish genes along the lines of Dawkins (1989), then all species in the evolutionary process can be viewed as trying to pursue their lineage proliferation. The description of family modernization of Goode (1982) in fact can be viewed as a change from the biological drive of lineage prosperity to the cultural drive of various measures of family welfare. An early model of lineage prosperity can be found in Chu (1991), and a recent survey of various biological aspects of the family is in Cox (2007).
2. The relevant website is https://www.cia.gov/library/publications/the-world-factbook/.
3. See the Marriage Law of China, 1950, p. 1.
4. Robert Hauser, Cheng Hsiao, Ronald Lee, William Parish, George Tiao, Jim Vaupel, Arthur Wolf, and Cyrus Chu all served as members of the advisory group.
5. See the references in Chapter 8.
6. The first and second birth cohorts have some overlap with respect to their birth years since the first group was interviewed one year earlier as a pilot project. But the overall distribution of the combined sample is similar to the population in terms of age, gender, and education.

2

Social Backgrounds of China and Taiwan

Conventional empirical models of family behavior, mainly focusing on the USA or countries in Western Europe, are often variations of a standard regression model. For instance, in the analysis of child education, the dependent variable is usually the child's education achievement, reflected either in the years of schooling completed, or measures of academic performance. The explanatory variables might include family- and individual-specific characteristics, and other socio-economic variables. In particular, researchers often pay attention to the influence of parental education or sibling structure on child education.

Before we start our empirical analysis on China and Taiwan, we shall provide some discussions about the societal contexts and economic backgrounds of these areas. Through these discussions, the reader may gain some rough understanding about the socio-economic situation in these areas. Furthermore, these discussions may help clarify the setting of the empirical models. Take the analysis on child education as an example: since sibship size is a standard control variable in regressions, background information of family planning practices would be helpful in model setting. Before we proceed to the analysis on child education, it is also necessary to get a full picture of the education system and the relevant regulations in the societies in question. This chapter gives an overview of the socio-economic background in the past few decades, for both Taiwan and for China. Readers who are interested in more detail may go to the references cited.

2.1. Economic Transitions in the Past Sixty Years

In this section, we examine several macro statistics for China and Taiwan, and with these figures we hope to give the reader a quick glimpse of the

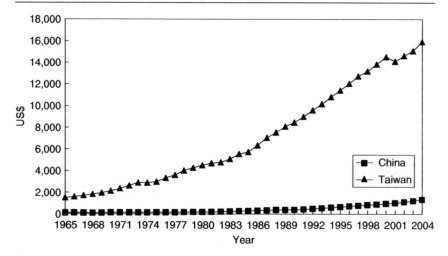

Figure 2.1 Per capita GDP (in constant 2000 US$)

Source: Taiwan, Directorate General of Budget, Accounting and Statistics (DGBAS), the Executive Yuan; China, World Development Indicators, 2006.

changing societal backgrounds. To save space, in most cases we shall skip numerical details but discuss the general trend instead.

The first economic indicator we present is the per capita gross domestic product (GDP), roughly indicating the economic capacity of the average individual or household. It can be seen from Figure 2.1 that the per capita GDP in Taiwan is consistently higher than that of China during the time span observed. The per capita GDP of Taiwan shows a steadily increasing trend, except for year 2001–2. The Chinese economy grew slowly before 1980, but an upward trend prevails since the early 1990s. Until 2007, a significant gap persisted between Taiwan and China in terms of per capita GDP, but it has been shrinking rapidly in recent years.

It is well known that China has been experiencing very rapid economic growth in the past several decades, implying that the Taiwan–China difference shown in Figure 2.1 is shrinking. However, China also suffers from a huge rural—urban gap, which will be discussed later in Section 2.3.

Concerning the demographic features, Figure 2.2 presents the crude death rates and the crude birth rates in China and Taiwan. The death rates in Taiwan had been low before 1960, partly because sanitation had already been improved during Japanese colonial rule (1895–1945). The trend of decreasing mortality rates can also be found in China except for the early 1960s, when famine followed the Great Leap Forward (1958–60). Since the political turmoil subsided, the death

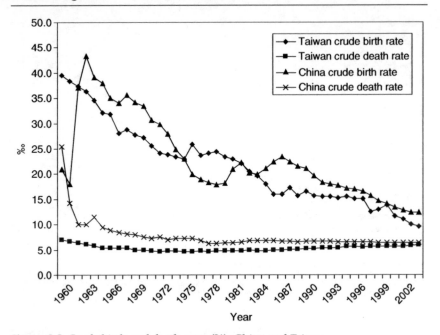

Figure 2.2 Crude birth and death rates (%): China and Taiwan
Source: Taiwan, Directorate General of Budget, Accounting and Statistics (DGBAS), the Executive Yuan; China, World Development Indicators, 2006.

rates in China have been declining steadily. The crude birth rates in Taiwan show a clear declining pattern, whereas those in China had a huge rise in the early 1960s. The birth rates in China have since shown a decreasing trend, but it is difficult to see distinctly the roles of demographic policies behind the trend. Therefore, we shall provide more analysis about the family planning programs later. As we shall explain, the one-child policy implemented after 1979 has had a tremendous impact on various dimensions of the family in China.

The life expectancies for both genders in Figure 2.3 show a steady increase in China except for the early 1960s; this again is attributed to the turmoil mentioned above. The life expectancies of Taiwan exhibit a much smoother pattern.

Other than the general socio-economic measures mentioned above, there is one more dimension worth exploring for family-related analysis, which is the system of education. Since the scenario is more complicated, and since education is a very important parental investment in children in Chinese societies, we shall discuss this in more detail later.

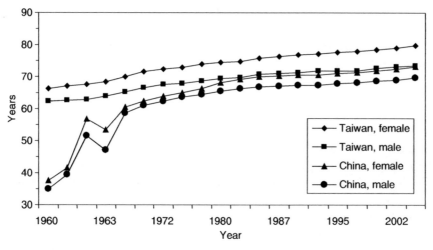

Figure 2.3 Life Expectancies at birth (in years): China and Taiwan

Source: Taiwan, Directorate General of Budget, Accounting and Statistics (DGBAS), the Executive Yuan; China, World Development Indicators, 2006.

2.2. Frequent Changes in China's Education System

Our purpose in this section is to lay before the readers the possible differences in education environment between Taiwan and China, in order to facilitate their understanding of the analyses to be presented. As we shall see shortly, the education scenario in China for the past fifty years is much more complicated than that in Taiwan. It is not that the traditional family background or sibling structure was not important in explaining child education in China, but that the macro environment was so volatile and influential that the importance of the micro family might be largely eclipsed, or even distorted. When it comes to child education, parents' preferences and decision patterns in China are not significantly different from those observed in Western countries, but there were often institutional changes and regulations that placed serious constraints on parental decisions *per se*. Because such regulations are relatively severe in China, in the following we shall pay less attention to the case of Taiwan.

Researchers often separate the Chinese society in the People's Republic of China into three stages (Hannum 1999). The first was from 1949 till 1965, the second from 1966 till 1977, and the third from 1978 until now. Each stage is sometimes further divided into several sub-periods, separated by respective events. In the early stage immediately after the Communist Party took power, there was a ten-year period of healthy development of the education environment. According to Hannum (1999: 195), the expenditure on public education doubled from 1949 to 1965, the number of schools increased, and related capital investment grew tenfold. Data from the Ministry of Education of China show that the primary school enrollment rates increased steadily, from 24.4 million in 1949 to 64.3 million in 1957. However, the glory days ended with the start of the Great Leap Forward in 1958, which soon led to a serious famine that lasted several years. Within the short period between 1960 and 1962, the primary school enrollment rate dropped sharply from 93.8 per cent to 69.2 per cent.

During the period 1949–65, the progression for juvenile education was mainly performance based; this practice was independent of the famine that began in 1958. There was severe competition in school entrance exams, which was also related to the existence of different school tracks. Usually, parents prefer to have their children go to regular schools rather than vocational ones. Among regular schools, there were *key-point* schools that were well known for their good records of student progression. Since sending children to such key-point schools was almost a guarantee of further education progression, competition to get into these schools was fierce.

As the economy gradually recovered from the famine in the early 1960s, the Chinese education system suffered another setback in the aftermath of the Cultural Revolution starting in 1966. One central element of the Cultural Revolution in fact was to promote a radically different educational agenda. The Cultural Revolution tried, among other things, to narrow the gap in education opportunities between the peasantry and the rest of the population. During the period of the Cultural Revolution, the exam-based progression criterion was replaced by political recommendation and class background in order to redress the handicap suffered by the children of peasants in education opportunity. Of course, the key-point schools, known for their exam-based selection of entrant students, were also abolished in this period.

During the Cultural Revolution period, the school tracking system was also abandoned. Vocational education, which was mainly for rural students in the past, nearly stopped, and most students entered the regular track. The years of schooling for primary/junior high/high school education also changed into a 5–3–2 system from the original 6–3–3. The curricula in schools during the Cultural Revolution period were very ideology oriented. In general, the quality of education in this period has been recognized to be very poor (Lewin et al. 1994). As one can imagine, this change in the macro environment had a significant impact on the micro education achievement of children in any family.

In 1978, one year after the death of Mao Zedong, China moved toward its third education regime, with a renewed emphasis on competition, quality, and talents. School progressions based on political and ideological considerations were abolished, the exam-based progression was reinstated, and key-point schools were revived. This third stage also coincided with a period of fast-paced economic reform in China. The increasing importance of the market economy also played a role in guiding the allocation of education resources. As the concern for rural–urban or agricultural–industrial equality was put on the back burner, the discrepancies among social classes and across regions in education widened in this third stage (Hannum 1999).

It is true that from time to time any society experiences important events or institutional changes. But in human history, to our knowledge, there has not been any education reform that was more ideology based, or any society which was placed under stricter authoritarian control, than was the case in the People's Republic of China during 1949–79. In fact, the impact of these events and changes on education was dramatic; individuals were literally forced into radically different education environments as the Cultural Revolution waxed and waned. In the eleven years during which the Cultural Revolution reigned supreme (1966–76), the criteria of climbing up the educational ladder, as we mentioned, were class origins and political ideology, whereas before and after these eleven years advancement in education was based on merit. If we define school-age children to be those between ages 7 and 16, then the Cultural Revolution period covers cohorts born between 1950 and 1970. When the education progression criterion has been distorted for such a large group of cohorts, as in China during this period, we are not sure how the usual empirical models on years of schooling or academic achievement could be applied. Of course, some talented people were able to pick up their education after the turmoil was over, but those cases are presumably exceptions rather than rules. To be frank, no one knows how serious the distortion was. One should exercise extra caution in analyzing educational achievement in China by taking into account the significant differences in social background across cohorts.

2.3. Heterogeneous Geo-economic Conditions

China is a large country and, as we mentioned, its rural–urban differences are very significant in various aspects. Many Chinese rural adults, for the sole purpose of pursuing better opportunities for work and child education, have tried to move to urban areas. A strict system of household registration control in place before the 1980s kept this migration under tight regulation.

2.3.1. Regional Economic Differences in China and Taiwan

To illustrate the significance of area differences in China, we present in Table 2.1 the per capita consumption statistics from Kanbur and Zhang (2001), who summarized and decomposed the inequality measures in China. In terms of the *level* of inequalities, we see from the rural–urban decomposition that most of the inequalities are *between* rural and urban rather than *within*. In terms of the *change* in inequalities, we find a fast-growing divergence between coastal and inland provinces since 1980. As is well known, much of the economic development and public construction in China since the 1980s has taken place in coastal provinces, while inland areas have been relatively left out in the boom. The coastal–inland divergent trend we observe in Table 2.1 is consistent with the time pattern when China opened up its economy. The same trend also appears in the rural–urban differentiation, although the figures are not as significant.

Table 2.1. Inequalities and decompositions of per capita consumption, 1952–1999, China

		Within		Between	
Year	GE	Rural–urban	Inland–coast	Rural–urban	Inland–coast
1952	0.084	0.027	0.078	0.057	0.006
1956	0.087	0.025	0.084	0.063	0.003
1960	0.162	0.030	0.159	0.132	0.004
1964	0.106	0.024	0.104	0.082	0.002
1968	0.094	0.017	0.092	0.077	0.002
1972	0.106	0.014	0.104	0.091	0.002
1976	0.127	0.017	0.123	0.110	0.004
1980	0.106	0.016	0.100	0.091	0.006
1985	0.076	0.017	0.071	0.058	0.005
1989	0.083	0.024	0.075	0.059	0.008
1993	0.107	0.029	0.090	0.078	0.017
1997	0.121	0.044	0.092	0.076	0.028
1999	0.159	0.065	0.124	0.094	0.034

Source: Kanbur and Zhang (2001), where GE refers to the generalized entropy index.

Table 2.2. Per capita annual disposable income of rural and urban areas, China and Taiwan

	China (RMB; %)			Taiwan (NTD; %)		
Year	Rural households (A)	Urban households (B)	(A)/(B)	Farm households (C)	Non-farm households (B)	(A)/(B)
1964	—	—	—	3,682	5,212	70.64
1968	—	—	—	4,487	7,807	57.47
1972	—	—	—	7,140	11,624	61.42
1976	—	—	—	16,440	24,601	66.83
1980	191.3	477.6	40.05	35,199	52,682	66.81
1982	270.1	526.6	51.29	42,110	63,747	66.06
1984	355.3	651.2	54.56	48,838	72,886	67.01
1986	423.8	899.6	47.11	57,339	80,415	71.30
1988	544.9	1,181.4	46.12	71,488	101,874	70.17
1990	686.3	1,510.2	45.44	91,031	131,469	69.24
1992	784.0	2,026.6	38.69	117,380	163,901	71.62
1994	1,221.0	3,496.2	34.92	146,294	199,846	73.20
1996	1,926.1	4,838.9	39.80	165,826	217,505	76.24
1998	2,162.0	5,425.1	39.85	171,075	240,028	71.27
2000	2,253.4	6,280.0	35.88	184,730	255,340	72.35
2002	2,475.6	7,702.8	32.14	177,121	248,080	71.40
2004	2,936.4	9,421.6	31.17	187,526	261,075	71.83
2005	—	—	—	189,009	268,728	70.33

Source: China Statistical Yearbook, 2005; Report on the Survey of Family Income and Expenditure, Taiwan, 2005.
RMB, renminbi; NTD, new Taiwan dollar.

In contrast the coastal–inland distinction is vague in Taiwan, which is a small island. The rural–urban gap in Taiwan is not as serious as in China. We do not have statistics for Taiwan equivalent to those of Table 2.1, but in Table 2.2 we try to make some comparisons between Taiwan and China on a similar basis. We list the per capita disposable income for rural–urban households in China, and for farm–non-farm households in Taiwan. As one can see, the rural–urban difference in China is large, whereas the farm–non-farm difference in Taiwan is much smaller. This indicates that the relative disadvantage of the farmers in China in economic opportunities is more pronounced as compared to Taiwan. In any event, the reader should keep in mind that locations of residence may play a more significant role in China than in Taiwan. In the context of education, this translates into the fact that education opportunity for youngsters in China was very much limited by the education resources of their place of residence.

2.3.2. Rural–Urban Differences and Education Opportunity in China

The notorious Cultural Revolution has been condemned by many histor-
ians from various angles. However, as Hannum (1999) pointed out, it did
contribute to a narrowing of the rural–urban differences in education.
During the period of the Cultural Revolution, many new schools were
established in the countryside, and many teachers were forced to serve in
poor rural areas, which would not have happened otherwise. The school
enrollment rate for primary, junior high, and high schools in rural areas
increased tremendously during 1966–77. According to Hannum (1999), the
enrollment rate for rural junior high schools increased from 35 per cent to
70 per cent and for high schools from 9 per cent to 66 per cent between
1965 and 1971. But these rates dropped sharply after the Cultural Revolution ended, eventually down to less than 63.7 per cent for junior high and
below 24 per cent for high schools in 1990. It is evident that without the
authoritarian intervention of the government, the rural–urban difference
would in all probability have remained large in the 1960s and 1970s. Of
course, the existence of rural–urban and coastal–inland differences does
not in any sense justify the authoritarian intervention of the state, even less
the serious political distortions brought to the sphere of education during
the Cultural Revolution, which led to the general deterioration of education quality in both rural and urban areas.

How serious was the influence of a poor village environment on the
education of an adolescent? A case study by Andreas (2004) using coun-
try-wide data was instructive. Andreas took a detailed look at the historical
enrollment rates of a small farming village in the Hebei Province as well as
the overall situation in China. He compared the enrollment data for primary, junior high, and high schools for three years, namely 1966, 1976, and
1981. Recall that 1966 was the year when the Cultural Revolution started,
1976 was the year it ended, and 1981 was four years after the entrance
examinations for school progression were reinstated. Andreas found that
the school completion rates were much higher in 1976 than in 1966 and
1981. We collected data from other sources and listed the entrance rates
and progression rates for selected years in Table 2.3. From this table one can
see how significantly the Cultural Revolution changed school attendance
in China, and how quickly the unequal *status quo ante* returned after the
government stepped aside. These figures together with the evidence
provided by Hannum (1999) suggest that the changes in overall enrollment
rates were mainly attributable to the changes in rural areas, especially in the
higher tiers of education.

Table 2.3. School entrance and progression rates of China in selected years (%)

Year	Primary entrance rate	Primary progression rate	Junior high progression rate
Before the Cultural Revolution			
1957	61.7	44.2	39.7
1962	56.1	45.3	30.0
During the Cultural Revolution			
1970	—	71.2	38.6
1975	96.8	90.6	60.4
After the Cultural Revolution			
1978	95.5	87.7	40.9
1982	93.2	66.2	32.3
1986	96.4	69.5	40.6
1990	97.8	74.6	40.6
1994	98.4	86.6	46.4
1998	98.9	94.3	50.7
2003	98.7	97.9	60.2
2004	98.9	98.1	62.9
2005	99.2	98.4	69.7

Source: Chinese Natural Resources, Environment, Economic and Population Database (http://www.naturalre sources.csdb.cn/index.asp).

In terms of rural–urban disparities in teacher quality and school progression ratios, Hannum (1999) found patterns similar to that in Table 2.3. In short, the emphasis on rural–urban equality during the Cultural Revolution has made a significant difference in the macro environment of education for several decades. Under a changing system like this, one can imagine how little the rural families can do at the micro level to effect meaningful changes in their children's education.

The problem of geographic differences was aggravated after the 1980s, with the spread of the market economy. According to Adams and Hannum (2005), the market economy has caused a shrinking of the profit of public enterprises, which in turn decreases the revenue of the central government. Under financial pressure, since the 1980s (in some places since the early 1990s) China has gradually started to promote the policy of educational decentralization, which renders the local governments responsible for most of the expenses of their schools, including primary, junior high, and high schools. Although colleges could still obtain financial subsidies from the government, their impact on rural education is not important, for the simple reason that college education is beyond the reach of most rural children anyway.

Adams and Hannum showed that even after controlling the family background variable, the income levels of the *village* of residence were significant in explaining the education achievement of individuals. This effect was not evident toward the end of the 1980s, but became evident in the 1990s, which is consistent with the gradual worsening of local government finances we just mentioned. The negative impact of village financial constraint was less significant for primary schools than for junior high schools. Moreover, girls are affected more by this constraint than boys (Hannum 2003). This pattern is in fact consistent with the findings of Heyneman and Loxley (1983), who argued that in poor areas, the provision of *basic* instructional materials was very important for education success.

The rural–urban difference in China also has a compounding effect on parents' gender-specific differential treatment in education resource allocation among children. In the context of gender differences in child education, there have been two hypotheses with respect to the impact of economic development. The first is the modernization hypothesis, which says that economic development can help eliminate the gender disadvantage against girls. The second hypothesis suggests that economic development provides market incentives for school-age girls, which in fact may induce them to drop out of schools. Using the 1988 and 1992 UNICEF survey data, Hannum (2005) found that Chinese families do follow the second hypothesis in the beginning period of development, but the long-term effect may be more compatible with the first hypothesis. As we can imagine, this conclusion may also be related to the rural–urban difference in question. Given that poor rural areas only marginally benefited from economic development, school-age girls in those areas are more likely to feel the lure of market incentives; in richer coastal urban areas, the gender perception may be more susceptible to the influence of Western norms as they benefit from economic development. Thus, the gender differences are expected to be more severe in rural than in urban areas.

2.3.3. One-Child Policy and Economic Reform in China

As we mentioned in the previous discussion, to tackle the problem of tremendous population pressure, the Chinese government imposed the well-known one-child policy in 1979. The rigidity of implementation varies across different years and different locations. In general the restriction was severe in the city, and weak in rural areas; stringent for the ethnic Hans and lax for ethnic minorities. According to Tsui and Rich (2002), more than 90 per cent of families with school-age children in cities had one child only. But this was not a pattern welcomed by parents. In fact, 82 per cent of urban parents in a 1990 national survey did express the wish to have two to three children instead of one. The same survey shows that the average years of schooling were 10.4 for male children and 9.4 for female children, indicating a small gender gap. Tsui and Rich attributed the small gender gap to the one-child policy.

The mandatory one-child policy in cities impacts parents' resource allocation decisions in least at three ways. First, for a young child who was the only offspring in his or her family, by definition there is no sibship effect to speak of. Second, parents have to devote all of their resources to their only child, for they have no other education investment target. Thus, there is no gender effect either. Third, since China does not have a comprehensive old-age social security system yet, the idea of "child as old age support" is still prevalent. Therefore, it is also in the parents' interest to invest in their only child, in the expectation that this child will eventually partly support them in their old age.[1]

Empirically, if the one-child policy was mandatory, then the change was like an ideal "natural experiment," and hence the number of siblings does not have the usual problem of *endogeneity* in statistical analysis. An analysis of Tsui and Rich (2002) based on survey data of the city of Wuhan found that, for families with only one child, the education achievement of boys and girls did not reveal any statistical difference, either in math scores or in parental aspirations. Indeed their analysis shows that this one-child policy has significantly changed the context of family decisions on child education.

The above conclusion of an equalizing gender gap may not hold uniformly across different geographical areas and time periods in China. As is well known, the economic development in China after 1978 affected the coastal areas first, before spreading inland. The inland–coastal difference has been widening ever since, as we have seen from Table 2.1. In this context, we can think of three differences between urban and rural areas. First, in urban areas the one-child policy is strictly implemented. Second, in urban areas mandatory education and enrollment can be practically implemented. Third, urban areas are influenced to a greater degree by modernization and economic development, and they also provide market opportunities for teenagers, either after graduation or as an attractive alternative to school attendance. This certainly has some impact on parents' education investment decisions. Thus, the one-child policy and the pace of economic development may have a combined influence on parents' education decisions for children, and presumably other family decisions as well.

2.4. Smooth Changes in the Education System in Taiwan

According to Chu and Tai (1996), education in Taiwan also experienced severe regulations after the Second World War. The regulations in Taiwan can be categorized into four types: establishing new schools, teacher licensure, issuance of diplomas, and school curriculum. We shall explain their roles as we proceed. The following discussion is partly extracted from the study of Chu and Tai (1996).

2.4.1. Regulatory Practices in Taiwan's Educational System

A six-year mandatory education period had been implemented in Taiwan since the Japanese colonial period. After the Second World War, Taiwan was returned to the Republic of China by the Japanese government in 1945, and the six-year mandatory education term remained. Prior to 1968, the proportions of elementary school graduates allowed to enter junior high schools were less than 60 per cent (see Table 2.4). For most periods of the PSFD sample we are concerned with, the screening mechanism for education progression was the joint entrance examination (JEE). These exams were standard written tests, and students were ranked according to their total test scores. After the highest-ranked test-takers were allowed to choose their preferred schools first, usually the public (less expensive) ones, the

Table 2.4. Taiwan's education progression rates of various tiers (%)

Year	Primary	Junior high	Senior high
1950	31.78	51.15	39.76
1954	39.71	64.20	43.01
1958	51.07	71.57	36.85
1962	55.14	76.16	41.83
1966	59.04	75.80	38.62
1970	78.59	82.66	41.92
1974	88.03	67.57	39.68
1978	94.08	60.42	40.43
1982	97.96	71.52	46.03
1986	99.04	77.13	40.98
1990	99.77	84.70	48.58
1994	99.83	88.49	57.38
1998	99.60	93.94	67.43
2002	99.70	95.48	69.01
2004	99.42	96.03	80.05

Notes: Progression rate for tier j is calculated as the number of graduates of tier j +1 divided by the number of graduates of tier j.

The rates are only slightly different if graduates are replaced by admissions.

Source: Education Statistics of Taiwan, 2005.

lower-scored students would get to make their choices. There were always some students who had too low a score to be accepted by any school, as shown by the progression rates of various years in Table 2.4. The main channels of education progressions from junior high to high schools and from high schools to universities or colleges were also joint entrance exams.

With economic development, there was an increasing demand for education in Taiwan. Starting from 1968, mandatory education has been extended from six to nine years, i.e., from elementary to junior high, thus eliminating the joint entrance exam from elementary to junior high. Most elementary school graduates were assigned to neighborhood junior high schools, and only a small proportion of them attended the better-disciplined, more expensive private schools. Unlike in China, the 1968 policy change was about the only abrupt change in Taiwan's educational system that might have a tremendous impact on child education achievement.

Are there significant differences in school quality in Taiwan? How do students with high scores in the joint entrance exam choose their preferred schools? We shall explain below that in terms of measurable indices, there is not much difference in school quality in Taiwan. The teachers of schools of all tiers (excluding universities and colleges) in Taiwan have been under strict licensure control, which was deregulated only after 1995.[2] Before 1995, to become a schoolteacher, one had to be a graduate of a normal university or college, which by law is a public school. The teacher's training was fairly standardized, and the curriculum was almost uniform. Graduates of the normal colleges were distributed to different schools based on the candidates' applications, and the admission criteria include location convenience, family considerations, and sometimes bureaucratic lobbying. Moreover, schoolteachers as well as university professors are all treated as civil servants, so that their salary is mainly seniority based. This uniform salary system also inhibits the development of variations that could have arisen across schools. In short, the quality of teachers does not differ much across schools.

Since Taiwan is a small island, the rural–urban discrepancy in school facilities is not as egregious as in China. Most students in Taiwan can reach a nearby high school by mass transit. Essentially all schools have indoor classrooms, textbooks, blackboards, and qualified teachers. Leaving aside the very few schools for the aborigines in the mountain, there are no significant objective distinctions across schools. Therefore the choices made by students who rank high in the JEE were mainly based on the students' subjective criteria. Usually, schools which have acquired a prior good reputation, such as the *first girls'* or *first boys'* high schools in the Japanese colonial period, would be the priority choice of most students. Because these good schools are often chosen by the highest-scored students, their progression ratio toward the next rung on the educational ladder is high, which in turn sustains their good reputation.

Before 1968, the year mandatory education was extended from six to nine years, there was fierce competition among senior students of elementary schools to get into their preferred junior high schools. After 1968, the education progression rates for elementary school students changed significantly, as one can see from Table 2.4. The competition thus shifted to the progression from junior high schools to high schools. The role of government regulation on new-school establishment then becomes apparent.

The establishment of new schools is regulated in almost every country. Conceptually, we expect the schools to have qualified teachers, some minimum space for physical exercise, and an appropriate curriculum that delivers common cultural values (Friedman 1982). In Taiwan, however, an application for the founding of a new school, even if it meets all the space-content requirements mentioned above, can be approved only if it passes the review board of the Commission for Economic Planning and Development (CEPD).

Taiwan's CEPD reviews applications for the creation of new departments in universities and the size of the freshman class of every university department, as well as applications for opening new schools of all tiers. The CEPD used to have the traditional concept of economic planning, and hence the approval of new schools had to be based on the theoretical match of estimated demand for and supply of graduates of all education tiers and occupations. Because the demand for highly skilled labor in Taiwan had been estimated to be low in the past, during the 1970s the CEPD approved many vocational high schools but few regular-track ones. However, as in China, most parents in Taiwan hope their children will proceed to higher education and hence prefer regular high schools. Given this scenario of a lopsided demand for regular-track education, in the past few decades there has always been severe competition for education progression.

The ratios of students attending regular high schools to vocational high schools decreased steadily, from 150 per cent in the mid-1960s to less than 50 per cent in the 1990s. This policy was relaxed in the late 1990s, and the ratios of high school students to vocational school students eventually increased to over 100 per cent in the twenty-first century. Because there was a significant barrier to switching between regular and vocational tracks, most parents in

Taiwan prefer their children to attend regular high schools rather than vocational ones, so that their children can have a better chance to be admitted to universities. This regular-track preference is very much the same as that in China (Andreas 2004). The CEPD policy in the establishment of new schools resulted in stiff competition at the stage of high school entrance examinations after 1968. Table 2.4 shows that before 1990, less than 80 per cent of junior high school students could progress to high schools, regular and vocational combined. The fact that there were more vocational school admissions than regular ones evidently intensified the competition.

2.4.2. *Impact of Taiwan's Educational Regulation*

We mentioned in the previous subsection that other than the regulations on school establishment and the training of teachers, there are also controls on diplomas and school curricula, which we shall briefly describe. Even as of 2008, all school diplomas, including those from universities, can be bestowed only with the approval of the Ministry of Education. This helps tighten the regulation of school establishment, for graduates from programs or schools that do not offer legal diplomas cannot participate in the joint entrance exams of the next tier, or the qualification exams for public service. With such limited *ex post* outlet expectation, "illegal" schools or programs are less welcome *ex ante*. Thus, diploma control is a subsidiary means to make the regulation of school establishment more effective. The regulation on school curricula responded partly to the need of the authoritarian control of the KMT government in an earlier period. This regulation was mainly aimed at thought control by limiting students' exposure to diverse viewpoints. However, it did not have much impact on the general child achievement that one usually measures.

Despite the tight regulation of education in Taiwan, the education system of Taiwan is significantly different from that in China in three aspects. The education progression ladder in Taiwan has always been based on examinations; there has not been any structural change that distorts the system into one based on political background or social classes, as was the case during the period of the Cultural Revolution in China. The stringent regulations on school curricula and teacher training together with the implementation of joint entrance examinations make the education progression process a very standard one. Facing such a uniform scenario of competition, it is common for parents to send their children to cram schools or provide after-school tutoring, in order to improve their children's competitiveness in the JEE.

In Taiwan, there were also some systemic changes in education, such as adjustments to the numbers of regular high school and of vocational high school students. Since such changes are mostly gradual, these structural factors can be easily controlled in the empirical analysis. The same cannot be said of China, where systemic changes were abrupt and unpredictable. The only sudden change in Taiwan was the extension of mandatory education in 1968. However, this may be a beneficial factor in our analysis instead of a detrimental one. The extension of mandatory education constitutes a natural experiment which can serve as an instrumental variable and help solve the estimation problem in our empirical models.

The regulation on teacher training was abolished in 1995, and the uniform school curricula for mandatory education were abolished in 2002. But since the joint entrance exam is still the main channel for education progression, none of these changes affects the macro educational background for our micro analysis. The admission rates to higher education tiers changed very slowly in the past. The college admission rate increased significantly after 1996 because many vocational high schools were allowed to upgrade to vocational colleges. However, few of our PSFD interviewees were affected by this late transformation.

The second factor that distinguishes Taiwan from China is the impact of geographic differences. Since Taiwan is a small island, geographic differences are never serious enough to limit the education opportunity of youngsters, except for the very few aboriginal communities. There are of course rural–urban differences; but such differences are mainly manifested in cultural and economic conditions, which are not the same as the barriers to school attendance often observed in China. In Taiwan, geographical locations matter more for college education, since there are no nearby colleges in some rural areas. But due to the regulation on tuition fees, most families in Taiwan can afford the living and tuition expenses of college attendance, thus the financial constraint issue would not be a serious problem in our analysis.

The third factor that facilitates a more convenient micro analysis of child education in Taiwan is the absence of a mandatory birth control program, in contrast to China. Families may have more or fewer children; but that's a decision parents make of their own free will. The family planning program in Taiwan only dispenses free contraceptive devices or advice, and never resorts to any compulsion. Even if the parents do decide to have only one child, they have their own reasons for that choice, which researchers may be able to control, explain, or test.

2.5. Conclusions

In this chapter, we tried to give the reader an overview of the socio-economic backgrounds of Taiwan and China in the past sixty years. We first highlighted some basic economic and demographic indices for both China and Taiwan in the past sixty years. Other than such basic backgrounds, we emphasized three features in China that are important to our later analysis.

The first feature is the frequent, abrupt changes in education system, mainly associated with some major upheavals, such as the Great Leap Forward, the Cultural Revolution, and the opening-up of the economy begun in 1978. The second is the tight fertility control and eventually the implementation of the one-child policy. The third is the significant rural–urban difference. These features impose constraints on regular family decisions, and also justify an important caveat on the empirical methodology and the interpretation of findings for China. In contrast, the scenario of Taiwan is more stable and similar to that of the West. This is also why, on a few occasions, we restrict our later analysis to Taiwan.

Notes

1. Because of the one-child policy, in some of our later chapters we have to confine our analysis to cohorts that are not subject to this policy.
2. Under the new law, teachers can also be trained by ordinary colleges offering a professional program of education. The change was too late to have any impact on our sample anyway.

3

Co-residence and Family Size

There seems to be a general impression that Chinese family members are closely attached to each other and extended family co-residence is more widespread than in Western societies. A traditionally "ideal" big Chinese family, according to Gallin (1966) and Cohen (1976), is composed of a married son's parents and sometimes his married brothers.

Despite the fact that this impression is by and large correct in ancient times, the uniqueness of Chinese families in a historical perspective was recently challenged by Thornton and Fricke (1987), who argued that many changes that occurred in family structure have been similar across cultures. Thornton (2005: 5) also found that prior to the latter half of the nineteenth century, the attachment between family members in England and north-west European societies was also strong. The household size then was large, and children, parents, grandparents, aunts, and uncles all lived together. Most people married at a young age and individualism was not common at that time. This "sideways" look at European family history generates some common features in family development dynamics. Nevertheless, toward the end of the twentieth century, large family size and extended household structure were more likely to be observed in Chinese societies.

The pattern of extended Chinese families had been predicted to change imminently and fundamentally by Levy (1949) sixty years ago. His argument was mainly a version of the modernization theory, which says that urbanization, rising living standards, industrialization, and the opening of women's market opportunities would reduce the likelihood of co-residence and make extended families less dominant. However, the evidence to be presented soon shows that this prediction has so far been belied by the fact that the proportion of co-residence at least in China is still very high.

One should note that the pattern of family is also related to marriage and fertility. Given the prevalent nuclear family pattern in the West, adult children can get married only after they are capable of establishing and sustaining a separate economic unit. Since economic capability can only be established when the child gets relatively old, the average age for marriage is older in the West, and hence fertility occurs later. The case was quite different for Chinese societies, where extended families were prevalent. Adult children then had little incentive to marry late given that they were going to stay in the extended family anyway. The starting age of giving birth therefore would be younger in Chinese families. This chapter will focus on the formation and pattern of households, and the discussion of marriage will be provided later in Chapter 5.

3.1. Some Earlier Evidence on Family Types

In order to categorize the complexity of family structure, scholars often classify families into several types. The first is the *nuclear family*, which consists only of the married couple and their unmarried children, and possibly includes relatives other than the parents of a spouse. The second type is the *stem family*, which consists of the couple and their children, one or more parents of the husband or wife, or a grandparent of the husband or wife. The third is the *joint family*, which includes one or more other married couples related to the respondent couple, usually of the same generation. The fourth category is the *joint-stem family*, which includes both the vertical and horizontal linkages described above. Sometimes researchers do not distinguish between joint and joint-stem, and call both types joint, or grand or extended families.[1] In what follows, we shall adopt such definitions in our analysis. The purpose of our discussion in this section is to provide background information concerning previous Chinese families. With this background in mind the reader can have a better understanding of the changes in family structure we shall present in later sections.

Freedman (1970) used field and survey data to estimate the family size of Singapore in the late 1940s. At the time of the survey, the ethnic Chinese accounted for 78.8 per cent of the population of Singapore. The survey was done with respect to this subpopulation only. It turns out that for urban areas, the average household size was 4.08, and for rural areas it was 7.33. Freedman further classified families according to the occupation of household heads, and found that household heads with professional and higher-income occupations tended to have larger families. This evidence prompted Freedman to conclude that large and complex families were only found among the elite.

Wolf (1985) used historical data of Taiwan (1906–46) to investigate Taiwanese family structure and size in that period. He provided a more refined definition about family structure, but here we only focus on the change of stem and grand families. Wolf (1985: 35) found that during the forty-year period in question, the proportion of stem families was quite stable, fluctuating between 29.0 per cent and 34.5 per cent. And the grand families showed an increasing trend, rising from 23.3 per cent to 30.0 per cent during the period. Concerning family size, the average number of residents in the family increased quite steadily, from 6.56 in 1906 to 8.10 in 1946. When classifying families according to economic status, Wolf (1985: 48) found that landlords or peasants with some land tended to have larger families.

Based on the above evidence, contrary to the findings of Freedman (1970) that large Chinese families were found only among the elite, Wolf (1985: 49) concluded that Chinese families were potentially large whenever material conditions allowed. A larger family size was determined not so much by elite class membership *per se* as by whether there were sufficient food and clothes to support more family members. This observation seems to be consistent with some later evidence we find, to be described below. However, as Goode (1963) pointed out, the transition from grand to conjugal families must be influenced by the trend of freedom of mate choice, the expanding opportunities in the labor market (especially for females), and the spread of individualism from industrialized societies. These factors may not be easily disentangled from the material support that Wolf referred to; but we shall try to accomplish that in later discussion.

In contrast to Singapore and Taiwan, no data were available for China until 1982. The first and second Chinese censuses were conducted in 1953 and 1964, respectively; but essentially no family statistics from these two censuses were published. Taiwan does have some high-quality survey data since the 1970s, which will be further discussed in later sections.

3.2. Statistical Descriptions

In this section we shift our focus to more recent data sets from China and Taiwan. To describe the realized or desired family structure, three statistics are often used, namely: (1) the average number of household members, (2) the distribution of families types (e.g., nuclear, stem, and joint), and (3) the couple's subjective willingness to co-reside with their parents, parents-in-law, or married children. Next, we shall summarize some evidence we find from the literature.

3.2.1. *Family Size*

There have been some area-specific surveys and field studies that provide us with figures of family size in different time periods and different areas of China. One can go to the collected papers edited by Davis and Harrell (1993) for more details. Here we only review evidence from larger-area surveys.

In 1982–3, a survey was conducted in five big cities of China, namely Chengdu, Shanghai, Nanjing, Tianjing, and Beijing, covering eight neighborhoods and 5,436 married women as respondents. The average family size summarized by Zang (1993) from these five cities is 4.08 and the corresponding number for urban China overall is 4.62, indicating that big cities do have smaller family size in general. A contribution by Zang was that he classified the observations into several periods defined by major historical events such as the Second World War, the Chinese Civil War, land reform, and the Cultural Revolution. He found that it was hard to establish any single year as the watershed with respect to the changes in age at marriage, freedom of mate choice, post-marital residence, and the nuclear-stem-joint family structure. This shows that the transformation in Chinese families in the past few decades has been a gradual process and was not triggered by any specific events.

The most thorough summary of household size in China was provided by Zeng and Wang (2003). They estimated that the average family size was 5.6 in 1930–40, 4.3 in 1953, and 4.3 in 1964, although they did not provide very much detail about how these numbers were obtained. Using the census data of 1982, 1990, and 2000, they were able to calculate the family sizes more precisely, with the estimates being 4.36, 3.94, and 3.45 (see Table 3.1a). The significant decrease in family size in the past twenty years reveals not only a shrinking birth rate, but also the influence of other factors. Concerning the rural—urban gap in the year 2000, they show that the average family size was 3.62 in rural areas, and 3.16 in urban areas.

In the case of Taiwan, numbers in later years, from 1949 to 1958, were summarized from Hermalin et al. (1994). Starting from the 1960s, the Ministry of Interior of Taiwan has supplied good records of family size. As one can see from Table 3.1b, the average family size steadily decreased, from 5.57 in 1961 to 3.21 in 2003. On the basis of the PSFD data, the average family size is also calculated for both Taiwan and China. It can be seen from the bottom rows of Tables 3.1a and 3.1b that the figures are 4.63 and 4.39 for China and Taiwan respectively. Compared to the figures from census or government statistics, the figures computed from PSFD seem to be higher.

Table 3.1a. Average family size, China

Source	Area covered	Year(s)	Average family size	Data source
Zeng (2001)	Country-wide	1990	3.97	Census with 1% sample randomly selected
		1995	3.7	Mini-census
Zeng and Wang (2003)	Country-wide	1982	4.36	Census
		1990	3.94	
		2000	3.45	
	Urban	2000	3.62	
	Rural	2000	3.16	
Calculated by the authors	3 coastal areas	2004	4.63	PSFD survey

Table 3.1b. Average family size, Taiwan

Source	Area covered	Year(s)	Average family size	Data source
Hermalin et al. (1994: Table 3.3, p. 48)	Island-wide	1949	5.55	Government statistics
		1952	5.45	
		1955	5.57	
		1958	5.56	
Calculated by the authors[a]	Island-wide	1961	5.57	Government statistics
		1964	5.63	
		1967	5.60	
		1973	5.43	
		1976	5.19	
		1979	4.87	
		1982	4.58	
		1985	4.42	
		1988	4.14	
		1991	3.94	
		1994	3.75	
		1997	3.50	
		2000	3.33	
		2003	3.21	
Calculated by the authors	Island-wide	1999–2003	4.39	PSFD

[a] Indicates the figures are from the Demographic Yearbook, Ministry of the Interior, Taiwan.

The main reason for this discrepancy is that the PSFD surveys exclude individuals aged over 68 as respondents; since older people are more likely to be empty nesters, the family size obtained may be larger in our PSFD survey.

3.2.2. Family Types: Area-Specific Evidence

Again, here we only review evidence from larger-area surveys. Zang (1993) used the five-city survey data of 1982 to calculate the family type composition. He classified the families according to periods in which the year of marriage occurred. It turns out that the proportion of nuclear families increased in these areas, from 60.4 per cent for the cohort married between 1900 and 1938, to 69.2 per cent for the cohort married during 1977–82. The proportions of stem and joint families both decreased. We find this change in family pattern to be consistent with the prediction of Levy (1949) and Goode (1963). An analysis by Tsui (1989) also used the five-city survey data, and the classification of samples is only slightly different from the one described in Zang (1993).

For the case of Taiwan, the earliest statistics (1906–46) were provided by Wolf (1985). Roughly speaking, the proportion of nuclear families decreased and that of joint families increased during this period. And the average proportions for nuclear, stem, and joint families were 41.1 per cent, 32.2 per cent, and 26.7 per cent respectively. Later, Weinstein et al. (1994) presented the distribution of family types for five discontinuous years, using data from the Knowledge, Attitudes, and Practice (KAP) survey conducted by the Taiwan Provincial Institute of Family Planning. From their data we find an increasing trend of nuclear families (from 34 per cent in 1965 to 56 per cent in 1985) and a decreasing trend of joint families (from 30 per cent in 1965 to 8 per cent in 1985), whereas the proportion of stem families remains the same. This pattern was obviously distinct from the period of 1906–46. In the earlier periods Wolf studied, he suggested that the family type was correlated with economic capability, whereas for the periods after the 1970s, changing conceptions and the spread of individualism in society might have begun to play a more important role.

As in the study of family size, Zeng and Wang (2003) also provided the most comprehensive evidence for recent trends in China. Instead of classifying families into nuclear, stem, and joint families, they separated families into one-generation, two-generation, and three[+]-generation categories. The data used by Zeng and Wang came from the 1982, 1990, and 2000 censuses, and thus had a large sample size. To facilitate comparison with

Table 3.2. Proportion of various family types by number of generations, China and Taiwan (%)

Year	One generation	Nuclear	Other two generations	Three+ generations
China				
1982*	13.92	66.02	1.26	18.80
1990*	13.52	67.27	0.90	18.30
2000*	22.28	55.86	2.86	19.00
Rural*	20.33	56.32	3.25	20.10
Urban*	26.54	56.87	2.28	14.32
2004	15.69	61.44	1.35	21.52
Taiwan				
2003	15.72	58.22	1.24	24.83

Source: * indicates that the figures are retrieved from Zeng and Wang (2003: Table 1, p. 101). Other figures are computed by the authors, based on the China and Taiwan PSFD surveys conducted in 2004 and 2003 respectively.

Zeng and Wang (2003), we employed the same categories to classify the sample of the PSFD survey. The results are summarized in Table 3.2.

From Table 3.2, we see that from 1982 to 2000, the proportion of one-generation families in China increased significantly with time, from 13.92 per cent to 22.28 per cent, and nuclear families sharply decreased from 66.02 per cent to 55.86 per cent. This pattern is certainly related to the decreasing number of children in most families: when the one-child policy was implemented in most areas, the probability that a household had a child residing in it evidently decreased, which in turn led to an increasing (decreasing) proportion of one-generation households (nuclear households). Nevertheless, the proportion of three-generation families did not change much in this period.

Area-wise, we see from Table 3.2 that the percentage of one-generation households was higher in urban areas than in rural areas. This is intuitive, for urban families are under stricter fertility control and are more likely to face an empty nest. The proportion of three+-generation families is much higher in rural areas. This is also intuitive: since rural society tends to be more traditional, its young couples are often economically less able to form an independent household, and also it has higher fertility rates. In 1990, the proportion of extended families comprising three generations or more was about seven times that in the USA (Zeng 2001).

The proportions for China and Taiwan computed from PSFD surveys are listed in the bottom rows of Table 3.2. We can see from these rows that the distributions of family types are similar across the Strait.

However, the proportion of nuclear families is relatively higher in China than in Taiwan, while an opposite pattern prevails for the three+-generation families. These patterns are consistent with the findings based on the traditional classification of families, which we discussed in the previous subsection.

3.2.3. Co-residence with Married Children, Preferences and Practice

Another measure of family structure focuses on the co-residence of parents and their adult children, either unmarried or married. In some surveys, parents are asked whether they hope to or *want to* co-reside with one of their children after the latter get married. The answer reflects the parents' subjective preferences. There are also some family surveys that ask about the *practice* of parental co-residence with adult children. We summarize some of the results in Table 3.3.

Using his own survey data, Unger (1993) listed the parents' preferences for living arrangements after their children have their own families. It can be seen that there were significant differences between the cities of Tianjin, Wuhan, and Shanghai during the period 1983–6. We have no strong presumption to explain the differences between these big cities, but some general comments will be provided later in the next section. Logan and Bian (1999) investigated nine cities of China and arrived at a percentage of co-residence preference roughly comparable to Unger's.

Comprehensive data from Taiwan on co-residence willingness can also be found in Weinstein et al. (1994). In Table 3.3 we listed the percentage of married women who "expect" to co-reside with married children in their old age. The percentage dropped sharply from 55.9 per cent in 1973 to 44.8 per cent in 1986, revealing a remarkable attitudinal change toward co-residence with children. Weinstein et al. (1994) also found that the percentage of married women who believed that the newly wed *should* live with the husband's parents dropped from 56.6 per cent in 1973 to 40.0 per cent in 1986, a pattern similar to the co-residence expectation we just described.[2]

In terms of practice (as opposed to preferences), Zeng and Wang (2003) did some interesting analysis using census data of China. They found that the proportion of elderly people (aged 65+) living with their children decreased significantly from 73.6 per cent in 1982 to 68.7 per cent in 2000. However, the same statistics for the oldest old (elderly people whose age was over 80) did not change much. In fact, the percentage increased slightly from 76.5 per cent to 79.9 per cent during 1982–2000.

Table 3.3. Willingness and actual practice of co-residence with children, China and Taiwan

Source	Area covered	Year(s)	Respondents	Co-residence expectation by aged parents, %	Co-residence practice as % of parents (P) or adult children (AC)
China					
Unger (1993: Table 2.6, p. 39)	Tianjin	1983	Married individuals with unmarried adult children	61	—
		1984		40	
	Wuhan	1985		48	
	Shanghai	1985–6		45	
Logan and Bian (1999: Table 1)	Nine cities	1987	Individuals aged 60+, with married children	47	—
Pimentel and Liu (2004: Table 1)	Beijing	1991	First-married women aged 30+	—	Young cohort, 75.6% of AC; old cohort, 65.7% of AC
Logan et al. (1998: Table 1)	Tianjin	1993	Individuals aged 21+	—	67% of P
	Shanghai		Married sons in 20s		52% of AC in first 5 years of marriage; 33% of AC in 5–10 years of marriage
Taiwan					
Weinstein et al. (1994: Table 12.9, p. 322)	Island-wide	1973	Married women aged 20–39	55.9	—
		1980		39.3	
		1986		44.8	
Hermalin and Yang (2004: Table 6, p. 436)	Island-wide	1989	Ever-married women aged 50+	—	61.9% of P
		1996			56.6% of P
		1999			53.3% of P

This might be due to the lack of a comprehensive social security system in China; most of the very elderly still rely on their children to take care of their remaining years. For the situation of the USA, the percentages of male and female elderly (65+) living with only a spouse in 1990 were 61.1 per cent and 33.6 per cent respectively. The contrast reflects the significant cultural difference between these two countries.

In Taiwan, the proportions for married women aged 50 or above who co-resided with married sons were 61.9 per cent in 1989, 56.6 per cent in 1996, and 53.3 per cent in 1999, as indicated by Hermalin and Yang (2004). The sharp decrease indicates Taiwan's fast transition in family structure.

3.3. Family Structure: Institutional Features of China

Goode's (1963) theory suggested that with economic development and modernization, the importance of the family network may gradually be replaced by various social networks. From this standpoint, one may suspect that the pace of modernization could be a factor which influences the family co-residence decision. This intuition may be right normally; but for the case of China, we shall affirm that other institutional factors may be much more important than modernization. In what follows, we shall present several special features of China that might have affected the pattern of family structure considerably. Our discussion calls for extra care in interpreting Chinese data and in conducting empirical analyses using the data. Some of our discussion below has been documented by Zeng (2001); details can be found therein.

1. Up until 1990, China had a restrictive system of regulations on household registration and residence permits. The document of household registration was called a "booklet." In the 1970s and early 1980s, the economy of China was poor in general and had to resort to a food rationing system (for both staple and subsidiary foodstuffs). Because such food rationing was based on household booklets, some families managed to register some of their family members under a separate household, despite the fact that they actually lived together for most of the time. This circumstance evidently inflated the proportion of one-person households as well as the proportion of old people living alone. Such a distortion was reduced only after 1990 with the dismantlement of the food rationing system.

2. Perhaps bound by the perception of lineage continuation, most Chinese couples have their first child soon after their marriage. As we shall see from Chapter 4, the average duration from marriage to first birth was 2.18 years for the China sample in the PSFD survey, and the corresponding figure for the Taiwan sample was 1.81 years. This led to a lower percentage of couple-only households.

3. As is well known, China has experienced since 1970 the sharpest fertility decline in human history. Related numbers are provided in Chapter 4 and will not be repeated here. Given such a drastic reduction in births, the average family size has shrunk radically. Moreover, because most families (especially those in cities) had only one child, the probability of observing a joint family was reduced. And as the number of siblings was reduced to zero, this only child had to bear the responsibility of parental care in adulthood, thus increasing the likelihood of co-residence. Finally, since this only child might be of either gender, the trend for senior parents to co-reside with their sons could not be sustained and as a result one began to observe an increase in cases of co-residence with married daughters. However, looser fertility control in rural areas also contributed to a sharp rural–urban divergence.

4. The divorce rate was low and remarriage rate high in China (Zeng and Wang 1993; Zeng and Wu 2000). This led to a low rate of single-parent households.

5. The stringent household registration system also increased the likelihood of having a parent living and working alone in the city or town. For instance, the fact that it sometimes took several years for the migration application of the spouse and children of a man who worked in the city to be granted led to a higher statistical record of one-parent households and grandparent–grandchild households, especially in rural areas. This pattern began to change only in the late 1990s.

6. As a result of the laxer enforcement of the one-child policy in rural areas as opposed to cities, extra births were relatively common in rural families. Since these extra births were sometimes illegal in any event, they must be hidden from the interviewer conducting household surveys. For this reason the accuracy of survey data about families, especially in rural areas, was to some degree questionable.

7. Housing constraints have been more severe in urban areas than in rural ones. This has led to a sharing of living quarters among married siblings. The spread of this arrangement resulted in an increased percentage of

extended families in cities. Distortions caused by the above-mentioned features are not difficult to understand; but the problem is that no one knows the extent of such distortions. For instance, Logan et al. (1998) showed that, when predicting co-residence, it was necessary to control whether the married son's work unit provided housing to employees. Logan et al. (1998) also argued that the sharp decline of the co-residence ratio in Tianjin during 1988–93 was partly due to relaxation of the area's housing restrictions. Institutional factors such as this were often too area specific to be taken as a general rule.

Even though the Chinese Communist Party has attempted to play down the role of the family and stressed the importance of loyalty to the state since they took power in 1949, there have been only minimal changes in the normative structures and living arrangements of families (Treas and Chen 2000, Whyte 2003). The above remarks about institutional factors made it more difficult to identify any trend in the context of family structure. Moreover, ever since the more recent market and social reforms in China, the government has re-emphasized the responsibility of adults in supporting their ageing family members and formalized the obligation into law (Zimmer and Kwong 2003). This might further change the practices of intergenerational living arrangements.

3.4. Determinants of Co-residence: Previous Literature

3.4.1. *Evidence from Non-Chinese Areas*

There has been some research on decisions about and patterns of intra-family living arrangements, but since the contexts of such research are very different from that of Chinese society, we shall only briefly present the background without getting into the details of the relevant literature.

For countries with poor economic conditions, family members usually have strong incentives to share public goods and use all sources of labor, hence the proportion of co-residence is usually very high. According to Kochar (2000), World Bank data documented that 85 per cent of elderly aged over 60 co-resided with adult sons in Pakistan in 1991–2. Since co-residence in these areas is the predominant arrangement, the focus of analysis is usually not on the *determinants* of co-residence, but on its related *implications*. In general, when the economic condition is poor, the *necessity* of co-residence plays an important role, and there will not be much room for family decision-making to be analyzed.

At the other extreme, for rich countries such as the USA, economic modernization and prevalent individualism have made the rate of co-residence decline continuously. According to Schoeni (1998), in the USA the share of elderly who live with their children dropped from 59 per cent in 1900 to 14 per cent in 1990. Note that this figure also covers co-residence with young or unmarried children, whereas the Chinese co-residence we are interested in is often with married children. Moreover, in US families, the economic power is often in the hands of parents, and young adults are unable to provide resources upward to their parents (Rosenzweig and Wolpin 1993: 87). Indeed, since parents in the USA control both the co-residence arrangement and the transfers of financial resources, the research by Rosenzweig and Wolpin mainly focused on the *joint determination* of these two decisions. This, as we shall explain below, is again different from the Chinese practices.

The two Chinese societies we study in this monograph are economically better off than Pakistan but not as rich as the USA. Thus, the decision of co-residence is a particularly meaningful one. Furthermore, since co-residence in Chinese societies often involves parents and a married child conscious of filial duty, the child is often expected to transfer resources to the parent. Thus, the decision context is significantly different from the USA. In particular, it may be the child's call whether or not to co-reside with the parents, instead of the other way around. As such, factors on the children's side may be important explanatory variables. Keeping such differences in mind, we shall discuss the evidence from the Chinese societies in more detail.

3.4.2. *Previous Findings on Chinese Societies*

There have been a number of relevant studies concerning China and Taiwan. Logan et al. (1998) analyzed two cities of China, namely Tianjin and Shanghai, and found that widowed mothers, parents with frail health, and a larger housing space all contributed to the practice of co-residence, whereas the probability of co-residence was reduced when the sibship size increased or when the parents had only daughters. They also suggested that the provision of public housing to young adults was a key to explaining the practice of co-residence. Lavely and Ren (1992) found that, among other things, literate husbands tended to co-reside with the parents. Their interpretation was particularly interesting: they suggested that literate husbands were the ones who accepted early fertility control, and hence literacy of the husband was a proxy variable for a smaller sibship size, which in turn increased the observed co-residence. One cannot be sure how good a proxy the husband's literacy was for small sibship size; but one can clearly see the intertwined effect of sibship size and education. This was an interpretation for which we can hardly find a counterpart in the Western literature.

Pimentel and Liu (2004) is the only study we found to focus on co-residence with the wife's parents, called matrilocal co-residence. Given the one-child policy, it is likely that some parents would not have any sons to co-reside with. This would certainly increase the proportion of parents co-residing with a married daughter. It was shown that the percentage of such matrilocal co-residence had increased to more than 30 per cent by 1988. Using a logit model, the authors showed that the probability of this kind of matrilocal co-residence decreased when the wife had brother(s) and increased when she had children of a young age. This last factor may be consistent with the practice of babysitting and care by grandmothers, which we commonly observe in Chinese families, as we shall see below. Finally, Pimentel and Liu's regressions show that a widowed mother or father tends to have a lower probability of co-residence. They did not provide an explanation for this finding. This, if we might hazard a guess, might be related to the practice of housing distribution.[3]

In Table 3.4, we use the data from PSFD to present the proportions of respondents who co-resided with their parent(s) or parent(s)-in-law. The table shows that about one-third of the married couples co-resided with the husband's parent(s), with the proportion being higher in Taiwan (40.51 per cent) than in China (32.08 per cent). However, the proportion of the sample who co-resided with the wife's parent(s) is much lower for both sides of the Taiwan Strait, with the figures being 3.96 per cent and 6.05 per cent for Taiwan and China, respectively. These preliminary findings are consistent with those found in past literature that parents are more likely to co-reside with sons than daughters (Davis 1993, Logan et al. 1998). In what follows, we adopt a probit model to analyze the determinants behind the co-residence decision.

Table 3.4. Co-residence between the couples and their parents (%)

	Couples with husband's parent(s) alive (1)	Couples with wife's parent(s) alive (2)	Couples co-residing with husband's parent(s) (3)	Couples co-residing with wife's parent(s) (4)	$\frac{(3)}{(1)} \times 100\%$	$\frac{(4)}{(2)} \times 100\%$
Taiwan	1,133	1,288	459	51	40.51%	3.96%
China	1,415	1,488	454	90	32.08%	6.05%

Source: Sample of Taiwan is from the first-wave surveys conducted in 1999, 2000, and 2003. The counterpart of China is from the 2004 survey.

3.5. Empirical Analysis in Taiwan and China

In this subsection, we use the PSFD data from Taiwan and China to analyze the co-residence decision between the married couples and their parents. The samples of Taiwan are retrieved from the first-wave surveys conducted in 1999, 2000, and 2003. To analyze the co-residence between the couples and the parents of either spouse, the sample is further confined to those who got married and had at least one parent alive on either side. And the samples of China are selected in like manner.

Before proceeding to the regression analysis, we first present the means and standard deviations of the variables by co-residence status. For the sample of Taiwan (China), we can see from Table 3.5 that the husbands' years of schooling tend to be lower for couples who co-reside with the *wife's* parents than for couples in other living arrangements. Table 3.5 also reveals that the wife's socio-economic status, either measured by years of schooling or income, tends to be the highest for couples who co-reside with the wife's parents, and the lowest for those who co-reside with the husband's parents. We will explore these issues further in the probit analysis.

Owing to the growing concern for matrilocal co-residence in China, matrilocal co-residence is analyzed in addition to the more common practice of patrilocal co-residence. The results of the univariate probit models for co-residence with the husband's parents and the wife's parents are presented in Tables 3.6 and Table 3.7 respectively. From Table 3.6, it can be seen that the effects of many explanatory variables, either in sign or in magnitude, are different between Taiwan and China. On the common parts, the couple is more likely to co-reside with the husband's parents if (1) the couple has children under age 3, (2) only the husband's mother is alive, and (3) the couple lives in a rural area. These findings are by and large consistent with the above-cited literature such as Logan et al. (1998).

Some interesting facts in Table 3.6 deserve special attention. First, while in Taiwan, the decision to co-reside with the *husband's* parents depends on the *wife's* resources, in China it depends on the *husband's* resources. If the wife's income is higher, the couple's tendency to co-reside with the husband's parents will be lower in Taiwan. As to the case of China, the higher the husband's income is, the higher the tendency to co-reside with the husband's parents. As suggested by Hermalin et al. (2003) and Cornman et al. (2003), Taiwan is more "traditional" than China with regard to family attitudes or family behavior. In such a tradition-laden society, Taiwanese married women have to rely on their resources to resist the traditional

Table 3.5. Means and standard deviations for the Taiwan and China samples: by co-residence status

	Taiwan's sample			China's sample		
	Co-residing with husband's parent(s)	Co-residing with wife's parent(s)	Not co-residing with any parent	Co-residing with husband's parent(s)	Co-residing with wife's parent(s)	Not co-residing with any parent
Any child of age ≤3 (1 = yes)	0.24 (0.43)	0.20 (0.40)	0.20 (0.40)	0.14 (0.35)	0.11 (0.31)	0.10 (0.30)
Living in urban area (1 = yes)	0.26 (0.44)	0.34 (0.48)	0.33 (0.47)	0.17 (0.37)	0.26 (0.44)	0.28 (0.45)
Characteristics on husband's side						
Husband's education (in years)	11.44 (3.21)	10.95 (4.86)	11.77 (3.49)	8.86 (2.82)	9.58 (3.88)	9.09 (3.38)
Husband's income (in thousand local currency)	44.10 (44.98)	37.20 (25.54)	53.29 (184.14)	1.36 (3.24)	1.23 (1.06)	1.30 (2.25)
Only husband's father alive (1 = yes)	0.09 (0.28)	0.12 (0.33)	0.10 (0.30)	0.11 (0.31)	0.07 (0.25)	0.09 (0.28)
Only husband's mother alive (1 = yes)	0.36 (0.48)	0.37 (0.49)	0.32 (0.47)	0.35 (0.48)	0.26 (0.44)	0.31 (0.46)
Husband's father being professional or manager (1 = yes)	0.07 (0.26)	0.10 (0.30)	0.10 (0.29)	0.07 (0.26)	0.12 (0.33)	0.09 (0.28)
Husband father's education, junior high or above (1 = yes)	0.12 (0.33)	0.17 (0.38)	0.15 (0.36)	0.06 (0.24)	0.11 (0.31)	0.09 (0.28)
Husband's number of siblings	2.51 (2.27)	2.39 (2.53)	2.39 (2.36)	2.78 (1.89)	2.64 (1.64)	3.00 (1.80)
Characteristics on wife's side						
Wife's education (in years)	10.72 (3.55)	11.10 (4.22)	11.02 (3.66)	7.28 (3.84)	8.68 (3.73)	7.77 (4.10)
Wife's income (in thousand local currency)	16.94 (20.56)	27.22 (42.16)	21.39 (43.71)	0.72 (0.98)	1.04 (1.49)	0.77 (0.98)
Only wife's father alive (1 = yes)	0.09 (0.29)	0.12 (0.33)	0.10 (0.30)	0.10 (0.30)	0.14 (0.35)	0.09 (0.29)
Only wife's mother alive (1 = yes)	0.26 (0.44)	0.41 (0.50)	0.27 (0.44)	0.23 (0.42)	0.29 (0.46)	0.27 (0.45)

(Continued)

Table 3.5. (*Continued*)

	Taiwan's sample			China's sample		
	Co-residing with husband's parent(s)	Co-residing with wife's parent(s)	Not co-residing with any parent	Co-residing with husband's parent(s)	Co-residing with wife's parent(s)	Not co-residing with any parent
Wife's father being professional or manager (1 = yes)	0.05 (0.22)	0.12 (0.33)	0.08 (0.27)	0.04 (0.20)	0.07 (0.25)	0.07 (0.26)
Wife father's education, junior high or above (1 = yes)	0.13 (0.33)	0.29 (0.46)	0.15 (0.36)	0.07 (0.26)	0.08 (0.28)	0.08 (0.28)
Wife's number of siblings	2.73 (2.46)	1.83 (1.91)	2.44 (2.42)	3.00 (1.80)	2.12 (1.62)	2.98 (2.04)
Number of observations	571	41	1,526	428	73	1,361

Note: Standard deviations are in parentheses.

Table 3.6. Probit models for co-residence between couples and the husband's parent(s)

	Taiwan	China
Husband's education (in years)	−0.000	0.016
	(0.014)	(0.014)
Wife's education (in years)	−0.003	−0.010
	(0.013)	(0.012)
Husband's income (in thousand local currency)	−0.001	0.029*
	(0.001)	(0.017)
Wife's income (in thousand local currency)	−0.004**	−0.008
	(0.002)	(0.040)
Any child of age ≤3 (1 = yes)	0.350***	0.507***
	(0.086)	(0.121)
Only husband's father alive (1 = yes)	−0.083	0.348***
	(0.116)	(0.131)
Only husband's mother alive (1 = yes)	0.183**	0.294***
	(0.075)	(0.082)
Husband's father being professional or manager (1 = yes)	−0.148	0.132
	(0.127)	(0.142)
Husband father's education being junior high or above (1 = yes)	−0.102	−0.210
	(0.106)	(0.148)
Husband's number of siblings	0.010	−0.071***
	(0.014)	(0.021)
Living in urban area (1 = yes)	−0.258***	−0.587***
	(0.075)	(0.102)
Constant	−0.196	−0.407***
	(0.141)	(0.143)
Log-likelihood	−979.373	−806.973
Pseudo R-squared	0.032	0.052
Number of observations	1,532	1,372

Notes: Standard errors are in parentheses. *, **, and *** denote 13%, 10%, 5%, and 1% significance levels respectively.

The sample is confined to spouses with the husband's parent(s) alive.

practice of co-residence with the *husband's* parents. This is why we observe a negative coefficient associated with the wife's income. In China, on the other hand, there is no such barrier of tradition to be overcome by wives, and the husband's income plays the ordinary role of resources on co-residence decisions.

Secondly, the presence of children under age 3 turns out to be a contributing factor of co-residence. Thus, co-residence may be more than an upward manifestation of filial piety by children, but also a downward transfer of time by grandparents. We also note that the corresponding coefficient is especially large in China. According to Tsui (1989), a private babysitter would cost about 90 per cent of a young mother's salary in China. Couples with young children may choose to co-reside with their parents to alleviate the financial and/or physical burden of child care. This result echoes the findings of Pimentel and Liu (2004) but is not consistent with Logan et al. (1998: 873), who found that the existence of pre-school-age children had no impact on the likelihood of co-residence.

Thirdly, the widowhood of a parent affects the living arrangement between the surviving parent and the married son. Compared to the sample with both parents alive, the one with a widowed parent is more likely to opt for co-residence. Furthermore, the probability of co-residence is significantly higher for widowed mothers than widowed fathers in Taiwan, which is consistent with the findings of Logan and Bian (2004) and Ha et al. (2006), that widows are more dependent on their children for financial and emotional support than widowers. But in China the relative tendency for widowed fathers to co-reside with their sons is higher than that of widowed mothers.

Finally, the structure of the husband's sibship affects the probability of co-residence with the parents in China, but not in Taiwan. To further investigate whether the sibship sex composition makes a difference, we separated siblings into brothers and sisters, and reran the regression. It turns out that, for either Taiwan or China, the number of brothers has a significantly negative influence on the likelihood of co-residence, yet the number of sisters turns out to be insignificant. This may reflect the fact that daughters are more likely to establish their own families once they get married and leave the duty of parental support to their brothers.

As to co-residence with the wife's parents, different results prevail across the Taiwan Strait, as one can see from Table 3.7. In the scenario of Taiwan, the couple is more likely to co-reside with the wife's parents when (1) the husband's income/education is lower, (2) only the wife's mother is alive, (3) the wife's father has higher education, and (4) the wife has fewer siblings. The negative coefficient of the husband's income/education in Taiwan also suggests that men with fewer resources tend to acquiesce in co-residence with their parents-in-law. And the positive coefficient corresponding to the education of the wife's father indicates that the parental socio-economic status is also an important determinant for co-residence with the wife's parents. Since co-residence with the wife's parents is not a traditional practice in Taiwanese society, the above two findings suggest that the resources of the husband (the socio-economic status of wife's parents) have to be lower (higher) to induce the couple to adopt an uncommon practice of co-residing with the wife's parents. Nevertheless, wives' resources are not significant in this regression, suggesting a similar pattern to the husband's co-residence decision. Other than the minor difference in the effects of children aged under 3 and the wife's sibship

Table 3.7. Probit models for co-residence between couples and the wife's parent(s)

	Taiwan	China
Husband's education (in years)	−0.047*	0.007
	(0.025)	(0.023)
Wife's education (in years)	0.030	0.025
	(0.027)	(0.022)
Husband's income (in thousand local currency)	−0.006**	−0.025
	(0.003)	(0.043)
Wife's income (in thousand local currency)	0.001	0.063
	(0.001)	(0.063)
Any child of age ≤3 (1 = yes)	0.038	−0.061
	(0.186)	(0.195)
Only wife's father alive (1 = yes)	0.324	0.363*
	(0.231)	(0.187)
Only wife's mother alive (1 = yes)	0.365**	0.206
	(0.158)	(0.136)
Wife's father being professional or manager (1 = yes)	0.139	−0.097
	(0.238)	(0.240)
Wife father's education, junior high or above (1 = yes)	0.489***	−0.104
	(0.187)	(0.227)
Wife's number of siblings	−0.063*	−0.156***
	(0.033)	(0.039)
Living in urban area (1 = yes)	0.015	−0.241
	(0.159)	(0.158)
Constant	−1.635***	−1.518***
	(0.285)	(0.231)
Log-likelihood	−175.514	−325.675
Pseudo R-squared	0.071	0.042
Number of observations	1,532	1,492

Notes: Standard errors are in parentheses. *, **, and *** denote 13%, 10%, 5%, and 1% significance levels respectively.

The sample is confined to spouses with the wife's parent(s) alive.

size, all other results are symmetric to those for co-residence with the husband's parents in Table 3.6.

In China, we find from Table 3.7 that all coefficients except the number of siblings and the father's widowhood status are insignificant, indicating that the matrilocal co-residence practice in China is less relevant to the socio-economic characteristics.

Summarizing the evidence given above, we find that in China the husband's and the wife's resources only have trivial effects on the decision of co-residence, but in Taiwan the spouse with more economic resources is less likely to co-reside with his or her parents-in-law. The latter finding seems to be in sharp contrast with Wolf's (1985) conclusion we cited in Section 3.1, that Chinese families tend to be large whenever material conditions are better than miserable. If a Taiwanese husband owns more resources, our analysis suggests that he tends to resist co-residence with his wife's parents;

and if the wife owns more resources, she tends to resist co-residence with her husband's parents. The period Wolf observed was between 1906 and 1946, when individualism was not yet widespread and female labor participation was not prevalent. Our analysis shows that the situation in the twenty-first century seems to suggest a completely different story, a story more consistent with the prediction of Goode (1963).

Finally, note that in Tables 3.6 and 3.7, the coefficients associated with the number of the husband's siblings or the number of the wife's siblings are significantly larger for China than for Taiwan. Indeed, when most aged people in China have no pensions or savings to rely on, they really do not have options other than co-residing with their children. This explains the significant difference in the coefficients of these two places. It is worth noting that our result is in contrast with Pimentel and Liu (2004: 832), who found that a widowed mother or father had a lower likelihood of co-residence. Other than area differences, we have yet to come up with a plausible explanation for such conflicting findings.[4]

To account for the possible correlation between decisions for co-residence with the husband's parents and decisions for co-residence with the wife's parents, we estimate the two dependent variables jointly by a bivariate probit model, allowing the error terms of the two equations to be correlated. The estimates of the correlation coefficients are negative, which implies that the co-residence decisions should be considered jointly. The remaining results are qualitatively the same as those of the univariate probit models, and hence are not repeated here.

3.6. Conclusions

In this chapter we started out by providing a comprehensive review of the early scattered evidence with regard to co-residence and family size in Chinese societies. It is true that the subjective perception and objective practice in parents' co-residence with married children have been weakening with time.

Concerning the general pattern in the past few decades, we find that the scenario in China was much distorted. The regulations of household registration, food rationing, the one-child policy, and the low divorce rate all contributed to the change in observed family structure. Compared to China, the case of Taiwan reveals the gradual impact of the changing external environment on traditional perceptions. We concluded our discussion by presenting the results of probit models for both China and Taiwan.

Concerning co-residence with the wife's parents, the husband's income and the information regarding the wife's natal families are more important explanatory variables in Taiwan than in China. With regard to co-residence with the husband's parents, the wife's income is an important determinant in Taiwan, whereas the husband's income is only marginally significant in China. In summary, the husband's resources and the wife's resources are both important in the determination of the co-residence status, but the impacts are different between the husband-line and the wife-line, and also between Taiwan and China. While the husband's and the wife's resources are largely insignificant in China, a common pattern we observe in Taiwan is that the spouses endowed with more resources tend to avoid co-residing with their parents-in-law. Resources therefore play the role of a veto power in Taiwan, contrary to the prediction of Wolf (1985).

Notes

1. There are also other more refined definitions for family types, but we shall not go into details here.
2. To be coherent with the questions asked in other surveys, the results for the co-residence norm for the newly wed are not listed in Table 3.3.
3. Widowed mothers or fathers were in general older, which implied in turn that their children were likely to be older too. Since housing was more likely to be provided to senior (and hence older) adults, the older children were more likely to get their own housing and would not need to co-reside with their widowed parents.
4. Note that Pimentel and Liu presented the results for odds ratios, so that the impact is negative when the coefficient is less than one.

4

Family Fertility

Traditional analysis of family fertility has usually been separated into two strands, respectively focused on developed countries and on developing countries. For the former, the main concern is the tradeoff relationship between the quantity and quality of children, following the analysis of Becker and Lewis (1973). The dependent variable is usually the quality of children, often measured by their years of schooling, and the explanatory variables employed often include household income, the mother's employment status or wage, and an instrumental variable characterizing the quantity of children. For the latter, the quantity–quality tradeoff is less crucial to parental decisions, and more emphasis is put on the marginal gains of household production from an additional child's labor, due to the fact that child labor is more important in the developing countries. For references, see the two comprehensive survey chapters by Hotz et al. (1997) and Schultz (1997), respectively.

Of the two major Chinese societies we study, Taiwan, known for its rapid economic development, has now joined the ranks of developed countries. In contrast, at the threshold of the twenty-first century, most areas of China have just entered the initial stages of economic development. However, we shall argue below that other features in China and Taiwan may shift the usual focus of fertility analysis with respect to development stages.

There exist some issues which are relatively important in the West, but not so in Chinese societies. For instance, according to Lundberg and Pollak (2007: 5), 37 per cent of US births were out of wedlock in 2005. However, the statistic in Taiwan was much lower: 4.04 per cent in 2005 and 4.20 per cent in 2006.[1] We do not have much evidence about China, but we suspect that the figure is even smaller. Thus, we shall not put much effort into this line, although it is an important issue in Western families.

4.1. Some Features of Fertility in China and Taiwan

A common premise of the above-mentioned fertility analysis, both for developed and developing countries, is the degree of freedom in making fertility decisions. If most parents do not have such freedom of choice, then there is little point in conducting a choice-oriented analysis, which by definition stresses the systematic study of rational human decisions. Unfortunately, this seems to be the scenario of the fertility behavior in modern China. We shall give a more detailed explanation below.

4.1.1. *The Regulation Scenario in China*

In China, there were some family planning programs of limited scope in the periods 1956–8 and 1962–6. The first nation-wide fertility control policy went into effect during 1971–8, with the stated goal of "later-longer-fewer," meaning later marriage, longer child-birth spacing, and fewer children. In this period, peasant couples were still allowed to have up to three (later reduced to two) children. After Mao's death, the successive leaders were convinced that China's population had been growing far too fast, and the fertility rate needed to be further lowered to lessen the population burden and to improve the welfare of the country. Thus, effective from January 1979, China initiated its "one-child policy." The policy was soon modified for different areas and ethnic groups and, as we shall explain, later ramified into various fertility policy regimes. However, in cities and most densely populated areas of the country, the one-child doctrine was still the norm. Due to the Communists' authoritarian control, the enforcement of family planning programs has proved to be much more effective than in more democratic countries.

It may not be well known to some scholars that it is a *constitutional duty* for Chinese individuals to carry out family planning (Article 49 of the 1982 constitution). Similar provisions can also be found in the Family Law. Evidently, the constitution and other legal regulations give the Chinese government ample authority and support for the implementation of fertility-control programs. Furthermore, China has been known for its authoritarian family planning in the past several decades. As Greenhalgh (1994: 7) put it, childbearing in China is something decided by the state, not by the couple, and in the interest of the society as a whole, not for the utility of parents. Under the pressure of neighborhood committees, couples often have to exercise birth control even if they do not want to.

The most frequently cited evidence of such authoritarian control is the method used for birth control. According to Thornton and Lin (1994: 298), in Taiwan the percentage of IUD (intrauterine device) usage among all available contraceptive methods in the 1980s was about 50 per cent, but it was roughly 70–80 per cent in China according to Greenhalgh (1994: 14). The reason for the prevalence of IUDs was that their insertion and removal usually required surgery, which was difficult and risky for women to do by themselves but more reliable and amenable to government regulations. In contrast, the percentage of women taking the oral pill in China was extremely low, because its usage was hard for the neighborhood committees to control and monitor. The percentage of sterilization in the same period was high, roughly 18–23 per cent for China and 27 per cent for Taiwan, respectively. However, sterilization in Taiwan was mostly, if not all, voluntary, whereas in China it was often a result of "persuasion" by neighborhood committees. Moreover, sterilization was usually targeted at the "greedy" parents who had already had a certain number of children or a "satisfactory" composition of children (say a boy and a girl, or two boys).

The flexibility of the one-child policy varies across the regions of China. In general, the policy is more loosely implemented in places with less urbanization or higher concentrations of ethnic minorities. Guo et al. (2003) separated China into four areas by the levels of their "policy fertility rate," which was defined as the weighted average of the total fertility rates. The lowest fertility rates were observed in big cities such as Beijing, Tianjin, Shanghai, with policy fertility rates as low as 1.0–1.3 in 1990. The highest policy fertility rate was observed in Tibet, Inner Mongolia, Xinjiang, and several other places in southwest China. The policy fertility rate in these places was higher than 2.0. The policy fertility rates in the two remaining areas, mostly in the middle part of China, fell somewhere in between. In terms of population size, the area with the lowest policy fertility rates accounted for 44 per cent of the total population, the highest among the four areas. And the area with the highest policy fertility rates only accounted for 5 per cent of the nation's population. The national average policy fertility rate summarized by Guo et al. (2003) was 1.465. The gross reproduction rates (GRR) and the net reproduction rates (NRR) for China and Taiwan of selected years are listed in Table 4.1.[2]

4.1.2. *Interactions between Regulation and Social Norm*

The one-child policy and birth control in China did encounter resistance, particularly in rural areas. The one-child program was originally mandatory, but soon evolved into one that called for "cooperation" from couples. According to Zeng (1989), even in the 1980s, rural couples whose first child was a girl were allowed a second birth. The economic prosperity in the 1980s made possible the financial independence of many people, which undercut the "persuasive power" of neighborhood committees and the effectiveness of family planning economic incentives and disincentives. In rural areas, resistance to the one-child policy was especially strong, perhaps because the tradition of male-line lineage preservation was stronger there. In her field survey, Greenhalgh (1994) documented claims by many women that they got pregnant again because their IUDs had "fallen out." Although there were cases of forced abortion, it was not a prevalent practice. Generally the couple in question would be allowed to negotiate with the village cadres and eventually reach an agreement compatible with the community norm. Because the norms varied across areas and the attitudes of cadres were also diverse, the average fertility rates were different from place to place. For our PSFD respondents that resided in the southeastern coastal provinces, their resistance to the one-child policy was probably weaker than in the less developed areas in China due to the differences in outlook and economic conditions, and as a result they tended to have a lower fertility rate.

Other than the direct influence of community norms and cadre attitudes, the changes of related policies and environment also caused significant

Table 4.1. GRR and NRR (number of births) for China and Taiwan

Year	China		Taiwan	
	GRR	NRR	GRR	NRR
1953	2.96	1.84	3.15	2.73
1958	2.65	1.78	2.94	2.67
1963	2.72	2.10	2.59	2.40
1968	2.88	2.43	2.09	1.97
1973	2.31	2.04	1.55	1.49
1978	1.58	1.44	1.31	1.26
1983	1.21	1.11	1.04	1.01
1988	1.17	1.12	0.89	0.86
1993	0.91	0.84	0.84	0.83
1998	0.71	0.80	0.70	0.69
2003	0.66	n.a.	0.59	0.58

Sources: For China, China Population Statistics Yearbook, National Bureau of Statistics, China; China Statistical Yearbook, National Bureau of Statistics, China; Demographic Yearbook, United Nations; World Population Prospects, 2002 revision, United Nations; Demographic Yearbook, Historical supplement, United Nations. For Taiwan, Department of Statistics, Ministry of Interior, Taiwan.

variations in individual fertility. For instance, the age of marriage had been strictly regulated in certain periods. In our previous discussion we mentioned the later-longer-fewer policy during 1971–8, which was accompanied by the increase of the average marriage age from 20 to 23. After 1980, the relaxation of the marriage age regulation caused a marriage boom. Because China had very few out-of-wedlock births, the regulation on the age of marriage had a significant impact on overall fertility. According to Coale (1989), during 1950–81, the reduction in births due to the changes in the marriage age regulation was estimated to be 104 million, roughly 12 per cent of the total births in the same period.

Furthermore, China has experienced serious upheavals in periods such as the War of Resistance against Japanese Aggression (1938–45), the civil war between the Communists and the KMT (1946–9), the Great Leap Forward with the ensuing famine (1958–62), and the Cultural Revolution (1966–76). All these historical events have constituted severe checks on fertility.

From the above discussion we saw that in the past three decades, parental fertility "choices" in China were extremely constrained, if not completely frozen, by factors such as the degree of urbanization, the extent of one-child policy implementation, the minority ethnicity of a spouse, toughness of the neighborhood committee cadres, and the local norm of household composition. In contrast, popular variables in Western countries such as household income and female wage played a relatively minor role in determining family fertility in China. Since the freedom to choose fertility is limited for families in China, it is certainly hard to analyze family fertility empirically following the Western literature. Because each person's sensitivity to pressure exerted by external factors was different, the frequent changes in regulations and the environment also made it difficult to hold other things equal for the life cycle of a representative individual in China. This further complicates the life cycle modeling of fertility decisions.

4.1.3. *The Voluntary Scenario in Taiwan*

The fertility scenario in Taiwan, however, was quite different. In 1965, an extensive family planning program in Taiwan was introduced by the Taiwan Provincial Institute of Family Planning. The Institute sent out full-time (mostly female) workers to visit eligible women and to offer birth-control-related information and services. The contraceptive devices and advice were offered by qualified physicians free of charge or at a low cost. Contraceptive knowledge was also disseminated through postal mailings, schools, factories, hospitals, and the mass media.

Taiwan's achievement in family planning was extraordinary, especially when one recognizes the fact that the adoption of contraceptive measures by individuals in Taiwan was completely voluntary. Thornton and Lin (1994: 298) pointed out that the proportion of married women aged 20–44 who adopted a program-supplied contraceptive rose from 4 per cent in 1965 to 59 per cent in 1988, indeed a remarkable advance. The GRR and NRR statistics for Taiwan are summarized in Table 4.1.

In summary, given the above-mentioned policy intervention within China and the fact that such interventions have been deeply intertwined with regional, ethnic, political and socio-economic factors, it is very difficult to construct an empirical model to analyze the determination of Chinese family fertility in the past three decades. It is even more difficult to pool together the data of Taiwan and China in the empirical models for a systematic comparison of fertility behaviors across the Strait. In the following two sections, we shall follow Thornton and Lin (1994) and use statistics retrieved from the existing studies and the PSFD data to explore some facets of the fertility-related variables, both for China and for Taiwan. We expect to identify some variables correlated with parents' fertility in both China and Taiwan.

4.2. Comparisons between China and Taiwan

Despite the differences in economic and political structure between Taiwan and China, we try to identify several dimensions that are worthy of comparison in the following subsections. These statistics are to some extent independent of the regime restrictions we just mentioned.

4.2.1. *The Age of Marriage*

The marriage age certainly affects fertility, since earlier marriage means younger mothers; Coale's (1989) evidence showed that the impact was particularly large in China.

From the Taiwan and China PSFD data sets, we compute female respondents' average age at marriage and present the results in Table 4.2. To analyze any possible connection between women's marriage age and their socio-economic background, the figures in Table 4.2 are listed by women's education, urbanization of residence, and year of marriage. For simplicity, women's education was divided into "low" and "high" education levels, and place of residence was categorized into urban and rural areas.

Table 4.2. Average marriage age of females, China and Taiwan (in years)

Wife's education/urbanization			Year of marriage				
			1955–64	1965–74	1975–84	1985–94	1995–2004
High	Urban	China	21.42(31)	24.13(89)	26.09(332)	26.12(259)	25.56(115)
		Taiwan	21.40(77)	22.93(85)	25.00(164)	26.85(73)	27.60(82)
	Rural	China	20.63(8)	22.00(38)	22.85(165)	23.03(278)	24.50(150)
		Taiwan	20.36(148)	21.88(100)	23.81(220)	26.25(80)	27.61(118)
	Average	China	21.26(39)	23.50(127)	25.01(497)	24.52(537)	24.96(265)
		Taiwan	20.72(225)	22.36(185)	24.32(384)	26.54(153)	27.61(200)
Low	Urban	China	19.86(36)	22.02(43)	24.21(52)	25.35(20)	23.00(10)
		Taiwan	21.09(34)	21.85(156)	24.14(88)	24.54(103)	24.86(59)
	Rural	China	19.44(131)	20.63(269)	23.01(353)	22.76(204)	26.20(50)
		Taiwan	20.50(149)	21.17(381)	22.49(380)	24.08(378)	25.11(177)
	Average	China	19.53(167)	20.82(312)	23.16(405)	23.00(224)	25.67(60)
		Taiwan	20.61(183)	21.36(537)	22.80(468)	24.18(481)	25.06(236)

Notes: Numbers in parentheses are sample size. For Taiwan: Urban areas include the seven biggest cities. The sample is classified as low-education if education is less than elementary school in 1955–64; less than junior high school in 1965–74; less than senior high school in 1975–84; less than college in 1985–94 and 1995–2004. For China: Urban areas include big, medium, and small cities. Those who have elementary education or less are classified as low-education; complementary sample are in the other group.

Source: Year 2004 PSFD surveys.

Due to the gap in average education between China and Taiwan, we categorize education levels differently in these two areas. In China, those who have elementary education or below are classified as "low" education, and the others belong to the "high-education" group. In Taiwan, due to the rapid raise in average education, we choose not to stick to one fixed educational criterion across time, in order to avoid too few sample sizes in certain categories. We therefore separate the female sample into two roughly equal halves by the education level for each time interval. As to the urbanization of residence, the two biggest cities and the five provincial cities in Taiwan were classified as urban areas. The urban areas in China included big, medium, and small cities, which were distinguished according to the respondents' subjective judgement.

We can see from Table 4.2 that the average age for first marriage increased steadily in Taiwan in the past fifty years both in rural and urban areas. We also find that women with higher education tend to marry later than those with lower education. Holding the education levels equal, we see that, for most periods, the age of marriage was higher for the urban samples than for the rural samples. The above findings seem to be consistent with the conventional wisdom.

The findings for China are similar: the marriage age for females with higher education in the past few decades was higher than that for those with lower education, except that the pattern was reversed in the 1995–2004 period, probably due to the small sample size. For the high-education group, the rural–urban disparity in marriage age was in general more significant than that found in Taiwan. Leaving aside the case with a very small sample size (1995–2004 period in China), we see that the regional differences in marriage age may be as high as three years in China, whereas the largest difference in Taiwan was only 1.7 years. Concerning the changes with time, the average age of marriage in China had a significant jump during 1975–84 as compared to 1965–74, which is in line with the relaxation of marriage age regulation in the 1980s.

4.2.2. The Practice of Contraception

For the analysis of fertility control, one interesting variable is the percentage of married women who had ever practiced contraception. In the case of Taiwan, Freedman et al. (1994: 281) showed that these numbers, in the five time periods between 1965 and 1985, were 28 per cent, 56 per cent, 76 per cent, 82 per cent, and 90 per cent. These percentages clearly indicate the gradual spread of contraception knowledge in Taiwan. The percentage doubled from 1965 to 1970, showing an amazing achievement of Taiwan's family planning program. For further analysis, one can even study how such percentages changed across groups with distinct education backgrounds, child compositions, urbanization of residence, etc., as Thornton and Lin (1994) did.

The corresponding proportions for contraception usage in China, however, are hard to find and also less meaningful, partly because family planning in China was basically a mandatory program. Aside from rural and ethnic minority couples who have been granted exemptions, essentially every fertile woman has to adopt some kind of contraception. It would be unlikely to find a significant number of married women who have not yet practiced any birth control in China since the government policy of family planning was imposed.

The comparison across the Strait would be more meaningful with respect to the *methods* of contraception. We retrieve the statistics summarized by Freedman et al. (1994: 293) and Lin et al. (2002) about Taiwan and list the percentages of various contraception methods in Table 4.3. The table shows that the number of IUD users decreased steadily during 1967–98, whereas the proportion adopting sterilization increased significantly, a phenomenon consistent with most Western countries. We also note that in Taiwan the percentage of married couples taking oral pills or using condoms exceeded 20 per cent during 1980s and even attained 40 per cent in 1998. These two contraceptive methods are basically voluntary in nature and their usage is kept private.

Contrary to the findings of Taiwan, Greenhalgh (1994) pointed out that the IUD and sterilization practice in China accounted for the vast majority of contraceptive methods, but the practice of more voluntary methods such as pills and condoms was less than 10 per cent (1994: 15). Intuitively,

Table 4.3. Proportion using contraceptive methods, Taiwan (%)

Method	1967	1973	1976	1980	1985	1992	1998
IUD	57	50	44	32	25	27	25
Pill	8	10	11	9	7	5	4
Sterilization	17	16	18	25	33	34	24
Condom	5	6	6	12	18	24	37
Other	13	17	21	22	18	10	10

Note: For comparison, Greenhalgh (1994: 15) pointed out that pills and condoms account for roughly less than 10% in China.

Source: Thornton and Lin (1994), and Lin et al. (2002).

pills and condoms are not recommended by Chinese policy implementers because they cannot be monitored easily. Since all the IUD usage and 90 per cent of the sterilization practice are applied to women only, Greenhalgh criticized this phenomenon observed in China as particularly offensive to women.

4.2.3. Preferences for Having at Least One Son

Because of the mandatory nature of family planning in China, the fertility decisions of most Chinese couples were constrained in the past thirty years. Since most couples cannot have more than one child, it is somewhat difficult to obtain accurate answers from interviewees concerning what their *ideal* number and gender composition of children would be, if they were allowed to choose. However, it is a widely recognized fact that the traditional concept of lineage preservation has kept challenging the one-child policy, and has helped lead to its later modification in China. It is therefore interesting to compare how parents' perception of male-line lineage preservation changed through time, between China (which had mandatory family planning) and Taiwan (which had a voluntary program). In Table 4.4, we use the PSFD data to calculate the percentage of female respondents who agree that the traditional concept of male-line lineage preservation is important. The figures in the table are presented by the degree of urbanization of residence, education level, and the birth year of the women.

The pattern in Taiwan revealed by Table 4.4 is very clear: (1) those who had higher education had a weaker tendency to have the traditional concept of male-line lineage preservation; (2) given the same birth cohort and education level, women who lived in urban areas tended to have a weaker traditional concept; and (3) this traditional concept exhibited an evident declining trend, in both rural and urban areas. However, for less-educated women living in rural areas, the percentage remained high (around 50 per cent) even for the very young cohort.

In Table 4.4, roughly the same kind of pattern prevails in China, but there are still some delicate differences between Taiwan and China. First, the declining trend beginning in 1941 was not as drastic as in Taiwan, mainly because the initial values in early years in China were already very low. This might be due to the fact that the gender-equality doctrine was enunciated from the establishment of the Communist Party. Secondly, leaving aside the cells with small observations, the percentages did not change much for rural women born after 1941, whatever their education level. However, the

Table 4.4. Proportion agreeing with the concept of "having at least 1 boy for lineage preservation," China and Taiwan (%)

Wife's education/urbanization			Wife's birth year				
			1934–40	1941–50	1951–60	1961–70	1971–9
High	Urban	China	25.58 (31)	17.45 (149)	16.76 (370)	20.00 (190)	13.22 (121)
		Taiwan	70.13 (77)	43.81 (105)	34.83 (201)	36.29 (124)	31.94 (72)
	Rural	China	16.67 (6)	28.95 (38)	29.37 (126)	33.87 (310)	26.90 (171)
		Taiwan	58.87 (124)	42.20 (109)	38.31 (261)	43.86 (114)	34.38 (128)
	Total	China	21.62 (37)	19.79 (187)	19.96 (496)	28.60 (500)	21.23 (292)
		Taiwan	63.18 (201)	42.99 (214)	36.80 (462)	39.92 (121)	33.50 (200)
Low	Urban	China	39.13 (23)	34.85 (66)	15.91 (44)	16.67 (24)	36.36 (11)
		Taiwan	64.29 (42)	58.47 (183)	57.53 (146)	33.06 (121)	41.54 (65)
	Rural	China	47.76 (67)	48.76 (283)	41.41 (396)	48.39 (248)	53.85 (65)
		Taiwan	69.29 (140)	62.58 (489)	54.65 (538)	49.00 (449)	52.36 (191)
	Total	China	45.56 (90)	46.13 (349)	38.86 (440)	45.59 (272)	51.32 (76)
		Taiwan	68.13 (182)	61.46 (672)	55.26 (684)	45.61 (570)	49.61 (256)
Total		China	38.58 (127)	36.94 (536)	28.85 (936)	34.59 (772)	27.45 (368)
		Taiwan	65.54 (383)	57.00 (886)	47.82 (1,146)	43.94 (808)	42.54 (456)

Notes: The same as Table 4.2.

percentages for urban high-education groups showed a significant decline. This profile suggests that the concept of male-line lineage preservation might be affected by the external socio-economic conditions. Third, there seemed to be an evident resurgence of the traditional concepts for the high-education women during the 1960s; the change in percentage was quite significant, and we could not explain the phenomenon thoroughly.[3] Finally, by comparing the figures of Taiwan and China, it is difficult to conclude whether a mandatory family planning program or a voluntary one could more effectively change the traditional concept in people's minds; the changing pattern was more evident in Taiwan, whereas the eventual percentage of the traditional perception of male-line lineage was lower in China.

4.2.4. The Sex Ratio of Newborns

Another well-known measure related to gender attitude is the male–female ratio of newborn babies. For the time being we assume away infanticide, of which the official statistics are hard to obtain. Given the technology of ultrasound detection, it is more convenient nowadays to have abortion after the gender of the baby is detected. Chu and Yu (1998) argued that when the ultrasound technology was not prevalent, the societal male–female sex ratio of newborns was actually inversely related to the son preference of the society. This is so because women who have implicit characteristics (such as vaginal acidity) that predispose them to bearing girls tend to generate the "all-girl" outcome. If son preferences in the society are strong, these mothers often feel compelled to try more births. This in turn tends to generate more female newborns, because of their predisposition to bearing girls. Thus, a society with stronger son preferences usually winds up with a higher ratio of girl newborns.

When ultrasound detection is prevalent, however, the correlation would be reversed. Parents with strong sex preferences simply abort unwanted fetuses after the gender is confirmed. In China, as one can imagine, this happens mostly for girl detections. The male–female ratios of newborns in Taiwan and China provided by World Population Prospects are listed in Table 4.5. When the statistics of newborns are not available, we use the ratios of age 0–4 as proxies. As one can see from this table, the male–female ratio of newborns in China became significantly higher than Taiwan after 1980, perhaps due to the implementation of the one-child policy. Under the one-child policy, couples who bear a girl would have a stronger

Table 4.5. Male–female newborn ratios

Year	Taiwan	China
1955	—	1.0423
1960	—	1.0446
1965	—	1.0576
1970	1.0646	1.0591
1975	1.0610	1.0597
1980	1.0624	1.0666
1985	1.0623	1.0785
1990	1.1030	1.1074
1995	1.0799	1.1168
2000	1.0971	1.1139
2005	1.0904	1.1145

Source: China's data is from World Population Prospects, United Nations; Taiwan's data is from the Directorate General of Budget, Accounting and Statistics (DGBAS), Taiwan.

motivation to resort to abortion. As the ultrasound technology became financially affordable, the boy–girl ratio became higher, as shown in the rising figures after 1990. Ebenstein (2007) recently conducted a thorough analysis of the costs and benefits for parents in China in opting for an ultrasound detection and resorting to abortion if a girl pregnancy is detected.

4.3. Fertility Size and Birth Duration

4.3.1. *Fertility and Population Growth Rate*

In Table 4.6, we use data from various sources to calculate the GRR (gross reproduction rates), NRR (net reproduction rates), and age-specific fertility rates for China and Taiwan. The GRR is the average number of daughters each woman would have if she lives through the childbearing age subject to the prevailing age-specific birth rates. NRR is the GRR adjusted by the age-specific mortality rates. When mortality rates decline, the gap between GRR and NRR decreases.

From Table 4.6, one can find several facts about China. First, the gap between GRR and NRR was large in early years, and even in 1983 the difference was nearly 10 per cent. This means that mortality rates in China began to decline significantly only recently. Second, both GRR and

Table 4.6. Demographic statistics for China and Taiwan

		Gross reproduction rate (number of births)	Net reproduction rate (number of births)	Age-specific fertility rate						
				15–19	20–4	25–9	30–4	35–9	40–4	45–9
1953	China	2.96	1.84	94	278	280	n.a.	n.a.	n.a.	n.a.
	Taiwan	3.15	2.73	48	265	336	292	218	108	27
1958	China	2.65	1.78	72	260	269	241	n.a.	n.a.	n.a.
	Taiwan	2.94	2.67	43	248	336	281	199	90	14
1963	China	2.72	2.10	72	345	371	321	258	n.a.	n.a.
	Taiwan	2.59	2.40	52	252	337	231	139	60	10
1968	China	2.88	2.43	46	301	344	277	196	98	12
	Taiwan	2.09	1.97	41	256	309	161	68	26	4
1973	China	2.31	2.04	27	220	270	193	126	57	8
	Taiwan	1.55	1.49	33	203	250	105	37	12	2
1978	China	1.58	1.44	11	153	218	98	44	21	5
	Taiwan	1.31	1.26	36	194	213	73	20	5	1
1983	China	1.21	1.11	17	188	180	56	19	8	1
	Taiwan	1.04	1.01	26	154	174	62	13	2	0
1988	China	1.17	1.12	20	221	171	67	18	6	1
	Taiwan	0.89	0.86	16	111	164	64	13	2	0
1993	China	0.91	0.84	8	149	116	39	10	4	1
	Taiwan	0.84	0.83	17	91	149	75	18	2	0
1998	China	0.71	0.80	3	127	119	38	9	2	1
	Taiwan	0.70	0.69	14	66	116	73	21	3	0
2003	China	0.66	n.a.	5	123	102	38	9	2	1
	Taiwan	0.59	0.58	11	52	92	68	20	3	0

Source: For China, China Population Statistics Yearbook and China Statistical Yearbook, National Bureau of Statistics, China; Demographic Yearbook and World Population Prospects, United Nations. For Taiwan, Ministry of Interior, Taiwan.

NRR began to drop significantly after 1968, indicating the effect of China's fertility control policy. Third, the age-specific fertility rates of all ages started to decline after 1963; the only exception was in the 20–4 age group between 1978 and 1988. This may be due to the relaxation of marriage age regulation we mentioned earlier. Fourth, the fertility rate after age 35 dropped significantly after 1963, and became negligible in the 1990s. In fact, since 1990 most women finish their childbearing before they reach age 30; this is partly attributable to China's one-child policy.

In Table 4.6, we also provide the same statistics for Taiwan. As one can see, Taiwan's reproduction rates (GRR and NRR) started to decline as early as 1953. But there was a significant drop from 1963 to 1968, roughly coinciding with Taiwan's introduction of its family planning program. If we compare the figures of Taiwan and China, we find that the decrease in reproduction rates was about the same across the Taiwan Strait despite the significant distinction between mandatory and voluntary family planning programs. A major difference between Taiwan and China is that the fertility rates of the young women (20–4) in Taiwan began to drop as early as 1968, and women aged 25–34 became the main contributors to fertility in 2003, whereas in China the main cohort giving birth was females aged 20–9. The fertility rates of women aged 30–4 in Taiwan started to rise after 1983, but the same trend does not exist in China. In 2003, there was a significant proportion of women who gave birth in their late thirties in Taiwan. Again, that was not the case in China.

4.3.2. The Duration from Marriage to the First Birth

The average durations from marriage to first birth, for both China and Taiwan, are calculated by the PSFD data sets and listed in Table 4.7. Since highly educated women who tended to have better job market opportunities were more likely to delay their fertility, the first-birth durations were different for mothers with different education levels. Furthermore, since Davis (1955) and Freedman et al. (1982) argued that co-residing parents might push young couples to give birth earlier (so that the former can have a grandchild earlier), we also separate durations according to the co-residence status right after marriage.

In Table 4.7, we find several interesting facts for the sample of Taiwan. First, the groups with higher education tended to have longer first-birth duration except for the group of older women (married between 1955 and 1964). This pattern is especially prominent for the young cohort (born during 1995–2004); the difference in first-birth duration between the

Table 4.7. Average years from marriage to the first birth, China and Taiwan

			Year at first marriage				
Wife's education/co-residence status			1955–64	1965–74	1975–84	1985–94	1995–2004
High ed.	Co-residing with parents	China	3.222(18)	3.117(81)	2.196(319)	1.807(424)	1.711(246)
		Taiwan	1.700(10)	1.530(33)	1.731(169)	1.945(229)	1.556(160)
	Not co-residing with parents	China	2.791(34)	3.089(73)	2.182(261)	2.062(267)	2.071(140)
		Taiwan	2.500(7)	2.061(57)	2.051(187)	2.051(227)	1.883(128)
	Average	China	2.943(52)	3.104(154)	2.188(580)	1.905(691)	1.842(386)
		Taiwan	2.029(17)	1.867(90)	1.899(356)	1.998(456)	1.701(288)
Low ed.	Co-residing with parents	China	3.682(165)	2.446(351)	2.155(455)	1.734(367)	1.790(100)
		Taiwan	2.212(243)	1.485(322)	1.455(243)	1.669(83)	1.286(28)
	Not co-residing with parents	China	2.924(66)	2.388(116)	2.170(180)	1.595(116)	1.741(29)
		Taiwan	2.006(79)	1.942(208)	1.652(178)	1.864(55)	1.200(10)
	Average	China	3.465(231)	2.432(467)	2.160(637)	1.701(483)	1.779(129)
		Taiwan	2.162(322)	1.664(530)	1.538(421)	1.746(138)	1.263(38)

Notes: Education classification is the same as Table 4.2. Average years from marriage to the first birth are computed as: [the year of the first birth] – [the year of marriage] + [0.5]. 0.5 is added because some couples marry and have their first birth the same year.

high- and low-education groups is six months. In China, we also find the same pattern except that the difference in duration between education groups was not as large as Taiwan in recent years. But a larger between-education-group duration difference (eight months) prevails for couples married during 1965–74. This might be due to the fact that the later-longer-fewer policy implemented in the early 1970s was more effective on urban residents, who tended to be more educated.

The second phenomenon in Taiwan worth mentioning is that women co-residing with parents or parents-in-law tended to have a shorter first-birth duration for most sub-samples, except for an early marriage (1955–64, low-education) group and the group married during 1995–2004. However, the relationship between birth duration and co-residence is not so apparent for the sample of China. The relationship only begins to reveal itself in China for the highly educated couples married during 1985–2004, but we cannot infer much from these simple statistics.

After the demographic transition, it might be true that the total number of children is not important for most families; rather, the sequential decision regarding whether to have another child is more interesting. The first-birth duration analyzed above was one example of such analysis; in the literature there were some studies concerning the birth duration of subsequent births. In Section 4.5 we shall study the duration between consecutive births.

4.4. The Quantity–Quality Tradeoff

Perhaps the best-known contribution by Gary Becker on family fertility is his theory of quantity–quality tradeoff. Along with the improvement of hygienic conditions, child mortality has declined significantly in the past two hundred years. The availability of modern contraceptive methods also allows parents to control the number of births. These two facts combined together have made fertility an effective decision for parents in most developed countries. The demand theory of children (Becker 1991: Chapter 5) suggests that parents would choose both the number and the quality of children as they maximize their utility. For instance, due to budget constraint, a couple may not be able to support too many children's college expenses. As a compromise, they may decide to bear fewer children and provide more educational resources for each child, instead of having many children and providing less education. The quantity–quality tradeoff indeed reveals this kind of calculation in the parents' mind.

To examine this tradeoff hypothesis, researchers often set up the following regression for the ith observation (see for instance Conley and Glauber 2006, and Ginther and Pollak 2004):

$$y_i = \alpha + \beta n_i + \gamma X_i + \varepsilon_i, \tag{4.1}$$

where y is the child quality, usually measured by the education achievement of the child, n is the number of siblings of the child, X is a vector of other explanatory variables, and ε is an error term. The quantity–quality tradeoff relationship is expected to be captured by the coefficient β: if β is significantly negative, then it suggests that there is indeed a tradeoff between the sibship size and education achievement. Because China has implemented the one-child policy for nearly thirty years, our quantity–quality tradeoff hypothesis in this section refers to the interaction among the PSFD survey respondents and their siblings rather than to that among their own children.

A typical problem with the estimation of (4.1) is that, since the quantity (n) and the quality (y) are both determined by parents, there may be some correlation between n and ε. For instance, if couples care very much about the education achievement (quality) of their children, they would be more sensitive to the budget constraint they face and be careful not to let their education resources be diluted by too many children. As such, other things being equal, one tends to observe both high child education and low fertility for this type of parents, indicating a negative correlation between n and ε. As is well known, this will make the ordinary least squares (OLS) estimator of β in (4.1) biased and inconsistent (Greene 2003: 75). The problem caused by the correlation between n and ε is also called the endogeneity problem, since it is related to the endogenous nature of the explanatory variable. Evidently, we cannot make much interpretation based on a biased or inconsistent estimate.

One simple way to deal with the above-mentioned endogeneity problem is to introduce an instrumental variable (IV) for n (see Hotz et al. 1997: 326). Specifically, we try to find a variable, say, Z, which is correlated with n but uncorrelated with ε. In the literature there are two popular solutions for the endogeneity problem of quantity–quality relationship: one is the appearance of twins and the other is the gender composition of the first few births. Here we adopt the second approach because information concerning twins is not available. The idea is the following: because Chinese usually exhibit strong son preferences, if a couple have all girls in their first few births, then it is likely that they will bear more and eventually achieve a larger family size. Thus, the gender composition of the first few births will be correlated with the sibship size. But since the gender of birth itself is a random outcome, it will not be correlated with the error term ε.

In our regression below, we follow Conley and Glauber (2006) and Ginther and Pollak (2004) and control the background variables of the respondent. They include the child's parental education and family background when she or he was aged 16. We also control the child's birth cohort so as to capture the differential educational opportunities among cohorts. Finally, we add the ethnicity dummies for Taiwan and area dummies for China in case families with different backgrounds may have different attitudes for child education. Such variables are mostly self-explanatory, and hence we shall skip their detailed definition here.

Concerning the regression model for child education, the main estimator we are interested in is the coefficient of n, the effect of sibship size on child education. In the regression, n (sibship size) is defined to be the number of children including the respondent. In our IV analysis, we adopt two sets of IVs. First, we include all samples in our regression and use the gender of the first-born as IV. The corresponding IV is a dummy variable, which equals 1 if the first-born is a girl, and 0 otherwise. In the second part analysis, we restrict the sample to families with sibship size greater than or equal to 2 and retrieve the information from the first two children to construct our IVs. In this case, the corresponding IVs contain two dummy variables indicating whether the first-born is a girl and whether the first two children are both girls. Given the prevalence of son preferences in Chinese societies, these are reasonable instrumental variables for sibship size since couples who failed to have a son in their first few births are more likely to make more trials in order to maintain their male-line lineage. The correlation coefficients also verify the positive connection between the sibship size and our gender-composition IVs; details are not specified here.

Our IV estimation results for Taiwan are summarized in Table 4.8, and those for China are summarized in Table 4.9. To save space, the first-stage regression results are not presented and only the results for the second-stage regression will be discussed. In Tables 4.8 and 4.9, we see that later-born cohorts and children with better-educated parents usually have higher education. These are consistent with our intuition and are also compatible with previous literature. New migrants in both China and Taiwan have higher education than second- or later-generation migrants. For instance, Mainlanders and Hakka in Taiwan arrived in the island later than Fukienese, and tend to be better educated. In China, children with a father of non-local origin also tend to be better educated. Our focus here is

Table 4.8. Sibship size on years of schooling, Taiwan

	All sample		Sibship size ≥2	
	OLS	IV	OLS	IV
Sibship size	−0.050*	0.985	−0.056**	−0.061
	(0.026)	(0.773)	(0.027)	(0.264)
Birth year dummies (<1946 as reference group)				
Birth year 1946–55	2.482***	2.559***	2.493***	2.492***
	(0.143)	(0.180)	(0.144)	(0.150)
Birth year 1956–65	3.984***	4.968***	3.998***	3.993***
	(0.160)	(0.759)	(0.162)	(0.318)
Birth year >1965	4.809***	6.707***	4.807***	4.798***
	(0.170)	(1.431)	(0.172)	(0.537)
Male (1 = yes)	1.392***	1.662***	1.390***	1.389***
	(0.102)	(0.235)	(0.102)	(0.118)
Father's years of school	0.265***	0.289***	0.263***	0.263***
	(0.017)	(0.028)	(0.018)	(0.018)
Mother's years of school	0.159***	0.218***	0.160***	0.160***
	(0.019)	(0.049)	(0.019)	(0.025)
Father's ethnicity dummies (aborigine as ref. group)				
Fukienese	1.417***	1.747***	1.428***	1.427***
	(0.374)	(0.510)	(0.374)	(0.381)
Hakka	2.211***	2.126***	2.190***	2.191***
	(0.399)	(0.480)	(0.399)	(0.401)
Mainlander	2.189***	3.243***	2.173***	2.168***
	(0.417)	(0.931)	(0.418)	(0.486)
Family background when the respondent aged 16				
Father being professional or manager (1 = yes)	0.540***	0.510**	0.532**	0.532**
	(0.194)	(0.232)	(0.195)	(0.195)
Father worked for gov't or public enterprise (1 = yes)	0.482***	0.642***	0.480***	0.479***
	(0.159)	(0.225)	(0.160)	(0.165)
Mother being working (1 = yes)	0.482***	0.165	0.489***	0.490***
	(0.103)	(0.267)	(0.104)	(0.135)
Living in urban area (1 = yes)	0.790***	0.961***	0.771***	0.771***
	(0.157)	(0.226)	(0.158)	(0.161)
Constant	2.703***	−4.118	2.733***	2.765
	(0.419)	(5.115)	(0.423)	(1.791)
R-squared	0.55	0.36	0.55	0.55
Number of observations	3,690	3,690	3,643	3,643

Notes: Standard errors are in parentheses. *, **, and *** denote 10%, 5%, and 1% significance levels respectively.

not to explain why this is so, although we would hazard a preliminary guess that it may be related to the tough environment new immigrants have to face. First-generation immigrants usually do not have much in terms of real estate or physical assets, and hence the only way they can help endow their children is through human capital investment.

Table 4.9. Sibship size on years of schooling, China

	All sample		Sibship size ≥ 2	
	OLS	IV	OLS	IV
Sibship size	−0.050*	0.258	−0.104***	0.471*
	(0.028)	(0.309)	(0.031)	(0.258)
Birth year dummies (<1946 as reference group)				
Birth year 1946–55	0.083	−0.104		−0.147
	(0.177)	(0.259)	0.039	(0.211)
Birth year 1956–65	1.596***	1.443***	1.568***	1.470***
	(0.174)	(0.233)	(0.183)	(0.195)
Birth year >1965	1.812***	1.894***	1.764***	2.060***
	(0.179)	(0.199)	(0.190)	(0.238)
Male (1 = yes)	1.359***	1.429***	1.379***	1.467***
	(0.101)	(0.124)	(0.104)	(0.115)
Father's years of school	0.191***	0.185***	0.183***	0.179***
	(0.017)	(0.018)	(0.017)	(0.018)
Mother's years of school	0.151***	0.174***	0.149***	0.186***
	(0.019)	(0.029)	(0.019)	(0.026)
Father's birthplace dummies (others as ref. group)				
Shanghai	−0.364*	−0.362*	−0.439*	−0.372
	(0.213)	(0.216)	(0.224)	(0.236)
Zeijiang	−0.502***	−0.500**	−0.559***	−0.478**
	(0.180)	(0.183)	(0.190)	(0.201)
Fujiang	−1.195***	−1.420***	−1.203***	−1.505***
	(0.183)	(0.291)	(0.191)	(0.241)
Family background when the respondent aged 16				
Father being professional or manager (1 = yes)	0.691***	0.724***	0.670***	0.716***
	(0.218)	(0.223)	(0.226)	(0.237)
Father worked for gov't or public enterprise (1 = yes)	1.121***	1.157***	1.168***	1.241***
	(0.164)	(0.170)	(0.169)	(0.179)
Mother being working (1 = yes)	0.354**	0.305*	0.445***	0.374**
	(0.146)	(0.156)	(0.149)	(0.159)
Living in urban area (1 = yes)	1.648***	1.691***	1.571***	1.620***
	(0.164)	(0.172)	(0.169)	(0.178)
Constant	5.214***	4.044***	5.571***	3.061**
	(0.251)	(1.193)	(0.276)	(1.154)
R-squared	0.35	0.33	0.34	0.28
Number of observations	4,131	4,131	3,849	3,849

Notes: Standard errors in parentheses. *, **, and *** denote 10%, 5%, and 1% significance levels respectively.

As one can see from Tables 4.8 and 4.9, the coefficients of sibship size in the OLS models are all negatively significant for both China and Taiwan, seemingly indicating a quantity–quality tradeoff. However, when the IV method is applied, the coefficients of sibship size become insignificant in Taiwan and even become *positive* in China, a result also found in some cases cited by Angrist et al. (2006). Since most of our adult respondents in China were impoverished during their juvenile period, the positive sibship coefficient found in China is in fact consistent with the interpretation given by Mueller (1984). Mueller argued (pp. 135–6) that children in a poor economy were sometimes helpers of household production and income. These household production activities may help ease the parents' budget constraint, and hence the relationship among siblings may not be a competing one. Thus, the quantity–quality tradeoff theory *à la* Becker might not hold in China, especially for the respondents' generation.

On the other hand, most Taiwanese respondents grew up in relatively well-off families, in which the quantity–quality tradeoff might be more relevant. However, when the endogeneity issue is taken into account, the *conditional* effect of sibship size becomes insignificant in Taiwan. If the quantity–quality tradeoff is more likely to prevail in developed countries, Table 4.8 seems to suggest that Taiwanese families in the period 1950–90 (which is roughly the period when the respondents were of school age) were not rich enough to verify the quantity–quality tradeoff hypothesis. The story revealed in Tables 4.8–4.9 seems to be consistent with the fertility theories for different stages of development.

Note that the analysis above only discusses the conditional overall effect of sibship size on child education. Detailed analysis concerning the unconditional impact of more refined sibling structure on child education will be discussed later in Chapter 8. The possibility that some families treat their daughters as helpers for family income will also be considered therein.

4.5. Factors Affecting Birth Durations in Taiwan

In this section we study the factors that influence the couple's birth duration, with special emphasis on the couple's status of co-residence with their parents. We also investigate the impact of the traditional conception of son preferences on women's fertility behavior. Since the interviewed cohort (born in 1935–76) in China's PSFD survey is subject to the one-child policy starting in 1979, the analysis on durations of the second and the third birth intervals is not meaningful in the context of China. Therefore, we exclude the respondents of China from our sample and focus on the case of Taiwan in the following analysis.

In order to analyze the dynamic features of sequential fertility decisions, we adopt the standard hazard regression approach and study the duration of consecutive births. Our empirical analysis also improves upon earlier studies by adopting a more accurate measure of co-residence and a better indicator of son preferences. To avoid tedious introduction to our technical model, we shall skip most of the econometric analysis, and only present the results. Details can be found in Tsay and Chu (2005).

In the PSFD questionnaire, we ask the interviewee how much she or he agrees with the perception that each family should have at least one son in order to sustain lineal succession. The answers are chosen from the 5-point scaled items. The son preference dummy (SP) variable equals 1 if the item chosen is at least 3, and zero otherwise. Other than the above subjective measure, we also consider whether the respondent's family has had all girls in previous births. Specifically, for $j = 1, 2$, $F_j = 1$ if the previous j births of the family in question are all girls; $F_j = 0$ otherwise. If parents have SP $\times$ $F_j =$ 1, which implies that they have the *subjective* desire of sustaining the lineage line as well as the *objective* evidence of failing in the past, then they are more likely to try more births, conditional on their previous j births. We believe that SP $\times$ F_j is a better measure for son preference with respect to fertility behavior than the ones used in past studies. For the duration between marriage and the first birth, since F_0 equals zero for all couples, SP $\times$ F_0 cannot be used to measure son preference. We include the working status (WS) dummy of the woman at marriage to characterize her opportunity cost of having a birth right after marriage.

To construct a more precise measure for the co-residence status before each successive birth, for $j = 1, 2$, we let CO_j be a dummy variable which equals 1 if the couple co-resides with the male's senior parents after the birth of their jth child, whereas CO_0 indicates the co-residence status at the time of the couple's marriage. Thus, if CO_j has a significant influence on the birth duration of the $j + 1$ birth, then we can firmly say that it is the *present* co-residence pressure, instead of the *previous* co-residence experience, that affects the couple's fertility decision.

Our analysis finds the following results: First, the duration of the first birth is shorter for women who married late, showing that these women tend to have births early, and more-educated females tend to have longer durations for all births. These findings are consistent with most previous literature. Second, we find that co-residence does indeed have a significant impact on shortening the spacing of the first two births, but its impact on the second-to-third birth duration declines sharply. Intuitively, co-residing parents may push the couple to have births sooner, because the former either want to assure the maintenance of the family line or are eager to have fun with their grandchildren. However, when one or two children have already been born, the infants begin to absorb the senior parents' time and energy, and by then it is unlikely that the senior parents would still exert pressure on the couple to have more children. Even if such pressure is sustained, the wife may have a strong excuse to resist it, for she has been obedient to their wishes for at least the two previous births. Third, the purely subjective preference for sons or the purely objective fact of having the first-born being a girl *alone* is not strong enough to expedite the wife's next birth, and only the $SP \times F_2$ variable preserves a significant influence. This suggests that the subjective desire for sons intertwined with the objective fact of having no son in their previous two births does force a wife to expedite her third birth.

4.6. Conclusions

This chapter studies the various aspects of fertility behavior in China and Taiwan. It is well known that China exercised authoritarian control under the Communist regime for most of the period of our study, and the mandatory family planning programs such as the well-known one-child policy have constrained severely the fertility decisions of most parents. Under this circumstance, it is hard for a typical regression model to capture the true behavioral pattern of family fertilities for younger generations. We therefore presented some comparisons between China and Taiwan through tabulation. We study the age of marriage, contraceptive practices, first-birth duration, fertility rates, sex ratio of newborns, and son preferences, sometimes cross-tabulated by rural–urban locations, women's cohorts, and women's education. It turned out that in terms of the age of marriage, the preferences for sons, and differences in fertility between rural and urban areas, the time-trend patterns in Taiwan and China are qualitatively the same. However, there are divergences between China and Taiwan in contraception practices and the duration from marriage to the first birth. Some of these differences do reveal the distinction between mandatory and voluntary fertility control schemes.

We then applied the standard quantity–quality tradeoff approach to both China and Taiwan. It turned out that for the respondents' generation, the OLS regression indicates a negative impact of sibship size on child education, but after adopting the instrumental-variable method, this negative effect disappears in Taiwan and even becomes a positive one in China. These seemingly contradictory findings are in fact consistent with the prevalent fertility theories for different stages of economic development.

Finally, we concentrate on the case of Taiwan and use the PSFD data to analyze the duration of consecutive births. In particular, we analyze how the birth durations are affected by the co-residence status with parents and the son preferences of the couple. We find that co-residing parents would shorten the first and second birth durations, but not the consecutive ones, and that parents would speed up the next birth only if they have both the subjective son preferences and the objective fact of having no son in previous births.

Notes

1. The figures are from the Department of Statistics, Ministry of Interior Affairs of Taiwan.
2. In theory, NRR should never be larger than GRR due to the mortality adjustment. However, this was not the case for some numbers in Table 4.1. The main reason is that we collect GRR and NRR from different sources, and it is hard to verify which data source is more accurate.
3. One explanation may be the following: Only after the implementation of the one-child policy (which affected mostly women born after 1960) did people having only one girl begin to realize that bearing one boy was such a desirable thing. Before the one-child policy, their at-least-one-boy desire was never suppressed and its importance was never realized.

5

Marriage Patterns

In traditional Chinese society, as we suggest in Chapter 1, lineage preservation is a main objective to family members, who are just instruments to achieve this objective. Evidently, lineage continuation hinges upon marriage and fertility; therefore marriage itself also plays an important role in the accomplishment of lineage preservation. This chapter will discuss marriage patterns in China and Taiwan.

5.1. Conception and Tradition

As Fan and Huang (1998: 229) pointed out, marriage in a Chinese society serves five functions: (1) to continue the family line, (2) to increase the family labor (the wife being a new worker joining the family), (3) to extend the social network (by tying together the families of the bride and groom), (4) to provide old-age security, and (5) to facilitate the transfer of some economic resources (through brideprice or dowry). Note that none of the above involves any individual concerns or spousal decisions. Given that marriage was considered a means of lineage continuation in historical China, it was predominantly arranged and facilitated by the parents of the bride and groom. Furthermore, since one purpose of marriage is to form a strong social network, it is likely to be an assortative one, with the bride and groom usually from families of comparable class, wealth, socio-economic status, etc. The implications of assortative mating will be further discussed as we proceed.

On the one hand, if parents found a potential ideal match for their child, they might want to clinch the marriage early, to avoid possible disturbances or uncertainties in the future, and also to extend the family's social network earlier. This led to the custom of child betrothal. On the other hand, when a child was not expected to help the family wealth in the foreseeable future, this child, usually a girl, might be "sold off," probably as child labor or a betrothed child bride. There were of course cases where the family backgrounds of the groom and bride did not match well. In such cases, brideprice or dowry could serve as compensation for the background mismatch. In general, brideprice and dowry could also play the role of signaling, of showing off the economic power of the groom's or bride's family. Finally, since limited information was usually available about the potential bride or groom and his or her family, the professional matchmaker filled the gap by providing information, arranging meetings between the families, negotiating the brideprice and dowry, and clinching the final details. These were the practices of marriage in traditional China.[1]

Because traditional Chinese society was dominated by males, lineage preservation by definition implied male-line preservation. With such a legitimate excuse, polygamy and concubinage were practiced in traditional Chinese families, as long the husband could afford it. This tradition was prevalent even in the early twentieth century in Chinese communities in Singapore (Freedman 1970) and Taiwan (Saso 1999).

The above discussion provides a rough linkage between the marriage practices in traditional China and the functions of marriage mentioned by Fan and Huang (1998). As one can see, the key concept behind marriage was the interest of the lineage instead of the individuals involved. This is also why Engle (1984) argued that marriages in traditional China were not individual contracts but family contracts.

5.2. Changes in Marriage Customs and Restrictions

On both sides of the Taiwan Strait, many marriage-related phenomena have changed in the past fifty years. The patterns of change were, however, quite different between Taiwan and China. We shall discuss them one by one next, and highlight the corresponding implications for empirical studies.

In 1948, the Communist Party led by Mao took power in China. Two years later, the Marriage Law was promulgated. Under this new 1950 law, the old customs of polygamy, concubinage, professional matchmaking, and child betrothal were all prohibited. The legitimate age of marriage was 18 for women and 20 for men. Any pecuniary transfers in connection with marriage, such as brideprice and dowry, were also banned.[2] The ideology behind the prohibition of polygamy and concubinage was of course gender equality. The regulation on marriage age imposed an additional restraint on child betrothal. The Marriage Law also emphasized the individual decision aspect of a marriage, recognizing that adults could decide for themselves whether and with whom to marry.

In the 1980 revision of the Marriage Law, there were two major changes. One is the imposition of the joint obligation of the husband and the wife to implement family planning (clause 12). Another change was in the age of marriage. Despite the regulation in the 1950 Marriage Law that the minimum marriage age was 18 for women and 20 for men, according to Coale (1989), most marriage applications in the 1970s were denied if the woman was younger than 23 (25) in rural (urban) areas. The 1980 Marriage Law incorporated this *de facto* marriage age into the law to facilitate marriage (and hence fertility) control measures.

Concomitant with the change of the Marriage Law, the Chinese government under the Maoist doctrine encouraged women to join the labor market. It was believed that a good way to liberate women was to increase their participation in the labor force (Fan and Huang 1998: 230). According to Bauer (1992), China then was the country with the highest female labor force participation rate in the world. Empowered by their own labor income, women were financially more independent, and, at least hypothetically, more likely to make truly independent decisions in marriage.

Despite the fact that all the above changes were institutionalized by law, and that the Chinese government was known for its authoritarian control in the years before 1990, Chinese culture was not as easy to change as one might think. In fact, rigid regulations could easily be circumvented by superficial obedience, and the appearance of compliance often belied the reality. For instance, Tien (1983) showed by retrospective survey data that the marriage age for females should have increased to 22.8 (24.6) in the rural (city) area by 1970, but the officially recorded ages were close to 20, and this actually facilitated the amendment of the marriage age to 20 in 1980. The difference between the officially recorded age and the age inferred by the data was a result of either fake reporting by individuals, or concealment by officials. Furthermore, Wolf (1984: 227) described that all interviewees in her field study, when asked how they had met their husbands, assiduously avoided the answer "arranged by parents," for that was prohibited by the Marriage Law. But Wolf often got different answers from rural interviewees, who were usually more candid. All this evidence illustrates that the quality of marriage-related data was questionable, and the statistics from some early research were doubtful.[3]

It was relatively easy for civilians to deliberately misstate their age of marriage. But given the rigid household registration system and food rationing in the 1950s and 1960s, polygamy and concubinage were difficult to sustain. The poor performance of the economy between 1949 and 1980 also rendered the practice of brideprice and dowry impractical, with most people struggling to make ends meet. A remaining question is: has the custom of brideprice and dowry vanished after decades of privation and the prohibition by the Marriage Law? According to Zhang (2000), it did not turn out to be the case. The data from northern Chinese villages showed that during the period from 1984 to 1993, as the economy of China gradually improved, the practice of dowry and brideprice was actually revived. The dowry or brideprice was not only a compensation for mismatches, as we mentioned above, but also a matter of "face" for the couple's families. According to Zhang (2000: 62), some parents even had to borrow money to cater for a sizeable wedding banquet. And brideprice and dowry were sometimes necessary support from parents to finance the expenses of the new couple.

As far as empirical analysis is concerned, the practices in China also restrict the scope of our analysis. A meaningful analysis of marriage decisions is predicated upon the assumption that people can search around, find their ideal marriage partners, and then make the relevant choice. This in turn is meaningful only if there is a large enough geographical area in which the search for a marriage prospect can be conducted. Fan and Huang (1998: 230) noted that most rural Chinese in the 1980s found a marriage partner within 25 kilometers of their home. This implies that the marriage matching in China was geographically constrained, and this limitation may further restrain the degree of social mobility. In general, given the widespread poverty and strict regulations in China, the context of most marriage decisions in the relevant period had very limited economic implications. This difficulty should be borne in mind when we study assortative mating in China.

Another factor affecting the search for a mate has recently manifested itself in China: the emerging imbalance in sex ratios. Because the mindset of male-line dominance has not changed, the spread of ultrasound technique has motivated more couples to use it to detect the fetus gender so that they could abort an unwanted baby during the early stages of pregnancy, which is allowed under the one-child policy. As a result, Ebenstein (2007: Table 1) estimated that, for individuals aged 0–18, there was an 8.37 per cent deficit of females relative to males in 2000, whereas the same measure was 2.80 per cent in Taiwan and –0.78 per cent in the USA. This certainly affects the efficiency of marriage matching in China.

In a comparison of Taiwan and China, one observes some similarities and some differences. The traditional practice of polygamy has been prohibited by law in Taiwan as well. In addition, Taiwan's economy has been growing at a stable pace in the past fifty years, and its income and wealth have increased steadily; this experience matches well with the observation of China in the last three decades in the southeast coastal area of China. In general, the absence of authoritarian control and the better economic conditions in Taiwan have contributed to more flexible and more independent marital decisions.

The traditional customs of matchmaking, brideprice, and dowry have never been banned in Taiwan, but they have evolved with the changing times. Matchmaking as a search mechanism is an option available to individuals. But as the society became more open, as we shall see, more and more adults in Taiwan chose their partners on their own, and arranged marriage was no longer a common practice. Brideprice and dowry are still popular among traditional-minded families; but since few marriages are now arranged by parents or matchmakers, their role as price signal has faded. Rather, brideprice and dowry are now more like parental subsidies to the newlywed couple. Below we shall use both descriptive statistics and regression analysis to investigate the marriage practices of Taiwan and China. The data of Taiwan are from the first-wave PSFD surveys conducted in 1999, 2000, and 2003 respectively. And the counterpart of China is from the 2004 survey. In the following analysis, the married couples refer to the respondent and his or her spouse in the survey data.

5.3. Descriptive Trend Analysis

5.3.1. Who Makes the Marriage Decision

The Chinese tradition of marriage arranged by parents (or indirectly through matchmakers) instead of by the potential bride and groom themselves has certainly changed gradually as time goes on. The trends in Taiwan and China can be seen from Table 5.1, where we list the decision-making patterns across different years of marriage. As one can see from this table, the traditional type of marriage in Taiwan, arranged by relatives or family members, declined from 39.12 per cent for marriages occurring before 1970, to 6.44 per cent for marriages occurring after 1990. The "modern" type of marriage, in which the couple have met either in schools or in the workplace, increased significantly, from 12.44 per cent to

Table 5.1. The ways the couples met: by year of marriage (%)

Channels	Taiwan: year of marriage				China: year of marriage			
	≤1970	1971–80	1981–90	>1990	≤1970	1971–80	1981–90	>1990
Got acquainted in school	0.56	3.45	6.21	11.41	2.10	1.07	2.68	3.84
Got acquainted in workplace	11.88	20.58	24.69	30.74	12.45	14.06	16.27	17.98
Introduced by relatives or friends	31.73	34.59	40.68	37.18	28.95	31.33	32.80	32.12
Arranged marriage								
Arranged by relatives or friends	27.91	18.46	10.40	5.23	6.01	5.58	4.62	3.33
Arranged by family members	11.21	8.01	2.17	1.21	8.39	6.87	5.56	4.04
Arranged by matchmakers	—	—	—	—	36.64	34.01	29.85	24.75
Others	16.70	14.91	15.84	14.23	5.45	7.08	8.23	13.94
Total	100.00	100.00	100.00	100.00	100.00	100.00	100.00	100.00
Number of observations	892	899	644	745	715	932	1,494	990

Notes: The items in the questionnaire are slightly different between Taiwan and China. The "arranged by matchmaker" item is not available in the Taiwan questionnaire, because it was rarely heard of in the past several decades.

42.15 per cent in the same period. However, one also notes that there was always a significant proportion of couples who were introduced to each other by relatives and friends. Although such first encounters might not be as formal as an "arranged meeting with marriage in mind," relatives and friends, interested in the future development of the relationship, might exert some pressure on the new acquaintances.

Trends in China exhibited similarities to as well as differences from those in Taiwan. Compared to the case of Taiwan, the proportion of respondents in China who reported having met their spouse on their own showed a relatively mild increase, from 14.55 per cent for respondents married before 1970, to 21.82 per cent for those married after 1990. The proportion of respondents reporting that their marriages were arranged by relatives or family members, on the other hand, declined from 14.40 per cent to 7.37 per cent, which is similar to the pattern in Taiwan. Nevertheless, it is surprising to find that there was still a large proportion of marriages arranged by matchmakers in China: the percentage declined only mildly in the span of twenty years, from 36.64 per cent for marriages before 1970 to 24.75 per cent for marriages after 1990.

Another feature of marriage decisions in China is the regional differences. Since China had significant rural–urban disparities, Riley (1994) identified the difference in marriage decisions among six areas of China, which were categorized by the degree of urbanization. We follow a similar approach and use the PSFD data to make the comparison. It turns out that in China the proportion of marriages decided by the couple themselves (who met in schools or at the workplace, or were introduced by relatives and friends) was significantly higher in urban (59.81 per cent) than in rural areas (39.41 per cent).[4] This shows that traditional arranged marriages fade away at a slower pace in rural China. This rural–urban distinction has an intuitive explanation: compared to individuals residing in rural area, urban dwellers were more likely to have better educational and work opportunities, and consequently were more likely to meet marriage prospects in schools or at the workplace. In addition, urban residents tended to enjoy greater financial independence and had more freedom in their choice of spouses.

5.3.2. Changes in the Age of Marriage

Age of marriage is one of the important aspects of marriage-related characteristics. Zhang (2000) summarized the mean age of marriage for some village populations in northern China, and found a clear inverted-U pattern of marriage age during the period 1959–90+, both for men and for women. This trend matched well with the amendment of the minimum age of marriage prescribed by the Marriage Law and the related regulations we described in Section 5.2. However, Zhang did not report the original values of average age of marriage, and hence we do not know the exact numbers behind his U-shaped figure.

Thornton and Lin (1994) showed that the change in marriage age in Taiwan is similar to the trend in Western countries, where the age of marriage has increased steadily in the past few decades. They provided some statistics up to 1989. Concerning the correlation between education and marital status, it is usually expected that the higher the level of education, the higher the probability of being married. However, Yang et al. (2004) found that this positive correlation applies only partly to Taiwan: for men older than 30, the probability of remaining single is low irrespective of education levels; but the probability for a woman older than 30 to remain single was very high for the highly educated. This indicates that there is still a conceptual barrier against "marrying highly educated women" in Taiwan. Details can be found in their paper, and will not be repeated here.

In Table 5.2, we use the PSFD data to calculate the average age of marriage by education level and year of marriage. As one can see from Table 5.2, except for the inverted-U pattern observed for couples married during 1955–94 in China, the age of marriage showed an increasing trend in both China and Taiwan, and for both the low- and high-educated respondents. The marriage age is higher in Taiwan than in China, and higher for the high-education group than for the low-education group. Since the marriage age increases with economic development and job opportunities, we expect the gap in marriage age between Taiwan and China to shrink, if the economy of the latter gradually catches up with the former.

Table 5.2. Average age of marriage (in years)

		Year of marriage				
		1955–64	1965–74	1975–84	1985–94	1995–04
Taiwan	High-ed.	20.72	22.36	24.32	26.54	27.61
	Low-ed.	20.61	21.36	22.80	24.31	25.06
China	High-ed.	21.26	23.50	25.01	24.32	24.96
	Low-ed.	19.53	20.82	23.16	23.00	23.67

Note: There was a change in the legal minimum age of marriage in 1980 in China.

5.4. Theories of Assortative Mating

There is a growing body of evidence showing that "likes tend to match with likes," indicating the phenomenon of assortative mating (Dalmia and Lawrence 2001). The characteristics of potential spouses emphasized in past literature include education, age, ethnicity, and other socio-demographic variables. To establish meaningful empirical implications for assortative mating for the above-mentioned characteristics, one needs some theoretical hypotheses. Below we briefly introduce two of them.

The search theory of marriage considers a dynamic scenario, where single individuals continuously meet potential partners, and married individuals continuously face the random events of marriage breakup. The theoretical framework is like the job market, with the unemployed paralleling the singles, the employed paralleling individuals with spouses, and layoffs paralleling marriage break-ups. Each unemployed person may find a job at any time, just as each single may find a marriage partner at each moment. Similarly, an employee may be fired at any moment, just as a marriage may break up at any moment. It is usually assumed that at any point of time, a single individual faces a chance of contact governed by a probability distribution. The person whom they meet has characteristics drawn randomly from a societal pool. An individual weighs the pros and cons of remaining single or marrying with the one they meet. If the pros outweigh the cons in the latter case, then they get married; otherwise the search goes on. Once they marry, at each time instant there is another given probability that they may end the marriage and become single again.

Treating marriage as a dynamic game described above, one can derive the optimal search strategy which instructs the individual whether or not to marry a person with certain characteristics.[5] Koopmans and Beckmann (1957) showed that as long as the friction of search is not very high, i.e., the rate of encounter is high enough and the discount rate is low (people being impatient), then the optimal searching rule implies *positive assortative mating*, that is, likes tend to match with likes.

An alternative theory of marriage matching views marriage as an assignment game, where each man is "assigned" to a woman according to a certain rule. Each man and woman is endowed with a vector of characteristics, including age, ethnicity, income, education, etc. The equilibrium of an assignment game is to find an assignment rule such that, under this rule, no two persons can form a new marriage in which they jointly produce an output more than compensating the sum of their individual returns originally.

Similar to the search theory, Becker's theory of marriage also predicted assortative mating, although his prediction derives from a particular assumption, that individual characteristics are *complementary*. However, if the individual features are substitutive in production, Becker's theory would predict negative assortative matching. For instance, a man with job market achievement may match well with a woman specialized in housework, because these two features are substitutive. Another implicit assumption behind the assignment-game theory of marriage is *conditional transferable utility*. Given this assumption, it is the *total* output of a couple that matters; how this total product is to be divided between the couple does not affect the equilibrium of the assignment game.

5.5. Empirical Analysis of Marriage Matching

In summary, both the theory of search and the theory of assignment game need some assumptions to establish the prediction of positive assortative mating. Furthermore, neither theory provides an implication that can be tested against the other one. Thus, in most empirical studies, a statistical model is proposed to see whether there is assortative matching, rather than testing whether the matching practice is supported by the dynamic search theory or the assignment-game theory. In this section we proceed to discuss the empirical evidence, leaving the reader to choose his or her preferred theory to interpret the result.

There have been several papers focusing on assortative mating in Taiwan. Yi and Hsung (1994), Tsai (1994), Wong and Lu (1999), and Yang et al. (2004) have analyzed Taiwan's assortative marriage patterns. They found that there has been assortative mating based on education, age at marriage, ethnicity, and income. According to Yang et al., there has always been a practice of men marrying women younger than themselves; the proportion of couples with equal ages or women older than men, although increasing slightly from the 1970s to the year 2000, has never exceeded 9 per cent. The same pattern of "male superiority" also applied to education in the past. And again, cases in which women's education equalled or surpassed that of the men have increased gradually, which is consistent with the more equalized education opportunities in Taiwan. However, Yang et al. (2004) also found that, in terms of education levels, the "female superiority" pattern never prevailed for women who attained the graduate school level. For women who possessed master's or PhD degrees, Yang et al. found that only a small proportion of them would marry men with lower education levels. This suggests that men in Taiwan are more or less unwilling to marry women who are very highly educated. Or, to put it another way, the very highly educated women in Taiwan would hesitate to marry men with lower education. As to the case of China, to our knowledge the only rigorous analysis was provided by Raymo and Xie (2000). Their main purpose, however, was to rebut an earlier argument in the literature, that there was an inverted-U relationship between economic development and educational homogamy.

In this section we shall use the PSFD data to analyze assortative mating in China and Taiwan. For the case of Taiwan, we focus on three variables: age, education, and ethnicity. For the case in China, we study age, education, and "social class." More details will be provided as we proceed.

5.5.1. Empirical Formulation

We shall apply the model of Choo and Siow (2006a), which was a model adapted from Qian (1998). The refinement made by Choo and Siow was mainly to take into account the population remaining single. Choo and Siow explained that this consideration is necessary when the utility from marriage matching of a type-i man and a type-j woman is dependent on the number of persons remaining single in these two groups.

Our regression is derived from the expression in Choo and Siow (2006b: 467). Let μ_{ij} be the number of marriages between a type-i man and a type-j women, μ_{i0} (μ_{0j}) denotes the number of type-i men (type-j women) who remain single, and m_i (f_i) refers to the total number of males (females) of type i (j). Following the setup of Choo and Siow (2006a, 2006b), the marriage matching function is written as

$$\log\left|\frac{\mu_{ij}}{\sqrt{\mu_{i0}\mu_{0j}}}\right| = \log\left|\frac{\mu_{ij}}{\sqrt{m_i - \sum_k \mu_{ik}} \cdot \sqrt{f_j - \sum_l \mu_{lj}}}\right| \equiv \pi_{ij}. \qquad (5.1)$$

Choo and Siow show that the left-hand side of (5.1), $\mu_{ij}/\sqrt{\mu_{i0}\mu_{0j}}$, is the ratio of the number of (i, j) marriages to the geometric average of those types who are unmarried. Its log value could be interpreted as the total systematic gains to marriage per partner for any (i, j) pair relative to the total systematic gains per partner from remaining unmarried. In our later empirical analysis, we slightly transform (5.1) to forms adopted by most demographers, and then estimate the transformed equations to analyze assortative mating in education and other characteristics.

5.5.2. *Assortative Mating for Age at Marriage*

It is observed almost universally that men usually marry women a couple of years younger (Bergstrom and Bagnoli 1993). Empirically, this can be analyzed and tested using formula (5.1), as suggested by Choo and Siow (2006a). However, if we want to analyze the changes of age homogamy through time, we would need several waves of survey data to differentiate *cohorts* from *periods*, as was done in Mare (1991). Unfortunately, neither PSFD nor other survey data in China have long enough panels, and hence cohorts and periods could not be distinguished following the approach of Mare. Of course we can use a sequence of census or cross-sectional data sets to do such analysis, but to make our analyses compatible with other chapters, we decide to use our PSFD data and adopt a different approach.

In order to differentiate the cohort and period effects, we separate our samples into four groups according to the year of marriage of our respondents, for both China and Taiwan. For each year-of-marriage group, we cross-tabulate the couples by the age at marriage of husband and wife, with the age at marriage classified into five categories for both the husband and the wife. The results for Taiwan and China are respectively listed in Tables 5.3a and 5.3b, in which each matrix contains 25 (5 × 5) combinations of husband's and wife's marriage age. From these tabulations, one can easily see the pattern and trend of assortative mating across different marriage age groups.

Since the numbers in Tables 5.3a and 5.3b are self-explanatory, we will simply summarize the results as follows. (1) The average age of marriage in Taiwan is older than that in China. For instance, for marriages taking place after 1990, the proportion of Taiwanese women married after 28 is 31.05 per cent, whereas in China it is only 12.15 per cent. For men, the proportion married after 28 in Taiwan is 60.91 per cent, and the proportion in China is only 26.10 per cent. (2) There is an obvious age asymmetry in both China and Taiwan, with the husband's age older than or equal to the wife's. In the eight matrices in these two tables, the sum of percentages in the upper-right triangle (cases with wives being older than husbands) is never larger than 5.25 per cent. (3) Men are more likely to marry women of the same age range, or of the age category one tier younger; in addition, marriages crossing two or more age ranges happen with very low probability. This reveals an evident *crossing* barrier referred to by Mare (1991). (4) For a woman younger than 25, marrying a man from the next higher age category is more likely than marrying a man in the same age range. But for women aged 25 or older, marrying someone in the same age range is almost always the dominant pattern, for both China and Taiwan, and for any time

Table 5.3a. Husband's and wife's age at marriage by year of marriage, Taiwan (%)

Year of marriage/ husband's age at marriage	Wife's age at marriage					
	≤ 20	21–4	25–8	29–32	>32	Total
Year of marriage ≤ 1970						
≤ 20	4.59	1.79	0.22	0.11	0.56	7.27
21–4	9.84	17.90	0.56	0.00	0.34	28.64
25–8	7.16	23.83	7.16	0.00	0.22	38.37
29–32	2.80	7.16	4.70	0.22	0.11	14.99
>32	3.58	4.03	1.90	0.22	1.01	10.74
Total	27.96	54.70	14.54	0.56	2.24	100.00 (894)
Year of marriage 1971–80						
≤ 20	1.22	1.00	0.11	0.00	0.00	2.32
21–4	4.98	11.62	1.66	0.00	0.33	18.58
25–8	5.09	25.77	15.82	0.55	0.88	48.12
29–32	1.66	8.85	8.08	1.55	0.22	20.35
>32	1.44	1.88	3.10	2.21	1.99	10.62
Total	14.38	49.12	28.76	4.31	3.43	100.00 (904)
Year of marriage 1981–90						
≤ 20	1.70	0.00	0.00	0.00	0.00	1.70
21–4	2.47	6.80	1.08	0.00	0.00	10.36
25–8	1.70	24.57	18.55	0.77	0.00	45.60
29–32	1.24	6.49	13.60	6.49	0.46	28.28
>32	0.00	0.93	3.86	6.03	3.25	14.06
Total	7.11	38.79	37.09	13.29	3.71	100.00 (647)
Year of marriage > 1990						
≤ 20	0.13	0.40	0.00	0.00	0.00	0.54
21–4	1.47	3.61	1.07	0.13	0.00	6.29
25–8	1.07	12.32	16.73	1.61	0.54	32.26
29–32	0.67	4.95	15.13	9.10	0.80	30.66
>32	0.40	3.35	7.63	7.63	11.24	30.25
Total	3.75	24.63	40.56	18.47	12.58	100.00 (747)

Note: Numbers of observations are in parentheses.

period. The above findings can be easily seen from the diagonal, lower and upper triangular parts of the matrices in Tables 5.3a and 5.3b.

5.5.3. *Assortative Mating for Education*

To further analyze the effects of education assortment, we transform equation (5.1) into a log-linear form following the approach of Qian (1998).[6] For the number of marriages between type-i men and type-j women, the basic log-linear model is as follows.

Table 5.3b. Husband's and wife's age at marriage by year of marriage, China (%)

Year of marriage/ husband's age at marriage	Wife's age at marriage					
	≤ 20	21–4	25–8	29–32	>32	Total
Year of marriage ≤ 1970						
≤20	10.60	2.23	0.56	0.00	0.42	13.81
21–4	27.89	11.85	0.84	0.00	0.56	41.14
25–8	12.55	14.50	5.02	0.42	0.56	33.05
29–32	3.91	2.93	2.37	0.42	0.00	9.62
>32	0.84	0.56	0.56	0.42	0.00	2.37
Total	55.79	32.08	9.34	1.26	1.53	100.00
						(717)
Year of marriage 1971–80						
≤20	4.13	0.53	0.42	0.11	0.21	5.40
21–4	11.96	13.54	2.22	0.11	0.42	28.25
25–8	6.35	21.48	15.77	0.42	0.32	44.34
29–32	0.63	4.34	8.25	3.39	0.53	17.14
>32	0.21	0.95	2.12	1.38	0.21	4.87
Total	23.28	40.85	28.78	5.40	1.69	100.00
						(945)
Year of marriage 1981–90						
≤20	3.87	1.54	0.07	0.00	0.13	5.61
21–4	10.68	19.83	1.27	0.00	0.13	31.91
25–8	3.67	20.49	16.42	0.47	0.33	41.39
29–32	0.93	2.80	7.74	3.94	0.27	15.69
>32	0.53	0.73	1.60	1.34	1.20	5.41
Total	19.69	45.39	27.10	5.74	2.07	100.00
						(1498)
Year of marriage > 1990						
≤20	0.70	0.20	0.00	0.00	0.00	0.90
21–4	3.82	18.67	2.81	0.30	0.30	25.90
25–8	3.01	23.09	20.08	0.60	0.30	47.09
29–32	0.50	4.52	6.53	1.71	0.10	13.35
>32	0.20	1.31	2.41	1.61	7.23	12.75
Total	8.23	47.79	31.83	4.22	7.93	100.00
						(996)

Note: Numbers of observations are in parentheses.

$$\log \mu_{ij} = \beta_0 + \log \sqrt{\mu_{i0}\mu_{0j}} + \sum_i \beta_i^M X_i^M + \sum_j \beta_j^W X_j^W, \qquad (5.2)$$

where the coefficient of $\log\sqrt{\mu_{i0}\mu_{0j}}$ is constrained to be 1, and X_i^M and X_j^W denote dummies of educational levels for men and women respectively. The educational levels are categorized into four groups: elementary or below, junior high, senior high, college or above. In our empirical analysis, "elementary or below" is taken as the reference group.

1	5	6	7
5	2	5	6
6	5	3	5
7	6	5	4

Figure 5.1 Marriage crossing of four education tiers

The basic model in equation (5.2) could be further extended to consider the *asymmetry effects* and *crossing effects* of men's and women's education. For the asymmetry effects, we create one dummy variable indicating whether the husband's education is higher than that of the wife. In past literature, researchers sometimes used two dummy variables, one indicating whether the husband's education is higher than the wife's, and the other indicating the opposite (reference group being the same education category). We choose only one dummy since the couples where the wife's education is higher are so few that they can be ignored, for both Taiwan and China.

For education crossing effects, since there are four education tiers, three dummy variables are created: different by one ladder, different by two ladders, and different by three ladders. The specification of the crossing effects is characterized by Figure 5.1. To observe the possible changes of crossing and asymmetry effects along with time, we allow the parameters to change across men's birth cohorts. As will be demonstrated later, men's cohorts are separated into three categories: born before 1950, born during 1951–60, and born later than 1960.

For log-linear models, likelihood-ratio chi-squared statistic (G^2) and BIC (Bayesian Information Criterion) statistic were widely used to measure the goodness of fit in related literature.[7] In Table 5.4, we list these statistics for models of education assortative mating. Model A is the basic model corresponding to equation (5.2). Education asymmetry effects are included in Model B, while crossing effects (also called education heterogeneity effects) are controlled in Model C. Model D adds the consideration of both education asymmetry and heterogeneity, and Model E further takes into account the interaction effect of heterogeneity/asymmetry with men's cohorts. The various goodness-of-fit measures for education assortative mating models are listed in Table 5.4. It can be seen from the table that Model E fits best for both China and Taiwan. To contrast the findings for

Table 5.4. Goodness-of-fit measures for cohort and education assortative mating models

Models	Taiwan			China		
	df	G^2	BIC	df	G^2	BIC
A. Basic model	133	7997.42	7336.44	133	7046.32	6385.34
B. Basic model + education asymmetry	132	7103.25	6447.23	132	6446.71	5790.69
C. Basic model + education heterogeneity	127	6011.81	5380.65	127	5653.92	5022.75
D. Basic model + education asymmetry + education heterogeneity	126	5999.93	5373.74	126	5617.52	4991.32
E. Basic model + education asymmetry × men's cohort + education heterogeneity × men's cohort	112	4117.23	3560.61	112	4810.98	4254.36

Notes: G^2 and BIC denote likelihood-ratio chi-squared statistic and Bayesian Information Criterion statistic, respectively. And df denotes degree of freedom.

The Basic model contains marginal effects only.

The Education asymmetry model contains one dummy indicating whether men's education is higher than women's.

The Education heterogeneous model contains dummies measuring the degree of heterogeneity between men and women's education (6 dummies: both junior high, both senior high, both college or above, different by 1 education level, different by 2 education levels, and different by 3 education levels).

Taiwan and China, we present the results corresponding to Model E in Table 5.5.

To save space, in Table 5.5 we concentrate on the interaction terms of education-related variables and cohort dummies, and have omitted the coefficients for cohort and education dummies from the table. It can be seen from Table 5.5 that the education asymmetry effects across cohorts show slightly different patterns between Taiwan and China. In the case of Taiwan, the tendency of asymmetry of men having higher education than women is declining with men's cohorts, whereas the trend is not obvious in China. This may be partly due to the lasting effect of the chaotic educational system during the Cultural Revolution period. Indeed, as we mentioned in Chapter 2, during the period of Cultural Revolution, education progression in China was often based on political background and ideology rather than school performance, and hence the meaning of education in marriage screening is lessened. Since only a small proportion of our adult respondents' education was not affected by the Cultural Revolution

Table 5.5. Selected estimated parameters for cohort and education assortative mating models

Variables	Taiwan		China	
	β	$\exp(\beta)$	β	$\exp(\beta)$
Education asymmetry				
Men with higher education				
Men's birthyear ≤1950	1.417**	4.125	0.874***	2.397
	(0.240)		(0.205)	
Men's birthyear 1951–60	0.560**	1.751	0.219***	1.245
	(0.212)		(0.183)	
Men's birthyear >1960	0.089***	1.094	0.537***	1.711
	(0.197)		(0.174)	
Education heterogeneity				
Both junior high				
Men's birthyear ≤1950	−1.872***	0.154	−1.313***	0.269
	((0.268)		(0.219)	
Men's birthyear 1951–60	−0.142***	0.868	−0.344***	0.709
	(0.273)		(0.207)	
Men's birthyear >1960	3.666*	39.104	0.642***	1.901
	(0.511)		(0.203)	
Both senior high				
Men's birthyear ≤1950	−2.784***	0.062	−1.335***	0.263
	(0.227)		(0.200)	
Men's birthyear 1951–60	−0.188***	0.828	−0.423***	0.655
	(0.213)		(0.171)	
Men's birthyear >1960	3.712*	40.968	−0.183***	1.201
	(0.486)		(0.166)	
Both college or above				
Men's birthyear ≤1950	−1.362***	0.256	−0.432***	0.649
	(0.216)		(0.257)	
Men's birthyear 1951–60	0.798**	2.222	−0.413***	0.662
	(0.216)		(0.272)	
Men's birthyear >1960	4.663*	105.967	−1.114***	3.048
	(0.487)		(0.213)	
Different by 1 level				
Men's birthyear ≤1950	−3.409***	0. 033	−2.183***	0.113
	(0.232)		(0.183)	
Men's birthyear 1951–60	−0.958***	0. 383	−1.151***	0.316
	(0.217)		(0.162)	
Men's birthyear >1960	2.749**	15.641	−0.712***	0.491
	(0.486)		(0.161)	
Different by 2 levels				
Men's birthyear ≤1950	−3.852***	0. 021	−2.867***	0.057
	(0.197)		(0.174)	
Men's birthyear 1951–60	−1.928***	0. 145	−2.201***	0.111
	(0.200)		(0.162)	
Men's birthyear >1960	−0.681***	1.975	−2.015***	0.133
	(0.505)		(0.158)	
Different by 3 levels				
Men's birthyear ≤1950	−5.289***	0. 005	−4.017***	0.018
	(0.288)		(0.310)	
Men's birthyear 1951–60	−3.295***	0. 037	−3.523***	0.030
	(0.325)		(0.337)	
Men's birthyear >1960	−0.040***	0.961	−3.694***	0.025
	(0.598)		(0.373)	

Notes: *, **, *** denote significance at 10%, 5%, 1% levels respectively. Standard errors are in parentheses.

(entering school after 1977 or leaving school before 1966), we may not be able to observe the complete picture of education–marriage interaction in China from our current sample. Moreover, the relatively low degree of modernization in China may also contribute to the rigidity of their assortative marriage. More evidence from later survey data is needed to draw a definite conclusion.

Treating elementary education or below as the reference group for the husband and wife, we see that marriages by people of the same higher education tiers and marriages across different education tiers both became more likely for *younger* men's cohorts. Since Taiwan has extended compulsory education from six to nine years for the cohort born after 1955, we can observe its impact from the coefficients of the relevant cohorts. For instance, the dummies for both spouses having junior high, senior high, college degrees, or above began to have positive coefficients in Taiwan for men born after 1960. Finally, we find that a one-level educational difference between the husband and the wife became likely (relative to the reference group of both having elementary school education) in Taiwan for men born after 1960. This is evidently related to the rapidly expanded education

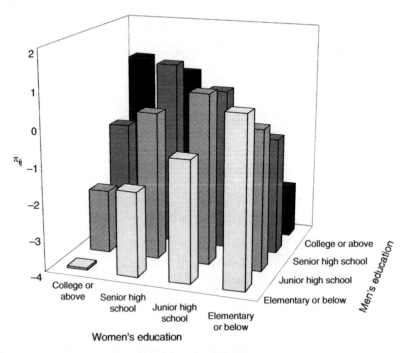

Figure 5.2 Total gains to marriage by education: Taiwan

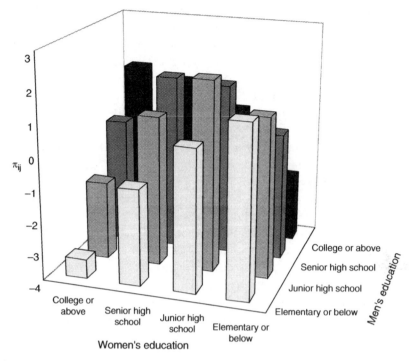

Figure 5.3 Total gains to marriage by education: China

of Taiwan. However, the same trend was not found in China, where all education heterogeneity coefficients except one are negative. The trend can be compared with that in the USA, as summarized in Schwartz and Mare (2005).

As we mentioned, the parameter π_{ij} in (5.1) could be interpreted as the gains to marriage for the (i, j)-type marriage. We can calculate the corresponding marriage gains for various combinations of education tiers. The figures are shown in Figures 5.2 and 5.3, for Taiwan and China respectively. It can be seen that same-education marriages always have the largest gain, and this is so for both China and Taiwan.

5.5.4. Assortative Mating for Ethnicity and Class

Some other aspects besides age and education deserve special attention in Taiwan and China. As noted by Jao and McKeever (2006), Tsay (2006), and other scholars, ethnic inequality is an important issue in Taiwan. It is worthwhile to analyze whether marriages across ethnicity have become more common in Taiwan. According to this rationale, the ethnic groups in Taiwan are divided into four categories: Mainlanders, Fukienese, Hakka, and others (including aborigines and foreigners). Relative to Taiwan, China has a more diverse ethnic mix. However, since the interviewees in the China PSFD survey are quite homogeneous in their ethnic background, we shall put the ethnicity assortative mating issue aside and focus on social class in China.[8]

The social classes in China used to be distinguished according to the background of husband's and wife's family of origin. For simplicity, we divide social classes into three categories: (1) the *lower class*, including labor, unemployed, and homeless (urban), and poor peasants or tenants (rural), (2) the *middle class*, including clerks in private companies, mid-rank government officials and staff (urban), and mid-ranked peasants (rural), and (3) *upper class*, including capitalists, high-ranking government officials of the KMT government (urban), and landlords and rich farmers (rural). In addition to the three wealth classes above, we have included a political *leading class*, which includes the revolutionary cadres, soldiers, and revolutionary martyrs. Of course, after 1978, the year China started its economic reform, this kind of social ranking gradually became obsolete.

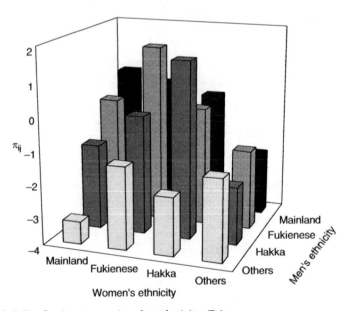

Figure 5.4 Total gains to marriage by ethnicity: Taiwan

Table 5.6a. Selected estimated parameters for cohort and ethnicity assortative mating models, Taiwan

Variables	β	$\exp(\beta)$
Ethnicity interactions		
Mainlander/Fukienese		
Men's birthyear $\leq$1950	−1.510***	0.221
	(0.120)	
Men's birthyear 1951–60	−1.138***	0.320
	(0.126)	
Men's birthyear >1960	−0.474***	0.622
	(0.109)	
Mainlander/Hakka		
Men's birthyear $\leq$1950	−1.971***	0.139
	(0.239)	
Men's birthyear 1951–60	−1.361***	0.256
	(0.225)	
Men's birthyear >1960	−1.033***	0.356
	(0.213)	
Mainlander/others		
Men's birthyear $\leq$1950	−1.977***	0.138
	(0.300)	
Men's birthyear 1951–60	−1.514***	0.220
	(0.301)	
Men's birthyear >1960	−1.401***	0.246
	(0.314)	
Fukienese/Hakka		
Men's birthyear 1950	−2.177***	0.113
	(0.128)	
Men's birthyear 1951–60	−1.773***	0.170
	(0.133)	
Men's birthyear >1960	−1.353***	0.259
	(0.122)	
Fukienese/others		
Men's birthyear $\leq$ 1950	−1.446***	0.235
	(0.121)	
Men's birthyear 1951−60	−1.745***	0.175
	(0.167)	
Men's birthyear >1960	−1.370***	0.254
	(0.156)	
Hakka/others		
Men's birthyear $\leq$1950	−2.068***	0.126
	(0.259)	
Men's birthyear 1951−60	−2.075***	0.126
	(0.324)	
Men's birthyear >1960	−1.692***	0.184
	(0.298)	

Notes: *, **, *** denote significance at 10%, 5%, 1% levels respectively. Standard errors are in parentheses. The coefficients of cohort and ethnicity dummies are omitted for brevity.

Skipping the comparison of goodness-of-fit measures across models and directly choosing the best-fitting model, we have presented the corresponding results for Taiwan in Table 5.6a. Note that in this model, couples with the same ethnicity are treated as the reference group. The Taiwan results indicate that marriages across ethnicity are in general more likely to exist for the younger cohort than the older cohort. The gain to marriage concerning ethnicity is drawn in Figure 5.4.

Similar to Table 5.6a, Table 5.6b shows the likelihood to marry across classes for China. Since the leading class is a political category, we will ignore it for the moment and look at the matching between the three wealth classes first. As one can see, relative to same-class marriages, matches across wealth classes become more difficult as men's cohorts become younger. This is a unique observation, perhaps due to the rural–urban, inland–

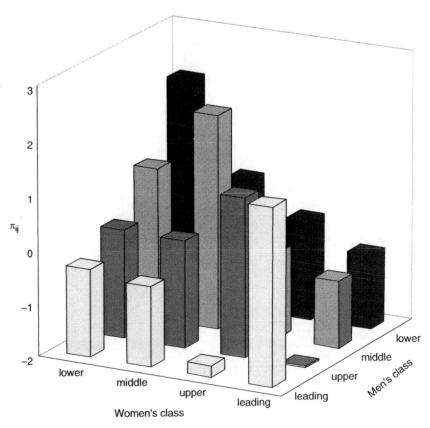

Figure 5.5 Total gains to marriage by social class: China

Table 5.6b. Selected estimated parameters for cohort and class assortative mating models, China

Variables	β	$\exp(\beta)$
Class interactions		
Lower class/middle class		
Men's birthyear ≤1950	−1.074***	0.342
	(0.083)	
Men's birthyear 1951–60	−1.477***	0.228
	(0.087)	
Men's birthyear >1960	−1.639***	0.194
	(0.082)	
Lower class/upper class		
Men's birthyear ≤1950	−1.180***	0.307
	(0.181)	
Men's birthyear 1951–60	−1.696***	0.183
	(0.200)	
Men's birthyear >1960	−2.012***	0.134
	(0.204)	
Lower class/leading class		
Men's birthyear ≤1950	−2.567***	0.077
	(0.336)	
Men's birthyear 1951–60	−2.109***	0.121
	(0.250)	
Men's birthyear >1960	−2.102***	0.122
	(0.225)	
Middle class/upper class		
Men's birthyear ≤1950	−1.002***	0.367
	(0.247)	
Men's birthyear 1951–60	−1.525***	0.218
	(0.278)	
Men's birthyear >1960	−2.090***	0.124
	(0.318)	
Middle class/leading class		
Men's birthyear ≤1950	−1.591***	0.204
	(0.336)	
Men's birthyear 1951–60	−1.932***	0.145
	(0.352)	
Men's birthyear >1960	−2.187***	0.112
	(0.351)	
Upper class/leading class		
Men's birthyear ≤1950	−0.736***	0.479
	(0.434)	
Men's birthyear 1951–60	−0.972***	0.378
	(0.434)	
Men's birthyear >1960	−1.227***	0.293
	(0.433)	

Notes: *, **, *** denote significance at 10%, 5%, 1% levels respectively. Standard errors are in parentheses. The coefficients of cohort and class dummies are omitted for brevity.

coastal uneven development in the past few decades; it may be the case that people of different wealth classes have found it more and more difficult to meet each other, not to mention marry each other. Concerning marriages between the leading class and other classes, it turns out that such matches become more difficult for younger men's cohorts, except for lower-class–leading-class matches. In any event, all coefficients in China are negative, showing that intra-class marriages are still the most popular type. One particularly surprising phenomenon is marriage between the political leading class (which was known as the "red 5 group" during the Cultural Revolution) and the wealthy upper class (condemned as the "black 5 group" during the Cultural Revolution). Marriages between them are supposed to be unlikely. This is indeed shown in Figure 5.5, where one can see the extremely low gain from marriages between these two classes.

5.6. Conclusions

In this chapter, we have discussed the various aspects of the custom of Chinese marriages, including whether the marriage is arranged by senior relatives, the age of marriage, and how the couple first meet. It turns out that the patterns are changing, in both China and Taiwan. The age of marriage is rising and the number of independent marriages is increasing, just as predicted by Goode's (1982) modernization theory. A major difference between China and Taiwan is that people in China still marry younger than in Taiwan, even for marriages taking place after the year 1990. Another interesting feature in China is that a significant proportion of people in China still had their marriages arranged by professional matchmakers, whereas the same pattern cannot be found in Taiwan.

We have also studied assortative mating with respect to various criteria. In Taiwan, the asymmetry of education (husbands being better educated than wives) has diminished as time goes by, and the crossing barrier (marriages between two persons with different educational tiers) is also getting lower. However, neither of these trends can be found in China. We also find that by and large the ethnicity barrier of marriage in Taiwan is falling, but the crossing barrier of social classes has been getting more serious in China. Finally, in terms of the "gains" to marriage, matches between members of the "black 5 class" and the "red 5 class" turn out to be extremely unrewarding.

The final remark we would like to make is about divorce. Stevenson and Wolfers (2007: 40) listed the annual divorce rate per thousand married couples around 2003 for seven Western countries. They are: USA (8.5 per cent), Canada (4.6 per cent), UK (6.9 per cent), France (5.1 per cent), Germany (5.7 per cent), Italy (1.3 per cent), and Sweden (6.8 per cent). For Taiwan, the divorce rate was 1.3 per cent in 2005, significantly lower than all but one of these Western countries. For China, there have not been any relevant data available; but the general perception is that the divorce rate is also low in most areas.[9] In any event, we have not yet had enough divorce samples to launch a quantitative study on related topics in Chinese societies. If the proportion of divorce cases increases in the future, our panel survey should be able to catch the fact, and we shall proceed with some parallel analysis then.

Notes

1. The professional matchmaker also plays the role of ensuring the match of the *fate or fortunes* of the couple and arranging the ritual details of a wedding. To avoid the possibility of bringing bad luck on the new couple because of the negligence of such details, parents of both bride and groom also tend to rely on a professional matchmaker.
2. See clause 3 of the Marriage Law, 1950.
3. As we all know, the one-child policy induced many fake reports for newborns. More discussion has been provided in Chapter 4.
4. The urban–rural classification is coded based on the question "what was the place where you resided for the longest period before the age of 16?" Those whose answer was "(small or large) cities or counties" are coded as urban, and those who answered "farming villages" are coded rural.
5. See Burdett and Coles (1999) for detailed derivation and references.
6. Log-linear models had been widely adopted to analyze marriage matching problem. See Kalmijn (1991a, 1991b), Mare (1991), Qian (1997, 1998), and Qian and Lichter (2001) for further examples. For detailed discussion of log-linear models, see Powers and Xie (2000: ch. 4).
7. The BIC statistic is defined as $BIC = G^2 - df. log(N)$, where G^2 is the likelihood-ratio chi-squared statistic, df denotes degree of freedom, and N is the total number of cells $(I \times J)$. The smaller the value of BIC or G^2, the better the model fits. See Powers and Xie (2000: ch. 4) for detailed discussion about these goodness-of-fit measures.
8. See the discussion of Bian et al. (2005) for the social class problem in China.
9. In a recent report on *Oriental Daily News* (25 January 2007), it is pointed out that in China there are only statistics for divorce numbers per 1,000 people, but there is no statistic for divorce numbers per 1,000 *married* people. Moreover, even the former statistics were believed to be inaccurate.

6

Housework and Household Decisions

Chinese society has been known for its male dominance. The traditional norm says that there should be three rules of submission in a woman's life: "submission to her father's authority before marriage, submission to her husband after marriage, and submission to her oldest son should her husband pass away" (Lang 1946). All three figures to whom a woman is supposed to submit are men, of course. Concerning the marriage relationship, terms such as "major marriage" (between adults), "minor marriage" (a girl adopted as a child bride to marry a boy of the family in the future), and "concubine" all connote male dominance. It was indeed against this background that the Communist government was eager to establish the new Marriage Law two years after it took power in Mainland China (Davis and Harrell 1993: 5). That law officially forbade concubinage and child betrothal, allowed women to sue for divorce, and advocated the right of a widow to remarry. However, marriage is just the starting phase of husband–wife interactions; whether this law has really created a more egalitarian scenario between the couple should also be examined by looking at empirical evidence after the marriage.

In general, male dominance is revealed in the forms of marriage and in various dimensions of family decision-making. Geographically, the phenomenon is observed not only in Mainland China, but also in many other Chinese societies. According to Freedman (1970), for Chinese families in Singapore, the control of most assets and earnings was in the hands of the male line (p.42); rich men sometimes practiced polygamy (p.130); and unwanted baby girls were often given away. According to Thornton and Lin (1994: 38), 50 per cent of marriages in Taipei before 1925 were polygamous. The evidence cited above may describe the practice before the Second World War, but it should be clear that not very long ago male dominance was indeed still a prevalent gender-role ideology. In Taiwan,

Thornton and Lin (1994: 27 showed that the major line of kinship was the male one); and most of the properties, labor, and resources were still controlled by males (p. 32).

In Chapter 2 we have described the economic development and social changes on Mainland China and Taiwan in the past sixty years; we now try to see whether such changes have created a different gender perspective within the household. In later chapters we shall have more discussion on parents' gender-differential treatment toward their children. In this chapter, we start with the couple's various *household decisions*.

6.1. The Couple's Role in a Household

To study the gender-role differences between spouses, social scientists usually focus on two types of variables. The first is "decision power," referring to the couple's relative opinion weight with respect to several important family decisions, such as career choice or change, child education, durable goods consumption, real estate purchase, etc. The second is the sharing of unpleasant household chores between husband and wife. The first approach was pioneered by Blood and Wolfe (1960) and Rodman (1967), and its most recent application to Taiwan can be found in Xu and Lai (2002). The second approach is more related to the concept of "household production," and can be traced back to Becker (1965) and Gronau (1977, 1980).

For empirical studies, the dependent variable for the first approach usually refers to a subjective scale, say 1–5, from a survey question, with 1 meaning husband dominance and 5 meaning wife dominance. The dependent variable for the second approach is the hours or shares of housework of the couple. Since economists prefer analyzing objective revealed decisions rather than subjective attitude scales,[1] most of the economics literature followed the latter approach. Our analysis that follows, however, will examine both dimensions.

In any household in question, the couple must negotiate the allocation of their time between market work, leisure, and housework, which includes cooking, laundry, cleaning, etc. The general perception is that cooking, cleaning, and laundry work is unremunerated and boring, and hence is something left to "weaker" or less important family members. Thus, those who do more housework are usually the ones who have an unfavorable family role.

Becker (1991), however, suggests that it might be more instructive if we leave aside the gender-role perceptional differences for a moment, and start with the neutral case when the spouses are exactly identical in most endowments. He argued that even if the husband and wife are by and large biologically comparable, for efficient family resource allocation, there should be a division of labor anyway—allowing the one possessing a comparative advantage in market (household) activities to exercise more market (household) work. However, the fact that there exists human capital specific to market and household activities creates a property of increasing return that tends to magnify a minor difference between males and females into a large one. For instance, if one wants to be more involved in market (household) activities, one needs to accumulate more market (household) human capital. Thus, a minor difference between the male and female tends to make the couple intensify their accumulation of market- or household-specific human capital, respectively. And as their respective capital starts to accumulate, the respective comparative advantages of the couple are reinforced, sometimes leading to a complete specialization of market versus household work. The above reasoning by Becker (1991: ch. 2) is indeed consistent with the evidence found in Warner et al. (1986).

Besides Becker's household production approach, the bargaining and exchange models also provide some insight concerning the effects of the couple's relative resources on housework allocation. The bargaining models emphasize the importance of threat points on the couple's decision outcomes (McElroy 1990, McElroy and Horney 1981). A spouse's "threat point" denotes his or her maximal level of utility attainable outside the marriage. It follows from the theory that the better one's alternative outside the marriage, or the worse his or her spouse's alternative outside the marriage, the better is one's bargaining position in the marriage relative to his or her spouse. This implies that the spouse who owns more resources would exhibit greater bargaining power in housework allocation. Another version of the bargaining model considers threat points internal to the marriage (Lundberg and Pollak 1993, 1996), not external as in the divorce-threat bargaining models. As suggested by Lundberg and Pollak (1993, 1996), the threat points internal to the marriage might be some non-cooperative solutions, with each spouse choosing actions to maximize his or her own utility. Under such a framework, family decisions are not dependent on relative resources after divorce, but on individual resources within the marriage.

As to sociological exchange theory, researchers often stress the power-dependence relations in marital relationship (Molm and Cook 1995,

Bittman et al. 2003). This theory states that if one is economically more dependent on one's spouse, one will give more and receive less in the exchange. Assuming that housework is not engaged in voluntarily, then both the bargaining and the exchange theories predict that the larger one's resources relative to one's spouse's, the more housework one will do, and the less one's spouse will do.

Note that the possible gender difference in the above-mentioned models may well be a conceptual one rather than a physical one. For instance, if the traditional norm of the society tends to treat women doing market work as "unusual," then this social pressure also contributes to women's cost or disadvantage in market work. Sometimes other seemingly unrelated circumstances also reinforce the comparative advantages. For another instance, if a large family size is common in a traditional Chinese society, then the payoff for the specialization of household work is higher (because the number of people served by housework increases), which in turn may aggravate the originally minor disadvantage of women in a family.

Another kind of compounding effect on gender role in a household results from the interaction between market and household. As Hersch (1991) and Hersch and Stratton (1994) pointed out, women more involved in housework tend to find jobs requiring little time commitment or overtime. This kind of slack job pays women lower wages, which in turn reduces their voice in the household, because their economic resources are fewer. As a result, women are more likely to be saddled with the unwanted housework at home, thus getting trapped in a vicious circle.

6.2. Household Power Structure: Descriptive Analysis

The theories of time allocation between couples mentioned in the previous section are basically gender-neutral: they state that the possible housework disparity between husband and wife is directly or indirectly (through the reinforcement of institutions and capital accumulation) due to differences in the couple's resources or endowments. They therefore imply that the difference will shrink or even disappear as the resource endowment between the couple is equalized. Sociologists call this argument the "resource theory" of housework allocation (Blood and Wolfe 1960), which in general predicts that the husband or the wife, whoever has more resource, tends to get a smaller share of the unpleasant housework.

6.2.1. *Theoretical Discussion*

The empirical evidence, however, does not support this gender-neutral resource theory. While it is true that with economic development, the market opportunities for females improve and the concept of gender equality achieves wider acceptance, we have not yet witnessed an obvious trend of housework equalization worldwide. In a survey article, Juster and Stafford (1991: 498) concluded that the relative wages of the couple could explain to some limited extent the sharing of their household chores, but "much of the division of labor is independent of wages and depends on the *identity* of the husband and wife" (italic added). Using Swiss data, Sousa-Poza et al. (2001: 599) also reported that the male's share of housework and child care was largely independent of changes in socio-economic factors. For instance, when female wage or education increased, it was found that the impact on the husband's housework was not that significant, in statistics as well as in magnitude. Such a trend was also found in Alenezi and Walden (2004).[2]

Economists and sociologists both noticed the interaction between gender role and resources in explaining housework allocation, but their approaches are quite different. Trying to identify the net effect of resources, some sociologists added a gender perception or ideology variable to capture the impact on the respondent (Ross 1987, Greenstein 2000, Bianchi et al. 2000, Zuo and Bian 2001, Xu and Lai 2002). This perception index is usually a scale measuring the respondent's attitude toward certain gender-norm descriptions. As we mentioned before, a criticism of this subjective index is that respondents tend to justify their own behavior by reporting a scale compatible with their family practice or with the perceived social norm. Economists, on the other hand, are reluctant to accept these self-reported perception indices from survey questions. Rather, along the lines of Samuelson (1948), they tend to identify and reveal the hidden preferences from observed behavior. However, since there are so many household decision aspects, sometimes revealing conflicting patterns, it is difficult to identify the hidden preferences from such conflicting patterns. We figure that this is a major reason why we do not find much counterpart economics literature analyzing household decision power. More analysis along the lines of revealed preferences will be provided in Chapter 7.

A more sophisticated hypothesis in sociology, suggested to capture the observation in the USA, is the theory of gender *display* proposed and elaborated by Brines (1994), Greenstein (2000), and Bittman et al. (2003). The hypothesis states that the relative resources of a couple can explain their housework load only when the husband–wife resource ratio is *higher* than some critical value; when the husband earns significantly *less* than the wife, "couples respond to this gender deviance by increasing the traditional outlook in the household" (Bittman et al. 2003: 187). Thus, if this hypothesis is valid, then we expect to see a non-linear relationship between relative resource and relative housework, and the turning point occurs when the necessity of "displaying gender" applies. The gender effect therefore interacts with resources and changes the coefficients of resource in different regions. Given that the Chinese are more attached to family members and less exposed to neighbors and peers (Fei 1992), we do not expect couples to have the necessity to "display" anything to outsiders, even if the wife owns more resources.

In this chapter we expect to examine several dimensions in Chinese societies. Do relative resources affect housework allocation? How sensitive is the housework allocation to individual status? Do households appear to exhibit more male dominance in Chinese societies than in the West? We first compare some empirical evidence from Taiwan, China, and other countries.

6.2.2. Housework Allocation Worldwide

In Table 6.1, we summarize the average hours per week of market work and housework of several countries. The data from the USSR, Japan, the USA, Norway, and Denmark are retrieved from Juster and Stafford (1991), and those of China and Taiwan are from the PSFD survey data and Taiwan's government statistics. As one can see from this table, the male–female proportion in housework time in China and Taiwan is roughly consistent with the other five countries: men are more attached to the market and women more attached to the household. Of course, some numbers have changed in recent years. For instance, the 2005 American Time Use Survey showed that married women reported an average of sixteen hours per week of household activities, compared to less than eleven hours for men (see Lundberg and Pollak 2007: 8).

In terms of the degree of difference, the housework load for males in China is close to the level of Western countries, whereas the figure is significantly smaller in Taiwan and Japan. The evident difference between China and Taiwan in the hours of male housework may reveal a cultural discrepancy. We conjecture that the Marriage Law that went into effect in 1950 and the doctrine of the right to work applied by the Communist regime might have changed the pattern of the division of labor in Chinese

Table 6.1. Time allocation practice in various societies (hours per week)

Area/year		Market work		Housework		Data source and data-collecting method
		Men	Women	Men	Women	
USSR	1965	54.6	43.8	9.8	31.5	Juster and Stafford (1991: 47), time diary
	1985	53.8	39.3	11.9	27.0	
Japan	1965	57.7	33.2	2.8	31.5	Same as above
	1985	52.0	24.6	3.5	31.0	
USA	1965	51.6	18.9	11.5	41.8	Same as above
	1981	44.0	23.9	13.8	30.5	
Norway	1971	37.8	13.3	15.4	41.3	Same as above
	1980	34.2	17.6	16.8	33.0	
Denmark	1964	41.7	13.3	3.7	30.1	Same as above
	1975	33.9	15.8	9.1	26.0	
	1987	33.4	20.8	12.8	23.1	
Taiwan	1987	37.0	21.8	1.5	22.7	Time Use Survey, time diary
	1990	33.4	19.7	1.5	21.8	
	1994	35.8	21.4	1.3	17.9	
	2000	31.8	22.8	2.0	15.3	
	2004	35.2	23.9	2.2	15.6	
	1999–2003	35.2	27.5	5.8	16.8	PSFD, self-reported
China	2004	47.4	45.3	9.6	20.0	PSFD, self-reported

Source: The statistics of Taiwan Time Use Survey are retrieved from the website of the Directorate-General of Budget, Accounting and Statistics (DGBAS), Taiwan (http://www.dgbas.gov.tw). The PSFD statistics for Taiwan and China are computed by the authors.

families, even if the male-dominance tradition may still lie latent in people's minds. On the other hand, the fact that Taiwan had been under Japanese colonial rule for more than fifty years before 1945 might also explain the similarity between Taiwan and Japan.

Another related comparison concerns the change in housework hours between marriage statuses. Gupta (1999) used National Survey of Families and Households (NSFH) data to show that as a man changes his marital status from single to cohabiting (married), his weekly housework decreases by 1.7 (2.4) hours, whereas when a woman changes her status from single to cohabiting (married), her housework load increases by 6.7 (2.4) hours. Gupta's numbers were constructed from panel data across two time points. Table 6.2 lists the situation in China and Taiwan, not from panel data, but across two marital-status groups of the same year. It shows that indeed marriage facilitates a division of labor that pushes women toward more domestic involvement.

Table 6.2. Average housework load across different marital statuses (hours per week)

	China		Taiwan	
	Men	Women	Men	Women
Single	10.99(311)	17.87(213)	7.94(185)	15.34(296)
Married	9.43(2,249)	20.28(1,886)	6.15(1,188)	19.80(1,273)

Notes: The data source is Taiwan and China PSFD Surveys. The numbers in parentheses are the sample size.

From Table 6.2 we see that in both China and Taiwan, the housework time is higher for men in the single status, whereas it is lower for women in the single status. Moreover, the difference in housework hours for men between statuses is less than that for women. Thus, it appears that not only is marriage a mechanism through which men shift part of their housework burden to women, but also it transforms part of men's original activities from market to household. For instance, originally men may often eat in restaurants, but after marriage they eat more often at home, and meals are cooked by females. Thus, the housework after marriages seems to involve both a *redistribution* between the couple and a *substitution* between home production and market alternatives.

Since a couple's housework hours are evidently related to their labor market involvement, as we consider the pattern of housework hours in China and Taiwan shown in Tables 6.1 and 6.2, it is necessary to take into account the background differences. In Table 6.3, we list the labor force participation rates of various years for both China and Taiwan. As one can see, while the male labor force participation rate is slightly higher in China than in Taiwan, the same rate for females is significantly higher in China, almost double the rate of Taiwan. This indicates a prevalent norm of working females in China, a background scenario we should keep in mind.

Table 6.3. Female labor force participation rates of selected years (%)

	Taiwan		China	
Year	Male	Female	Male	Female
1990	73.96	44.50	88.90	79.90
1995	72.03	45.30	89.60	80.30
2000	69.42	46.00	89.30	80.00
2005	67.62	48.40	87.80	75.80

Source: Taiwan's statistics are from the website of Directorate-General of Budget, Accounting and Statistics, Taiwan; China's statistics are from International Labor Office (2006), *Labour and Social Trends in Asia and the Pacific: Progress towards Decent Work*.

6.2.3. *Household Decision Power*

Now we shift to other dimensions of household power. In Table 6.4 we list several family decisions, and indicate the individual who is in charge of such decisions. Putting aside the small proportion of couples that leave the decision to parents and the large proportion of couples that claim to share the decision jointly between the couple, a comparison of the numbers in columns under husband-decision and wife-decision is itself interesting. As one can see from this table, other than in daily expenditure, the wife in Taiwanese families seems to have more power of decision-making.

The most interesting difference between China and Taiwan is that disciplining children seems to be the wife's job in Taiwan, but the husband's job in China. This leads us to wonder whether making such decisions is really a power or not: we figure that making decisions on matters such as family daily expenditure and insurance-buying in Taiwan may be less a "power" to be shared than some kind of tedious burden. Similarly, it is possible that mothers in Taiwan end up with the job of disciplining children because they spend more time with their children, and because husbands leave most of the nuts and bolts of household management to wives.[3] Expenditure on big-ticket items such as housing and high-price durables turns out to be the husbands' turf anyway, in both China and Taiwan.

6.3. Models of Unequal Housework Load

To explain why women have to do more housework, there are three prevalent theories. The relative resource model predicts that the spouse with more resources tends to do less housework (Hersch and Stratton 1994, Kroska 2004). The second model suggests that a spouse who spends more time on market work tends to do less housework. This "market constraint" hypothesis in fact is not incompatible with the relative resource model; all one should do is to take into account the market working hours of the couple. The third hypothesis is the gender-role model, which says that spouses with a more liberal attitude about gender roles tend to have a more equal division of housework.

Table 6.4. Proportions of various decision patterns, Taiwan and China (sample size and percentage)

Area/type of decision	Main decision maker(s)					
	Husband	Husband's parents	Husband and wife jointly	Wife's parents	Wife	Total
Taiwan						
Daily expenditure	488(17.4)	96(3.4)	1,387(49.5)	6(0.2)	823(29.4)	2,800(100.0)
Savings and investment	612(22.3)	38(1.4)	1,438(52.4)	3(0.1)	655(23.9)	2,746(100.0)
Housing and moving	557(20.2)	74(2.7)	1,793(65.0)	8(0.3)	326(11.8)	2,758(100.0)
Disciplining children	315(11.4)	13(0.5)	1,765(64.0)	5(0.2)	660(23.9)	2,758(100.0)
High-price commodities	519(18.6)	47(1.7)	1,741(62.4)	4(0.1)	481(17.2)	2,792(100.0)
China						
Daily expenditure	335(12.3)	40(1.5)	1,423(52.1)	8(0.3)	927(33.9)	2,733(100.0)
Savings and investment	482(18.2)	30(1.1)	1,836(69.3)	3(0.1)	299(11.3)	2,650(100.0)
Housing and moving	428(16.1)	38(1.4)	2,032(76.4)	5(0.2)	158(5.9)	2,661(100.0)
Disciplining children	351(13.1)	14(0.5)	2,084(77.8)	2(0.1)	227(8.5)	2,678(100.0)
High-price commodities	384(14.4)	23(0.9)	2,080(78.1)	5(0.2)	170(6.4)	2,662(100.0)

Note: The sample sizes are different among types of decision since the numbers of respondents who responded to the questions are different.

Most previous empirical work found a negative correlation between the couple's housework share and their relative resources.[4] For example, Hersch and Stratton (1994) used Panel Study of Income Dynamics (PSID) data to investigate the effects of relative earnings on the division of housework time between husband and wife. They found that the husband's income share had a negative effect on the husband's housework hours and share, while the effect on the wife's housework hours was positive. However, as Hersch and Stratton (1994) noted, the uncovered negative correlation may be spurious, and the reason may be related to the gender-role hypothesis mentioned above. Specifically, suppose a husband tends to abide by the traditional gender norm, and has more attachment to the market. Then, we tend to find he has long market working hours, high earnings, and low housework load all at the same time. If this is the case, then both housework hours and relative resources are correlated with this person's gender norm, and there is actually no causality between relative resources and housework load. Technically, the error term of the housework regression may be correlated with the explanatory variable (in particular, economic resources), and the usual ordinary least squares regression may generate an inconsistent estimator. This is the endogeneity problem we mentioned in Chapter 4. We shall come back to this point later.

Suppose the gender norm within a family is invariant with respect to time. One way to isolate the effects of relative resources from gender norm is to apply a fixed-effects model to estimate housework regressions using panel data. Ignoring the possible endogeneity problem for a moment, we propose the following pair of housework equations for our analysis: For the ith family at time t, consider the following housework time equations for the wife (w) and the husband (h):

$$h_{it,w} = \beta_{i,w} + \beta_{s,w} s_{it} + X_{it}\beta_{x,w} + u_{it,w}, \tag{6.1}$$

$$h_{it,h} = \beta_{i,h} + \beta_{s,h} s_{it} + X_{it}\beta_{x,h} + u_{it,h}, \quad i = 1, \ldots, N, \ t = 1, \ldots, T_i, \tag{6.2}$$

where s_{it} denotes the share of income contributed by the wife, and X_{it} denotes other explanatory variables. In the above equations, $\beta_{i,w}$ and $\beta_{i,h}$ are family-specific fixed-effects parameters, which could help capture the time-invariant characteristics of family i. Thus, the estimates of $\beta_{s,w}$ and $\beta_{s,h}$ represent the effects of the wife's relative resources on the housework time of wife and husband, given that other family-relevant factors are controlled.

As we mentioned above, if there is an endogeneity problem, the error terms ($u_{it,w}, u_{it,h}$) in (6.1) and (6.2) may be correlated with the explanatory variable. However, as long as these error terms can be written in an additive form, so that the family-specific factor can be captured and isolated by the fixed-effects parameter ($\beta_{i,w}$, $\beta_{i,h}$) as in (6.1) and (6.2), then the endogeneity problem can be removed or at least lessened.[5] In Section 6.5 we shall use our PSFD panel data to estimate the parameters, according to the fixed-effects setting in (6.1) and (6.2).

6.4. Empirical Results for Household Decision-Making

To study the decision power of household members, we also run ordered probit models for four out of the five decisions in Table 6.4. The one we leave out is disciplining children, which, as we explained, may involve different meanings in reality. The corresponding categorical dependent variable for each question is specified as:

$$z_i = \begin{cases} 1, & \text{if husband (or husband's parent) is the main decision maker,} \\ 2, & \text{if wife and husband make decision jointly,} \\ 3, & \text{if wife (or wife's parent) is the main decision maker.} \end{cases}$$

The models are applied to Taiwan's as well as China's data. The Taiwan data are retrieved from the first-wave surveys conducted in 1999, 2000, and 2003. To run such regressions, we delete the respondents who were single at the time of the survey.

From Table 6.4, it can be seen that the proportions of respondents who regarded "husband's parent(s)" or "wife's parent(s)" as the main decision-maker(s) are quite small, for both Taiwan and China. In addition, the distributions are centered on the category of "joint decision," with the proportion being higher for China than for Taiwan. However, we have to go to refined statistical analysis to isolate the influence of each factor. Finally, to control for ethnic or regional difference, we include ethnicity dummies in the Taiwan regression, and include area dummies in the China regression.

In Tables 6.5 and 6.6 we present the results for Taiwan and China respectively. As one can see from these tables, an increase in the wife's resources, either in her income or in her education, always increases her decision power in the family. This is true both for China and for Taiwan. Furthermore, co-residing with the husband's parents always decreases the wife's power at home, and this seems to be intuitive as well. However, co-residence with the wife's parents only partly helps the wife's power in Taiwan but not in China. Indeed, matrilocal co-residence in Chinese

Table 6.5. Ordered probit models for wife's relative power, Taiwan

Type of decision	Daily expenditure	Savings and investment	Housing and moving	High-priced commodities
Wife's share of income (0–1)	0.184**	0.347***	0.271***	0.166**
	(0.079)	(0.080)	(0.082)	(0.080)
Combined income of husband and wife (thousand NTD)	2.61E–05	7.83E–06	8.57E–05	−6.820E–06
Wife's weekly hours of working	−3.95E–04	0.001	−1.76E–04	−2.929E–04
	(9.03E–05)	(9.10E–05)	(9.72E–05)	(9.490E–05)
Husband's weekly hours of working	0.001	0.003**	0.001	−0.001
	(0.001)	(0.001)	(0.001)	(0.001)
Wife healthy (1 = yes)	−0.088	−0.117	0.001	0.036
	(0.081)	(0.082)	(0.084)	(0.082)
Husband healthy (1 = yes)	−0.014	−0.072	−0.055	−0.164**
	(0.081)	(0.083)	(0.085)	(0.083)
Any child of age ≤6 (1 = yes)	−0.038	−0.045	−0.032	−0.043
	(0.041)	(0.042)	(0.043)	(0.042)
Co-residing with husband's parents (1 = yes)	−0.351***	−0.150***	−0.220***	−0.169***
	(0.052)	(0.052)	(0.054)	(0.053)
Co-residing with wife's parents (1 = yes)	0.225	0.296**	0.272*	0.218
	(0.138)	(0.137)	(0.142)	(0.140)
Husband's birth cohort dummies (before 1941 as ref. group)				
1941–50	0.159**	0.107	0.070	0.035
	(0.070)	(0.071)	(0.073)	(0.071)
1951–60	0.108	0.052	−0.019	−0.026
	(0.074)	(0.075)	(0.078)	(0.076)
1961–70	−0.023	0.006	−0.070	−0.147
	(0.090)	(0.090)	(0.093)	(0.091)
after 1970	−0.255**	−0.119	−0.191	−0.201*
	(0.117)	(0.118)	(0.122)	(0.120)

Husband's years of schooling	0.005	−0.013*	0.004	0.005
	(0.008)	(0.008)	(0.008)	(0.008)
Wife's years of schooling	0.020**	0.027***	0.011	0.017**
	(0.008)	(0.008)	(0.008)	(0.008)
Any dowry when married (1 = yes)	0.083	0.002	0.077	0.062
	(0.050)	(0.051)	(0.052)	(0.051)
Any brideprice when married (1 = yes)	−0.068	−0.068	−0.040	−0.018
	(0.053)	(0.054)	(0.055)	(0.054)
Husband's ethnicity dummies (Aborigine as ref. group)				
Mainlander	−0.051	0.007	0.014	−0.031
	(0.115)	(0.115)	(0.119)	(0.117)
Fukienese	−0.127	−0.090	−0.092	−0.148
	(0.098)	(0.098)	(0.101)	(0.099)
Hakka	−0.131	0.016	−0.047	−0.088
	(0.114)	(0.114)	(0.118)	(0.116)
Having at least one son (1 = yes)	0.138**	0.023	0.061	0.101
	(0.061)	(0.061)	(0.063)	(0.062)
Log likelihood	−2832.50	−2759.46	−2373.84	−2542.96
Number of observations	2,800	2,746	2,758	2,792

Notes: Standard errors are in parentheses. *, **, and *** denote 10%, 5%, and 1% significance levels respectively. The two intercept terms corresponding to the ordered probit model are omitted for brevity.

Table 6.6. Ordered probit models for wife's relative power, China

	Type of decision			
	Daily expenditure	Savings and investment	Housing and moving	High-priced commodities
Wife's share of income (0–1)	0.071	0.430***	0.357**	0.338**
	(0.125)	(0.134)	(0.142)	(0.143)
Combined income of husband and wife (thousand RMB)	0.006	0.012	0.004	0.002
	(0.009)	(0.010)	(0.010)	(0.010)
Wife's weekly hours of working	−0.001	−0.001	4.44E-04	−0.002
	(0.002)	(0.002)	(0.002)	(0.002)
Husband's weekly hours of working	−0.002	−0.003*	−0.003**	−0.002
	(0.001)	(0.002)	(0.002)	(0.002)
Wife healthy (1 = yes)	0.509***	0.324**	0.239*	0.286**
	(0.110)	(0.118)	(0.123)	(0.125)
Husband healthy (1 = yes)	−0.440***	−0.412***	−0.533***	−0.375***
	(0.106)	(0.113)	(0.120)	(0.118)
Any child of age ≤ 6 (1 = yes)	0.014	−0.015	−0.051	0.016
	(0.079)	(0.084)	(0.089)	(0.089)
Co-residing with husband's parents (1 = yes)	−0.209***	−0.156**	−0.205***	−0.142**
	(0.056)	(0.059)	(0.063)	(0.063)
Co-residing with wife's parents (1 = yes)	0.064	0.057	0.143	0.141
	(0.102)	(0.107)	(0.115)	(0.117)
Husband's birth cohort dummies (before 1941 as ref. group)				
1941–50	0.023	0.056	0.021	−0.016
	(0.089)	(0.097)	(0.103)	(0.103)
1951–60	0.072	0.055	0.014	0.097
	(0.093)	(0.100)	(0.106)	(0.107)
1961–70	0.031	−0.005	0.014	0.010
	(0.099)	(0.107)	(0.113)	(0.114)

after 1970	-0.114	-0.115	-0.048	-0.109
	(0.128)	(0.137)	(0.145)	(0.146)
Husband's years of schooling	-0.006	-0.022**	-0.016*	-0.018**
	(0.008)	(0.008)	(0.009)	(0.009)
Wife's years of schooling	0.033***	0.036***	0.029***	0.029***
	(0.007)	(0.007)	(0.008)	(0.008)
Any dowry when married (1 = yes)	0.115*	0.023	-0.022	0.056
	(0.062)	(0.066)	(0.070)	(0.071)
Any brideprice when married (1 = yes)	0.064	-0.090	-0.033	-0.038
	(0.063)	(0.067)	(0.072)	(0.072)
Regional dummies (Zhejiang as ref. group)				
Shanhai	-0.138**	0.128*	0.048	0.102
	(0.066)	(0.071)	(0.075)	(0.076)
Fujian	0.108**	-0.072	-0.181***	-0.144**
	(0.050)	(0.053)	(0.057)	(0.057)
Having at least one son (1 = yes)	0.065	-0.063	-0.044	-0.035
	(0.052)	(0.055)	(0.058)	(0.059)
Log likelihood	-2619.65	-2105.90	-1757.77	-1706.16
Number of observations	2,733	2,650	2,661	2,662

Notes: Standard errors are in parentheses. *, **, and *** denote 10%, 5%, and 1% significance levels respectively. The two intercept terms corresponding to the ordered probit model are omitted for brevity.

societies is usually treated as an exception rather than a norm, and hence it sometimes reveals the objective necessity of sharing insufficient resources, instead of a factor that determines the family power. This may dilute the resource–power connection we normally expected. For instance, under a strict family planning policy in China, matrilocal co-residence is sometimes an unavoidable arrangement when the parents' only child is a girl. As a result, co-residing with the wife's parents may not reveal the wife's influence in the household at all.

The husband's education in China plays the role of enhancing the husband's power rather than enlightening him in the idea of gender equality, but this factor is not significant in Taiwan. The health status of the couple helps their respective power in China, but the coefficients are barely significant in Taiwan. In both Taiwan and China, the husband's birth cohort does not seem to have any effect on the wife's power. There are two possibilities: either the egalitarian perception of husbands in these two societies has not changed much, or the possible impact has been captured by the relative resource variables, such as education. The amount of working hours of the husband seems to play the part of a constraint on the husband's role of decision-making in saving and investment in Taiwan, whereas in China it increases the weight of the husband's decisions in the areas of saving/investment and housing/moving. Finally, in Taiwan or China, neither dowry nor brideprice plays any role in explaining family decision power.

6.5. Fixed-Effects Regression on Housework in Taiwan

The fixed-effects analysis here partly follows Hersch and Stratton (1994). As we explained in Section 6.3, if the error terms of the husband–wife regression equations are additive, then the fixed effects model can remove or at least lessen the endogeneity bias. The data we use in this section are constructed from the panels of the 1999–2005 Taiwan PSFD surveys;[6] the corresponding data in China have been collected only for one year at the time of writing this monograph, and will be ready for similar analysis only in the future. For the 1953–64 birth cohorts first interviewed in the year 1999, a panel is obtained by linking the serial number of the respondents. And panels for respondents born in 1934–54 (first interviewed in 2000) and 1964–76 (first interviewed in 2003) are obtained likewise, except that the numbers of waves are different for surveys started in different years. The number of families in the combined panels is about 3,600, and the number of observations is about 25,200.

Since very old couples may be seriously sick or handicapped in some way, which hinders the usual division of housework, in this section we restrict our samples to married spouses both born later than 1941 (aged 66 or below at the time of this analysis). The samples left after the above manipulation contain 5,460 observations, which pertain to 1,440 families. Among such households in which the couples have less volatile ages, we include their health status to control the physical constraints on housework load.

The information of housework time is gathered from the response to the question "About how many hours do you (your spouse) spend on housework in a typical week?" As to the health status dummy, it is coded as 1 if the health condition of the husband (wife) is fair, good, or very good. Otherwise, it is coded as 0. The combined income of husband and wife is recorded on a monthly basis, with the units being thousand NT dollars. The definitions for other variables can be easily understood from Table 6.7. The means and standard deviations of selected variables are also listed in the same table.

Hersch and Stratton (1994) separated their regressions according to two groups, wife working and wife not-working, and we can make some comparison along these lines. From Table 6.7, it is interesting to see that non-working wives tend to do more housework, but the wives of non-working husbands also do more housework. This also suggests that we need to control for the health status of the couple, otherwise we may be misled by the unusual housework division in families with an unhealthy or handicapped member, who happens to be classified as "not-working."

A variable used by Hersch and Stratton (1994) but not in our model is the spouses' education. In their model, education may capture the perception of gender equality. In our model, any family-specific variables are captured by the fixed-effects parameters, and hence cannot be identified independently.

Our main fixed-effects regression results are listed in Table 6.8. In this regression, the explanatory variables include the share of wife's income, combined income of husband and wife, working hours of husband and wife, health condition dummies for husband and wife, a dummy variable indicating the presence of any pre-school child (aged 0–6) and dummies indicating co-residence with husband's or wife's parents.

From Table 6.8, it can be seen that the wife's housework time decreases as the share of her income increases, which is consistent with the findings of the relative resource hypothesis. However, the effect of the wife's income share on the husband's housework time is not significant, which is different

Table 6.7. Means and standard deviations for variables, Taiwan

		Subsample			
	All sample	Husband working	Husband non-working	Wife working	Wife non-working
Wife's share of housework time	0.770	0.774	0.735	0.742	0.822
(0–1)	(0.239)	(0.236)	(0.263)	(0.235)	(0.239)
Wife's share of income (0–1)	0.241	0.220	—	0.370	—
	(0.284)	(0.241)		(0.276)	
Wife's weekly hours	19.034	18.811	21.020	15.411	25.812
of housework	(13.977)	(13.843)	(14.985)	(10.605)	(16.735)
Husband's weekly hours	5.221	4.908	8.011	5.433	4.826
of housework	(7.408)	(6.97)	(11.116)	(7.149)	(7.865)
Combined income of the couple	62.416	68.050	12.329	70.269	47.727
(in thousand NT dollars)	(178.641)	(186.968)	(45.411)	(120.503)	(253.259)
Wife's weekly hours of working	26.190	26.853	20.293	40.190	—
	(25.080)	(25.030)	(24.779)	(20.064)	
Husband's weekly hours	37.397	41.604	—	39.088	34.235
of working	(23.528)	(20.995)		(22.612)	(24.851)
Wife healthy (1 = yes)	0.936	0.942	0.882	0.949	0.913
	(0.244)	(0.233)	(0.323)	(0.220)	(0.282)
Husband healthy (1 = yes)	0.935	0.950	0.795	0.941	0.922
	(0.247)	(0.217)	(0.404)	(0.235)	(0.268)
Any child of age ≤6 (1 = yes)	0.176	0.208	0.033	0.192	0.154
	(0.497)	(0.532)	(0.240)	(0.507)	(0.480)
Co-residing with husband's	0.249	0.252	0.219	0.248	0.252
parents (1 = yes)	(0.433)	(0.434)	(0.414)	(0.432)	(0.434)
Co-residing with wife's	0.021	0.021	0.022	0.020	0.024
parents (1 = yes)	(0.145)	(0.145)	(0.146)	(0.140)	(0.154)
Number of observations	5,460	4,908	552	3,558	1,902
Number of families	1,440	1,400	302	1,161	775

Note: Standard deviations are in parentheses.

from the finding in Hersch and Stratton (1994). It suggests that the husband's housework hours are less sensitive to his holding of resources, perhaps revealing the strong gender mindset in Chinese families. The combined household income does not have any significant impact on the couple's housework.

The results of Table 6.8 also indicate that one's market working hours have a negative effect on one's own housework load, but there is no cross-influence on the other partner. If the wife is healthy, she tends to do more housework, and her husband does less. However, if the husband is healthy, the wife's load is not lessened despite an increase in the husband's housework load. This again shows an asymmetry consistent with the male-dominance gender role in a Chinese society.

The presence of pre-school children increases the mother's housework load, but not that of the father, a pattern different from that in Hersch and

Table 6.8. Fixed-effects models for wife's and husband's housework time, Taiwan

	Housework time		
	Wife's housework	Husband's housework	Wife's share of housework
Wife's share of income	−2.961***	0.260	−0.0378***
	(0.772)	(0.454)	(0.0134)
Combined income of the couple	0.001	−8.890E–05	0.0000
	(0.001)	(0.001)	(0.0000)
Wife's weekly hours of working	−0.080***	0.006	−0.0007***
	(0.009)	(0.005)	(0.0002)
Husband's weekly hours of working	−0.001	−0.027***	0.0007***
	(0.008)	(0.005)	(0.0001)
Wife healthy	1.151*	−0.866**	0.0357***
	(0.678)	(0.399)	(0.0118)
Husband healthy	−0.954	0.859**	−0.0264**
	(0.712)	(0.419)	(0.0124)
Any child of age ≤6	1.635***	0.506	−0.0193*
	(0.635)	(0.373)	(0.0110)
Co–residing with husband's parents	1.426*	−0.507	0.0117
	(0.727)	(0.427)	(0.0127)
Co–residing with wife's parents	−0.665	0.001	−0.0152
	(1.709)	(1.005)	(0.0298)
Constant	21.429***	6.263***	0.7573***
	(0.922)	(0.542)	(0.0161)
F-statistic for family fixed-effects df = (2203, 5312)	2.07***	1.98***	2.21***
R-squared	0.060	0.017	0.036
Number of observations	7,525	7,525	7,525
Number of families	2,204	2,204	2,204

Note: Standard errors are in parentheses. *, **, and *** denote 10%, 5%, and 1% significance levels respectively.

Stratton (1994), who found that both the husband and the wife increase their housework significantly in response to an increased number of young children, although the wife's load is heavier. This indicates that pre-school children are mostly the mother's burden in Chinese society. This evidence actually echoes with our previous finding that disciplining children is mainly the mother's job in Taiwan.

The co-residence status has an asymmetric impact: the presence of the husband's parents increases the wife's workload, but the presence of the wife's parents does not have any significant impact. The finding is also consistent with the paternalistic society of Taiwan, in which the husband's parents can command the wife, whereas the wife's parents cannot command the husband. Overall, the evidence shows that the presence of parents-in-law does indeed bring pressure on the wife. Again, this evidence echoes with our finding in Chapter 3 that wives with more economic resources tend to avoid co-residence with parents-in-law, which would increase their housework load, as we have just shown.

The last column of Table 6.8 lists the regression with respect to the wife's *share* of housework. The results are consistent with those for housework *time* in the previous two columns, and do not require additional discussion. Finally, the test statistic on the overall significance of the fixed-effects parameters shows that the null hypothesis of no fixed effects is rejected, which implies that the family-specific parameters are variant across families.

Basically, for the case of Taiwan, the results in Tables 6.5 and 6.8 are consistent, indicating that the power structure (measured by either housework share or decision pattern) in Taiwan can be understood in a coherent way. Area-wise, there are some minor differences between Taiwan and China in family power structure. The lack of panel data in China has prevented us from running a counterpart regression of housework load. We hope that we can accomplish that job in the not too distant future, as the panel accumulates.

6.6. Conclusions

In this chapter we have studied the division of family decision power and housework in Taiwan and China. Conceptually, housework is usually treated as boring, non-creative, routine, and often unpleasant chores. In societies with more traditional gender perceptions, the housework load is usually put more on the wives' than on the husbands' shoulders. Previous studies by Juster and Stafford (1991) indeed reveal such a pattern worldwide, and the same pattern also appears in both China and Taiwan, where male-dominance conceptions are expected to be stronger. Concerning family decisions, there are routine ones and crucial ones, and in this chapter we have seen different patterns for different types of decisions.

Comparing our housework statistics from PSFD with those of other countries, we find that the situation of China is more like that in the USA, Demark, or Norway, where the wife's housework time is about twice as much as the husband's. However, the situation of Taiwan is more like that in Japan, where the wife–husband housework ratio is about three. Given that they more or less share a common cultural origin, this difference between China and Taiwan certainly hinges on the societal economic background. Under the Communist regime in China, most women have a market job (Bauer et al. 1992), which certainly reduces the time they devote to housework; this is the time constraint hypothesis. On the other hand, the relative incomes of the couple also explain their housework differences, which is the prediction of the relative resource hypothesis. To disentangle these multiple explanations, we resort to the regression analyses.

Concerning family decisions, we find support for the resource hypothesis, that the wife's decision power is positively related to the share of her income and her education. Poor health in a husband or co-residence with his parents decreases his wife's decision power, a phenomenon consistent with the analysis of housework load. Basically, the scenarios in China and Taiwan are qualitatively the same. The only distinction is that the husband's education in China plays a role more in enhancing the husband's power of decision-making than in improving his egalitarian outlook. The same variable, however, is not significant in Taiwan. The interpretation of this result may require more research effort in the future.

To avoid the problem caused by the possible correlation between the explanatory variables and the unobservable characteristics of the family, we apply the fixed-effects model to estimate the household load in Taiwan. The results are by and large consistent with our intuition, that the couple's relative resources contribute to a decrease in their respective housework load, that the presence of pre-school children increases the wife's load, and that one's poor health status reduces one's load. A unique phenomenon we find is that co-residence with the husband's parents in Taiwan increases the wife's workload, but not that of the husband. This indicates that the presence of parents-in-law is still a source of pressure for the wife.

Notes

1. There is a measurement problem with respect to attitude scale variables. If a female respondent does most of the housework at home, she may tend to give an attitude scale that makes her current unfavorable position in the division of labor look "justifiable."
2. Other country-specific studies can be found in Gershuny and Robinson (1988), Solberg and Wong (1992), Jenkins and O'Leary (1995), and Alvarez and Miles (2003).
3. Our survey questionnaire does not provide us with enough information to pursue this question further. However, we can propose the following hypothesis: One dimension of modernization is of course the emphasis of the value of *diversity*. Given that the pace of modernization in China is slower than that in Taiwan, we suspect that the pressure on children to pursue the traditional educational progression in China is more severe, whereas in Taiwan diversified goals of children are more acceptable. In paternalistic Chinese societies, the sheer

pressure of educational progression is likely to be left to the authoritative father, and the mother is more tolerant and patient to the diversified needs of children.

4. For an overview see Shelton and John (1996) and Coltrane (2000).
5. See Hotz et al. (1997: 330) for more discussion.
6. We excluded the year 2003 observations, in which year the housework information was not requested.

7

Revealed Son Preferences

As we mentioned in previous chapters, male dominance has been the tradition of Chinese families for thousands of years, and is unlikely to change easily even with the spread of the market economy, or the promulgation of laws and regulations, such as the new Marriage Law in China. In order for the tradition of male dominance to continue, there have to be some *channels* which facilitate this transmission of male dominance. An analogy can be found in the analysis of discrimination: in order to sustain a form of discrimination, some elements have to spread from person to person. In the market context, for instance, employers have to treat minority employees unfavorably in order to sustain a stable equilibrium of discrimination against racial minorities. In the family context, parents must subject their boys and girls to differential treatment to sustain or reinforce male dominance. The focus of our analysis in this chapter is to investigate the existence and degree of parents' gender preferences in Taiwan and China.

Gender inequality in a family can be observed in various manifestations. For instance, the children of a family may customarily take the father's surname, so that the mother's role is more or less limited by the reduced significance of her surname. This is the nominal side of gender bias. More tangibly, the fathers may conform to the norm by transferring all their assets to sons but not to daughters, or bequeathing their assets in a very uneven way. Such an unequal division of bequests would leave the daughters in a relatively poor position to start with, which in turn further disadvantages the female line one generation after. In short, the custom of male dominance is in fact preserved through household decisions of unequal allocations. In this chapter we shall study how we can find evidence of such gender-specific preferences, and in the next chapter we study how gender preferences are implemented in education resource allocation.

7.1. Son Preferences: Theoretical Issues

In the economics literature, the existence or absence of son preferences (or male dominance) in a society is often taken for granted and is rarely tested or measured. Other social scientists tend to ask questions in their interview to check the gender attitude of their interviewees. The common questions include: (i) to what extent would you agree that "the family should have at least one son so as to preserve the lineage"; (ii) to what extent would you agree that "the husband's role is mainly to make money and the wife's role is to manage the household chores"; (iii) to what extent would you agree that a son should co-reside with his parents after his marriage? (iv) who (husband or wife) in your household is the major decision maker in purchasing durable goods?; or (v) for interviewees who have n successive girls, "do you plan to try another pregnancy in the near future?"

These are in fact questions asked in the PSFD survey in both China and Taiwan. Question (iv) is related to the family power structure, which we have discussed in Chapter 6. Question (v) is concerned with the preferences for a certain sex composition of children, and does not involve any unequal allocation of resources on the parents' part. This is a topic we studied in Chapter 4, and it will not be repeated here. The first three questions concern the attitude of respondents; a summary of the responses to these questions in Taiwan and China is listed in Table 7.1. As one can see, they do show a significant deviance from an ideal gender-neutral society. From Table 7.1, we find from such subjective attitude questions that people in Taiwan seem to exhibit more gender bias than those in Mainland China.

Attitude-related questions like (i)–(iii) above sometimes incur the critique that the interviewees may tend to provide answers compatible with their actual behavior or with the norm expectations of the society. For instance, if the wife wants to justify her excessive involvement in most of the housework, she may provide an answer consistent with her behavior in question (ii). Or, if a traditional wife realizes that the norm expectation is gender equality, then she may not want to reveal her "outmoded" thinking of lineage preservation in question (i). Thus, the answers to attitude questions may be challenged as a true revelation of preferences. Moreover, the above measures of son preferences or male dominance are more appropriate for ascertaining the existence of such preferences than for capturing their *intensity*.

Another way to identify the possible son preferences of parents is to look at their resource allocation behavior among children. For instance, if the parents send all their sons to college but discourage all their daughters from further study after mandatory education, then it seems to reveal the parents'

Table 7.1. Distribution of answers to gender-norm-related questions (%)

| | China | | | | | | Taiwan | | | | |
	Very unimportant 1	2	3	4	Very important 5		Very unimportant 1	2	3	4	Very important 5
Husband should make money, and wife should do domestic work	11.48	9.72	31.11	26.84	20.86		5.27	6.25	25.05	22.48	40.94
One should have at least one son to preserve the lineage	28.57	11.98	19.75	18.06	21.63		19.34	10.08	18.84	16.92	34.82
A son should co-reside with his parents after his marriage	22.64	15.93	26.26	19.50	15.66		20.32	12.55	30.64	14.47	22.02

Source: The figures for China are from the 2004 China PSFD survey and the figures for Taiwan are from the 1999, 2000, and 2003 Taiwan PSFD survey.

tendency of son preferences. Following Samuelson (1948), we call this *"revealed* son preferences." Economists favor the concept of revealed preferences because it could be examined empirically by observed behavior. However, evidence like this is often contaminated by the fact that parental decisions on child education are also dependent upon the rate of return from child education. For instance, if the marginal return to education for boys is better than that for girls, due to sex discrimination in the labor market, then parents may feel justified in investing more in boys. Therefore the evidence of unequal education investment alone does not necessarily imply son preferences. Empirically, one has to disentangle the tie between objective environment and subjective attitude in order to identify son preferences.

In addition to unequal allocations of education resources, unequal bequests or *inter vivos* transfers to children may also reveal some kind of son preferences. Given the fact that transfers and earnings are two complementary factors contributing to children's income, however, the prediction of gender preferences is still uncertain: parents who actually have equal preferences toward their children may still tend to bequeath more assets to the child who earns less, so as to compensate for the weaker earnings (Behrman et al. 1982). This tells us that in order to identify possible son preferences in Chinese families, one has to consider more than one allocation decision, such as parental educational investment and asset transfers simultaneously. As we shall explain shortly, the PSFD data set allows us to identify and test the *existence* as well as the *extent* of possible son preferences.

Intuitively, there are three factors determining the resource allocation to a child. The first is child ability; for instance, a smart kid naturally attracts more schooling investment from parents simply because this investment promises better returns. In any analysis using sibling data, the ability factor is usually assumed to be random across siblings. The second is the gender-specific difference in the market rate of return to education. This is a factor found in any society with sex discrimination in the labor market. In reality, the rates of return for males and females are different even in countries with relatively weak son preferences such as the USA (Card 1999). The third factor is differential preferences by parents. Distinguishing and isolating these three factors is key to identifying son preferences empirically.

In their classic paper, Behrman et al. (1986) used twin data to identify the roles of gender preferences and market differentials. In Behrman (1988), the author studied the case of nutrition allocation among children, given a particular specification of parental utility function. Davies and Zhang (1995) analyzed theoretically the comparative statistics with or without son preferences, and used the fixed-effects model to explore the empirical implications in the Philippines. The same data set has also been used by Estudillo et al. (2001) and the references therein; they found that in the Philippines sons tend to be endowed with more land whereas daughters tend to have more schooling years. In this chapter, we use the combined information of bequests and schooling to help identify son preferences. The key idea, as we shall explain shortly, is that the return to assets is predetermined by the market, whereas the return to education is variable across different children.

Conceptually, parents care about child incomes, which come from two sources: earnings and parental transfers (or bequests). It is well known that earning is a function of education, and as long as this function satisfies some technical condition, then an interior solution for child education could be obtained in the parental utility maximization problem. Then, parents who have equal concerns toward all their children will use their transfers to eliminate the difference in marginal utility from resource swaps between any pair of children, and also between family consumption and child transfers. Furthermore, it can be shown that poor families do tend to have zero bequests (a corner solution, see Ermisch 2003: ch. 5). When an interior solution of parental transfers is observed, microeconomic theory suggests an implicit relationship between transfers and child education investments, which can be tested empirically.

Empirical evidence shows that in a majority of Chinese families, both in Taiwan and in China, parents transfer *all* their assets to boys only, and girls often do not receive anything, in sharp contrast to the practice in the USA.[1] This fact alone seems to reveal that parents have a subjective weight difference toward their boys and girls. While it is possible that parents use such extremely unequal transfers to compensate for the low earnings of their boys, it seems an unlikely explanation for the phenomenon, for the labor markets in Chinese society do not appear to discriminate against males. Furthermore, even if there is a compensation effect, at most it should imply an *unequal* bequest distribution instead of a large proportion of families leaving *zero* bequests to girls. The information of unequal transfers among children together with the difference in education attainment of boys and girls can help us isolate parental son preferences from other factors.

7.2. Practices of Savings and Bequests in Chinese Societies

Taiwan is well known for its high savings rate (Tsai et al. 2000). If we compare the savings rates of China, Taiwan, Hong Kong, Singapore, with

Table 7.2. Savings rates across selected areas for various years (%)

	1986	1990	1996	2000	2004
China	35.9	38.7	41.1	39.0	44.7
Taiwan	36.9	27.6	25.7	24.3	23.4
Hong Kong	32.2	35.2	29.7	31.7	31.6
Singapore	38.0	43.3	51.1	47.4	48.0
South Korea	35.6	37.2	35.7	33.9	35.0
Japan	32.5	34.4	30.6	28.8	27.6
United States	16.5	16.3	16.6	17.7	13.8

Notes: The figures of China, Taiwan, Hong Kong, and Singapore are from the Asian Development Bank (http://www.adb.org) and those of Japan and USA are from Econstat (http://www.econstats.com/home.htm).

The statistics are computed as gross national savings in percentage of GDP.

that of the USA, as shown in Table 7.2, we find that Chinese families in southeast Asia do save a lot more than people in the USA.

There are several reasons for the behavioral differences in savings. The first is that pension systems in Chinese societies have not been prevalent in the relevant periods. For instance, in Taiwan, employees covered by pensions are mostly civil servants, who account for only 37.83 per cent in 2006.[2] Another cause of this high saving rate is the reliability of the family network. As we mentioned, family ties in traditional Chinese society are strong, and much of the risk in health, business failure, injury, and accidental longevity could be insured against within the family network. This makes market insurance less of a necessity, thereby reducing the importance of developing a pension system. This is also in contrast to the scenario mentioned in Kotlikoff and Summers (1981), where the authors show that only 20 per cent of US national wealth is due to life cycle savings, whereas 80 per cent is due to intergenerational transfers.

The high savings rate in Chinese families alone is not enough to give us a picture of the resource flow between generations; we need to know more about intergenerational transfers. In the PSFD survey, the interviewees were asked about the status of their parents' asset transfers, and the results are listed in Table 7.3. In this table, we restrict our samples to those who had at least one parent surviving at the time of the interview, so that the *decision* of parental transfers has a meaningful context. Depending on their parental surviving conditions, we cross tabulate the asset-transfer status into four cases, both for Taiwan and for Mainland China: all transferred, partly transferred, not transferred yet, and nothing to be transferred. It is surprising to observe that 24.88 per cent of Taiwanese families transferred *all* their assets when at least one of their parents was still alive, and the

Table 7.3. Distribution of families by parent-to-child asset-transfer status (%)

	China	Taiwan
All transferred	35.24	24.88
Partly transferred	5.78	5.00
Not transferred yet	24.99	35.75
Nothing to be transferred	33.81	34.39
Sample size	4,602	4,083

Source: The 1999, 2000, and 2003 Taiwan PSFD survey, and the 2004 China PSFD survey.

corresponding number for Mainland China is even higher (35.24 per cent). We consider this is a surprising statistic because, as we shall see in Chapter 11, any parents who want their children to heed their wishes would naturally want to keep some assets as lures instead of giving up all their leverage *inter vivos*. But Table 7.3 shows that a large proportion of Chinese parents did make the seemingly irrational decision of giving up such control. In Chapter 11 we are going to discuss more why Chinese parents tend to choose this seemingly irrational move; but right now let us investigate the gender inequality implication of these *inter vivos* transfers.

Because the Chinese used to treat the family as an end rather than a means, as we described in Chapter 1, parent-to-child *inter vivos* transfers are natural, as long as such resources are needed for the development of the children. Indeed, the PSFD data show that Chinese parents often provide resources for their children even after the latter finish schooling. The interesting phenomenon is: such *inter vivos* transfers are extremely unequal among children. As shown in Table 7.4, in Mainland China, less than 10 per cent of families give any assets to their daughters. In Taiwan, the proportion of families leaving positive bequests to girls is higher, but only

Table 7.4. Distribution of families by ways of transfer (%)

	China	Taiwan
Equally shared among son(s)	83.07	65.12
Unequally shared among son(s)	5.48	8.14
Equally shared among daughter(s)	0.64	1.25
Unequally shared among daughter(s)	1.50	0.42
Equally shared among son(s) and daughter(s)	6.07	11.88
Unequally shared among son(s) and daughter(s), larger share for son(s)	1.61	9.63
Others	1.61	3.57
Sample size	1,861	1,204

Source: The 1999, 2000, and 2003 Taiwan PSFD survey, and the 2004 China PSFD survey.

slightly more than 20 per cent. In most cases in Taiwan, girls still get less than boys, and only in 11.88 per cent of all Taiwanese families do parents make a truly equal allocation of parental assets. In Mainland China, the proportion of equal sharing is only 6.07 per cent, lower than that in Taiwan.

Because China has had a one-child policy for the past two decades, one may wonder whether our samples cover such one-child families, and, if so, whether the category "equal sharing among sons" is contaminated by the fact that there is only one son in the family. It turns out that this is not the case. As far as Table 7.4 is concerned, the average sibship size in question is quite large. In the equal-sharing category of Table 7.4, only 4.53 per cent of the China sample and 1.91 per cent of the Taiwan sample do not have any sibling in their family. Thus, the figures shown in Table 7.4 do reveal a "choice" of unequal division, and many girls indeed did not get any transfers from their parents.

In the next section, we shall propose a model of parental resource allocation. From the evidence of unequal sharing of parental asset transfers among children, we try to investigate the degree of parents' "revealed" son preferences.

7.3. Empirical Setting

Consider a family having several children, possibly including some boys and girls. The parents have the following family welfare function:

$$W = W(c_p, y_1, \ldots, y_n),$$

where c_p is the family consumption, and y_i is the income of the ith child ($i = 1, \ldots n$). The total number of children is assumed to be n. For child i, his or her income y_i is determined by $y_i = rt_i + \alpha_i S_i^\gamma \varepsilon_i$. In the above equation, r is the market interest rate, t_i is the parental transfer received by child i, a_i is the gender-specific rate of return to schooling, S_i is the schooling received by this child, $\gamma < 1$ is a parameter of the production function transforming schooling to earnings, and ε_i is the child's random luck or ability. The iso-elastic functional specification of S_i is assumed only to simplify our presentation; for general functional forms, the empirical setting should be understood as a log-linear approximation. We allow a to be possibly different across genders because the labor market rates of return are usually different for different genders. Suppose the total income of the parents is I. Other than family preferences, there is a budgetary constraint between transfers, schooling expenses, and family consumption. Subject to this budget constraint, the parents maximize their family welfare W.

Intuitively, as long as the marginal benefit of some minimum schooling is very large, then it is impossible to have a corner solution for the schooling investment in any child. However, it is possible to have a corner solution for *inter vivos* transfers, particularly when the parent is poor (constrained financially) or has a strong preferences toward some children. It is shown in Appendix 7.1 that family utility maximization generates the following equation for estimation:

$$\log\frac{W_j}{W_i} = (1 - \gamma)\log\frac{S_j}{S_i} - \log\frac{\alpha_j}{\alpha_i} + X_{ij}\beta - \log\frac{\varepsilon_j}{\varepsilon_i}, \qquad (7.1)$$

where X is vector of other explanatory variables, and W_i is the partial derivative of W with respect to its ith argument.

Equation (7.1) is the main equation for our estimation. Note that the ratio W_j/W_i reveals the parent's willingness to adjust incomes between child-j and child-i. Equation (7.1) characterizes the behavior of parents when they try to equalize the incomes of their children. Based on our previous discussion, we first consider the following set of gender dummies:

$$x_{1ij} = \begin{cases} 1, & \text{if } i \text{ is a boy and } j \text{ is a girl,} \\ 0, & \text{otherwise.} \end{cases}$$

$$x_{2ij} = \begin{cases} 1, & \text{if } j \text{ is a boy and } i \text{ is a girl,} \\ 0, & \text{otherwise.} \end{cases}$$

The reference group for the above two dummies refers to the case of both i and j being of the same gender. In equation (7.1), since the effects of the two dummies (x_{1ij} and x_{2ij}) should be symmetrical, we impose the restriction that the coefficients of these two variables are equal in magnitude but opposite in sign. As one can see, the coefficients of (x_1, x_2) reveal parents' son preferences.

Secondly, we consider the two more seniority dummies:

$$x_{3ij} = \begin{cases} 1, & \text{if } i \text{ is the eldest son,} \\ 0, & \text{otherwise.} \end{cases}$$

$$x_{4ij} = \begin{cases} 1, & \text{if } j \text{ is the eldest son,} \\ 0, & \text{otherwise.} \end{cases}$$

Similar to x_{1ij} and x_{2ij}, the symmetry constraint for x_{3ij} and x_{4ij} is imposed in the regression model. In sum, the vectors (x_1, x_2) and (x_3, x_4) capture two possible patterns of parental preferences.

Although W_j and W_i are not observable, using the transfer data presented in Table 7.4 we obtain some rough information concerning the magnitude of $\log(W_j/W_i)$, which may help us estimate the parameters in (7.1). For instance, we know that if children j and i receive positive and zero bequests respectively, then $W_j > W_i$ must be true. Furthermore, if both children get positive bequests, we also know that parents should make equal the marginal benefit from transferring to child i and child j, so that $W_j = W_i$. Below we shall make the following assumptions for W_j/W_i:

Assumption 1: If parents provide equal transfers to two children, it is prima facie evidence that the parents do not differentiate between these two children in their willingness to transfer.

Assumption 2: If parents provide unequal transfers to two children, it is *prima facie* evidence of differential willingness to transfer.

Assumption 3: If one of the children receives zero transfer, then the parents' differential willingness to transfer is assumed to be stronger than unequal positive transfers.

Let $z_{ij}^* \equiv \log(W_j/W_i)$. We shall consider three cases: First, if child i and child j receive equal positive transfers, then by assumption 1 we suppose that parents have roughly equal concern toward i and j. Thus, we should have z_{ij}^* close to zero. Second, if the parents transfer some assets to child j but nothing to child i, then, by assumption 3, this is prima facie evidence of a strong differential treatment. In this case, assumptions 2 and 3 tell us that z_{ij}^* should be a positive number. Similarly, if i receives a positive transfer whereas j receives nothing, then we say that child i is strongly favored, and z_{ij}^* should be a negative number. Third, if the parents transfer positive assets to child i and child j but one of them receives more, then by assumption 2 we suppose that there is some degree of differential preferences, but the case is less serious than the second case.

Now we can operationalize assumptions 1–3. In economics term, W_j/W_i is the marginal rate of substitution (MRS) of parents with respect to their children's incomes, which cannot be observed. But for those families that have transferred part or all of their assets, the above discussion suggests the following setting:

$$z_{ij}^* = X_{ij}\beta + \delta y_{ij} - a_{ij} + u_{ij}, \qquad (7.2)$$

where $y_{ij} \equiv \log(S_j/S_i)$, and $a_{ij} \equiv \log(a_j/a_i)$. More statistical details are given in Appendix 7.2.

The target of our analysis is to see whether parents have specific preferences among children. In our empirical analysis, the "parents" refers to the respondent's parents, and the "children" refers to the respondent and his or her siblings. First we shall drop those families which have no child or one child, for in these cases the parents by definition cannot have "preferences" among children. Second, our analysis focuses on the educational attainment of children, and hence we only keep families whose children are expected to have completed their education, namely aged 25 or older.[3] Third, since our analysis relies on the transfer of assets, we also drop families that do not have any assets to transfer. Fourth, for those families that have more than two children and have transferred some assets to them, we randomly select a pair of children as our (i, j) observation, namely child-1 and child-2.[4] Because the variables used here are not unique, we shall skip the tabulation of mean and standard deviation, and move directly to the regression results.

7.4. Empirical Results

We first present the ordered probit estimation results for the baseline model of equation (7.2), and in the next subsection we proceed with an analysis using an instrumental-variable approach.

7.4.1. Baseline Estimation

In Tables 7.5 and 7.6 we present three models for both Taiwan and China. In each model, the coefficient of $\log(S_2 / S_1)$ represents whether the parents tend to reward more the child with more schooling years, considered a point of merit; a positive (negative) coefficient indicates that parents treat more schooling as a merit point. It is clear that in all three models the coefficient is positive and significant. Moreover, its size is stable across various specifications, both for Taiwan and for China. Let us look at the Taiwan case first.

The baseline model (A) leaves all the difference in parents' willingness to swap (W_1/W_2) to schooling differences and the intercept terms. The parameters c_1–c_4 in Model A reveal the difference in intercepts, a result consistent with what one expects. The more interesting cases are Models B and C, where we include the gender and the eldest-son dummies as supplementary explanatory variables. As described earlier, we imposed the constraints that the coefficients for each set of dummies are symmetric. We see from Model B

Table 7.5. Ordered probit models for $\log(W_2/W_1)$, Taiwan

	Model A	Model B	Model C
$\log(S_2/S_1)$	0.331***	0.341***	0.328***
	(0.044)	(0.062)	(0.062)
Gender dummies (both siblings being same gender as ref. group)			
1st sibling male and 2nd sibling female		−2.993***	−2.838***
(1 = yes)		(0.110)	(0.116)
1st sibling female and 2nd sibling male		2.993***	2.838***
(1 = yes)		(0.110)	(0.116)
"Eldest son" dummies (neither being eldest son as ref. group)			
1st sibling being the eldest son (1 = yes)			−0.390***
			(0.097)
2nd sibling being the eldest son (1 = yes)			0.390***
			(0.097)
c_1	−0.907***	−2.508***	−2.574***
	(0.048)	(0.115)	(0.119)
c_2	−0.722***	−1.938***	−1.996***
	(0.046)	(0.102)	(0.107)
c_3	0.863***	2.052***	2.109***
	(0.048)	(0.107)	(0.111)
c_4	0.998***	2.471***	2.535***
	(0.050)	(0.115)	(0.120)
Log likelihood	−1099.47	−480.14	−471.83
Number of observations	929	929	929

Notes: Standard errors are in parentheses. *, **, and *** denote 10%, 5%, and 1% significance levels respectively. c_1–c_4 are constant terms corresponding to the 5-categorical ordered probit model.

The coefficients for the two gender dummies are equal in magnitude but opposite in sign. And a similar constraint is imposed on the two "eldest son" dummies.

of Table 7.5 that the male child is treated more preferentially in Taiwan, even after we have controlled the education differences. This preferential treatment is a direct characterization of the ratio of parents' marginal willingness to transfer to different children, as one can see from Appendix 7.1. Also note that this effect of gender difference is robust both in size and in statistical significance, even if we control the "eldest-son" effect in Model C.

Note that the implicit ratio of W_j to W_i is cardinal in nature, which indicates the parents' willingness to swap assets between two children. For instance, Model C of Table 7.5 says that if child 2 is a boy whereas child 1 is a girl, the estimated ratio of assets swap between them is larger at a magnitude of 17.08 ($=e^{2.838}$), compared to the case in which both children are of the same gender. This is indeed a very large discrimination scale. In contrast, the preference over the eldest son is not as large, at only 1.476($=e^{0.390}$). The marginal effect of reinforcing is also small: in comparison to the case of the same education, if a child has fifteen years of

Table 7.6. Ordered probit models for $\log(W_2/W_1)$, China

	Model A	Model B	Model C
$\log(S_2/S_1)$	0.364***	0.288***	0.288***
	(0.029)	(0.048)	(0.048)
Gender dummies (both siblings being same gender as ref. group)			
1st sibling male and 2nd sibling female		−3.530***	−3.477***
(1 = yes)		(0.093)	(0.101)
1st sibling female and 2nd sibling male		3.530***	3.477***
(1 = yes)		(0.093)	(0.101)
"Eldest son" dummies (neither being eldest son as ref. group)			
1st sibling being the eldest son (1 = yes)			−0.104
			(0.079)
2nd sibling being the eldest son (1 = yes)			0.104
			(0.079)
c_1	−0.800***	−2.359***	−2.367***
	(0.036)	(0.093)	(0.094)
c_2	−0.734***	−2.022***	−2.030***
	(0.35)	(0.085)	(0.086)
c_3	0.730***	1.961***	1.967***
	(0.035)	(0.083)	(0.083)
c_4	0.776***	2.227***	2.233***
	(0.036)	(0.090)	(0.091)
Log likelihood	−1769.34	−495.04	−494.17
Number of observations	1,605	1,605	1,605

Notes: Standard errors are in parentheses. *, **, and *** denote 10%, 5%, and 1% significance levels respectively. c_1–c_4 are constant terms corresponding to the 5-categorical ordered probit model.

The coefficients for the two gender dummies are equal in magnitude but opposite in sign. And a similar constraint is imposed on the two "eldest son" dummies.

education and his or her sibling has ten years, then the estimated swap ratio is 1.14 ($=e^{\log(15/10)\times0.328}$). Thus, the eldest-son effect and the reinforcing effect are both small, and the factor that contributes most to unequal asset transfers in Taiwan is gender. This seems to us serious evidence of son preferences in Taiwan.

In Table 7.6 we present the same analysis for China. The data manipulation procedure is the same as for Taiwan, and hence we skip the details. As one can see from this table, the son preferences are slightly stronger in China than in Taiwan, and the reinforcing effect in China is slightly smaller. Thus, the strong son preference revealed in Table 7.6 is not entirely consistent with the weak gender preference Chinese respondents provided as they answered the survey questions, shown in Table 7.1. The only qualitative difference between Taiwan and China is that the "eldest-son" dummy is insignificant in China but significant in Taiwan. It suggests that the seniority of boys is important only in Taiwan. It is well known that primogeniture is a custom in Japan but not in China (Chu 1991). It may be the case that the fifty-year Japanese colonial rule in Taiwan has made Taiwan's parents put more weight on the eldest son.

We further examine the robustness of our model by combining the response categories (the first and second as well as the fourth and fifth categories of the dependent variables in (a7.5) in Appendix 7.2) into one category. This combination of categories assumes that the case of a child receiving *no* transfer at all and the case of a child receiving *less* transfer than his or her sibling are indistinguishable. We find that in both China and Taiwan there is no significant difference before and after we regroup the categories. In summary, Tables 7.5 and 7.6 tell us that there does exist a gap in parents' marginal willingness to transfer to girls and their willingness to transfer to boys in the two Chinese societies we examine.

7.4.2. Instrumental Variable Estimation for Taiwan

For family i, let the two randomly sampled children be indexed 1 and 2 respectively. One critique of the estimation of (7.2) is, again, that the error term u may be correlated with $\log(S_2 / S_1)$. For instance, if the parents simply like child 2, then they will allocate more education investment as well as bequest to child 2, which sustains the correlation mentioned above. In this case, the estimate of δ would be biased and inconsistent. We shall use a unique instrumental variable for the case of Taiwan by applying the estimation method proposed by Rivers and Vuong (1988).

FIRST-STAGE ESTIMATION

In the first stage, we estimate the following equation:

$$\log(S_2/S_1) = X'\alpha + W'\lambda + \varepsilon,$$

where W includes variables that might be correlated with $\log(S_2 / S_1)$ but uncorrelated with z^*. Because the nine-year mandatory education period has been implemented in Taiwan since 1968, we use the information regarding the birth year of the siblings to construct our IV. We let W include the following dummies: (1) first sibling's birth year $\geq$1956, and second sibling's birth year <1956; (2) first sibling's birth year <1956, and second sibling's birth year $\geq$1956; (3) Both siblings' birth year $\geq$1956. And "both siblings' birth year <1956" is chosen as the reference group. From the first-stage estimation, we could obtain the corresponding residuals $\hat{\varepsilon}$ values.

SECOND-STAGE ESTIMATION

In the second stage, the residuals from the first-stage equation are added as one of the regressors in the ordered probit model:

$$z^* = X'\beta + \delta \cdot \log(S_2/S_1) + \theta \cdot \hat{\varepsilon} + u.$$

In the above model, the estimated $\hat{\theta}$ could be used to test the null hypothesis that $\log(S_2 / S_1)$ is exogenous.

The results of the second-stage IV estimation for the Taiwan sample are listed in Table 7.7. It can be seen from column 3 that "first sibling's birth year $\geq$ 1956 and second sibling's birth year <1956" has significant effect on $\log(S_2 / S_1)$, which means that the birth cohort dummy is not a weak IV. From column 2 of the same table, it can be seen that $\hat{\varepsilon}$ is not significant in the asset-transfers

Table 7.7. Instrumental variable estimation results, Taiwan

	2nd-stage estimation ($\log(W_2/W_1)$)	1st-stage estimation ($\log(S_2/S_1)$)
$\log(S_2/S_1)$	0.522	
	(0.537)	
Gender dummies (both siblings being same gender as ref. group)		
1st sibling male and 2nd sibling female	−2.799***	−0.168**
	(0.158)	(0.072)
1st sibling female and 2nd sibling male	2.799***	0.216***
	(0.158)	(0.078)
Seniority dummies (neither being eldest son as ref. group)		
1st sibling being the eldest son	−0.378***	−0.038
	(0.102)	(0.073)
2nd sibling being the eldest son	0.378***	0.134*
	(0.102)	(0.078)
Birth year dummies (both siblings' birth year <1956 as ref. group)		
1st sibling's birth year $\geq$ 1956 and 2nd sibling's birth year <1956		0.323***
		(0.105)
1st sibling's birth year <1956 and 2nd sibling's birth year $\geq$1956		0.012
		(0.100)
Both siblings' birth year $\geq$1956		0.086
		(0.065)
$\hat{\varepsilon}$	−0.198	
	(0.542)	
Log likelihood	−471.76	
R-squared		0.055
Number of observations	929	929

Notes: Standard errors are in parentheses. *, **, and *** denote 10%, 5%, and 1% significance levels respectively. The constant terms of the above two regressions are omitted for brevity.

In the $\log(W_2/W_1)$ equation, the symmetry constraints are imposed on the coefficients of gender and seniority dummies.

Table 7.8. Instrumental variable estimation results (symmetry constraints imposed on first-stage estimation), Taiwan

	2nd-stage estimation $(log(W_2/W_1))$	1st-stage estimation $(log(S_2/S_1))$
$log(S_2/S_1)$	1.227	
	(0.804)	
Gender dummies (both siblings being same gender as ref. group)		
1st sibling male and 2nd sibling female	−2.655***	−0.192***
	(0.199)	(0.049)
1st sibling female and 2nd sibling male	2.655***	0.192***
	(0.199)	(0.049)
Seniority dummies (neither being eldest son as ref. group)		
1st sibling being the eldest son	−0.331***	−0.085
	(0.110)	(0.051)
2nd sibling being the eldest son	0.331***	0.085
	(0.110)	(0.051)
Birth year dummies (both siblings being the same cohort as ref. group)		
1st sibling's birth year ≥1956 and 2nd sibling's birth year <1956		0.152**
		(0.069)
1st sibling's birth year <1956 and 2nd sibling's birth year ≥1956		−0.152**
		(0.069)
$\hat{\varepsilon}$	−0.907	
	(0.808)	
Log likelihood	−471.19	
Number of observations	929	929

Notes: Standard errors are in parentheses. *, **, and *** denote 10%, 5%, and 1% significance levels respectively. The constant terms of the above two regressions are omitted for brevity.

In the $log(W_2/W_1)$ equation, the symmetry constraints are imposed on the coefficients of gender and seniority dummies. And in the equation, the symmetry constraints are imposed on the coefficients of gender, seniority, and birth year dummies.

equation. This implies that $log(S_2/S_1)$ is exogenous in the second-stage IV model. In the asset-transfers equation, the coefficient of $log(S_2/S_1)$ is insignificantly different from zero; this is different from the finding of Table 7.5. It turns out that the reinforcing hypothesis no longer prevails after the endogeneity problem is taken into account. However, the gender and seniority dummies still remain significant, with their size roughly the same as those in Table 7.5. As one can see, the magnitudes of coefficients of the gender dummies in Tables 7.5 and 7.7 are only slightly different, indicating that our results of gender preferences are robust with respect to the IV adjustment.

In Table 7.8, symmetry constraints are imposed on gender, seniority, and birth year dummies in the first-stage estimation. Yet it turns out that the results are very similar to Table 7.7.

7.5. Conclusions

In this chapter we summarized some subjective as well as objective evidence of gender preferences in Chinese societies. The subjective evidence is usually captured by the interviewees' response to questions of typical gender-role perceptions. Data from our PSFD surveys indicate that a significant proportion of respondents are still strongly influenced by traditional perceptions such as "male-line lineage preservation" and "work is for the husband and housework is for the wife." We also found that this traditional ideology is more serious in Taiwan than in China. For objective evidence, we found that a large proportion of parents in Taiwan and China leave assets, either *inter vivos* or in the form of bequests, only to boys but not to girls. And even if the girls do receive some asset transfers, their shares are usually smaller.

Using the property that the marginal returns to education may be different across individuals whereas marginal returns to assets are the same in the capital market, we are able to estimate parents' marginal willingness to swap assets between two children. In both China and Taiwan, it turns out that this swap ratio is considerably more favorable to boys than to girls. The preference for the eldest son seems to exist only in Taiwan. The reinforcing effect, which states that parents tend to bequeath more to the better-educated child, is significant in a primitive model, but disappears after we have controlled for the endogeneity of the relative schooling variable.

APPENDIX 7.1 DERIVING THE ESTIMATION EQUATION IN (7.1)

Based on the utility maximization setting in Section 7.3, we consider the first-order conditions for the simple case of two siblings, indexed by i and j respectively. Denoting the partial differentiation by a subscript, the first-order conditions turn out to be

$$-W_c + rW_j \leq 0; t_j \geq 0 \qquad (a7.1)$$

$$-W_c + rW_i \leq 0; t_i \geq 0 \qquad (a7.2)$$

$$-W_c + W_j \cdot \alpha_j \gamma S_j^{\gamma-1} \varepsilon_j = 0 \qquad (a7.3)$$

$$-W_c + W_i \cdot \alpha_i \gamma S_i^{\gamma-1} \varepsilon_i = 0 \qquad (a7.4)$$

In (a7.3) and (a7.4) above, since γ is assumed to be less than 1, it is impossible to have a corner solution for schooling, and hence the first-order conditions are written as equalities.[5] In (a7.1) and (a7.2) however, we have complementary slackness conditions for t_j and t_i, because transfers may well be zero, especially for poor parents (see Ermisch 2003: ch. 5).

Now let us investigate the preferences of parents. If parents have equal preferences toward their children, the W function should be symmetrical with respect to the income (y_i) of all children. In case of an interior solution, bequests play the role of equalizing the marginal utility of transfers of every child's income. In reality, parents are likely to have more or less differential preferences toward their children, and the possible criteria may be health, smartness, gender, birth order, personality or character of the child, etc. We assume that the following factors influence the parental relative preferences for a pair of children (i, j): (i) the gender composition of (i, j), and (ii) whether one of the children is the eldest son in the family. This is basically consistent with the descriptions of possible preferences found in the literature (also see our discussion in Chapter 8).

For the time being suppose that the parents' marginal utility of their respective incomes, W_i and W_j, is known. From (a7.3) and (a7.4), we see that

$$\log \frac{W_j}{W_i} = (1 - \gamma)\log \frac{S_j}{S_i} - \log \frac{\alpha_j}{\alpha_i} - \log \frac{\varepsilon_j}{\varepsilon_i}. \qquad (a7.5)$$

If the two children i and j are of the same gender, then in (a7.5) $\log(\alpha_j / \alpha_i)$ should be zero. We also assume that the relative intelligence or ability of the two siblings follows a symmetric log-normal distribution, so that $u_{ij} \equiv \log(\varepsilon_j/\varepsilon_i) \sim N(0, \sigma_u^2)$. If parents have some special preferences, their willingness to transfer toward one child may be relatively higher, other things being equal. In this case, (a7.5) should be revised as

$$\log\frac{W_j}{W_i} = (1 - \gamma)\log\frac{S_j}{S_i} - \log\frac{\alpha_j}{\alpha_i} + X_{ij}\beta - \log\frac{\varepsilon_j}{\varepsilon_i}, \qquad (7.1)$$

where X is a vector of explanatory variable characterizing such preferences.

APPENDIX 7.2 STATISTICAL SPECIFICATIONS BEHIND (7.2)

In equation (7.2), even though the latent variable z_{ij}^* is not observable, we assume that its corresponding observable variable is ordered in the following sense based on assumptions 1–3:

$$
z_{ij} = \begin{cases}
= 1; & \text{if } t_i > t_j = 0, \\
= 2; & \text{if } t_i > t_j > 0, \\
= 3; & \text{if } t_i = t_j > 0 \quad \text{or} \quad t_i = t_j = 0, \\
= 4; & \text{if } 0 < t_i < t_j, \\
= 5; & \text{if } 0 = t_i < t_j.
\end{cases} \quad (a7.6)
$$

Thus the error term $u_{ij} = z_{ij} - (X_{ij}\beta + \delta y_{ij} - a_{ij})$ has the hierarchical structure accordingly:

$$
\begin{cases}
u_{ij} \in (-\infty, c_1); & \text{if } t_{1i} > t_{2i} = 0, \\
u_{ij} \in [c_1, c_2); & \text{if } t_{1i} > t_{2i} > 0, \\
u_{ij} \in [c_2, c_3); & \text{if } t_{1i} = t_{2i} > 0 \quad \text{or} \quad t_{1i} = t_{2i} = 0, \\
u_{ij} \in [c_3, c_4); & \text{if } 0 < t_{1i} < t_{2i}, \\
u_{ij} \in [c_4, \infty); & \text{if } 0 = t_{1i} < t_{2i},
\end{cases} \quad (a7.7)
$$

c_k $(k = 1, \ldots, 4)$ are unknown constants, with $0 < c_1 < c_2 < c_3 < c_4$. Assuming u_{ij} is standardized normally distributed, the regression described above is an ordered probit model with the symmetry constraints imposed on (x_1, x_2) and (x_3, x_4) respectively. Note that a_{ij}, the gender-specific difference in schooling returns, is society specific, and is not variant across families, but y_{ij} and X_{ij} are family specific. The regression does not have a constant term due to the assumption made for the latent structure of u_{ij}.

Notes

1. McGarry (2008) finds that equal division of bequests among children is the norm in the USA. Light and McGarry (2004) also found that 80 per cent of respondents in the National Longitudinal Survey intended to divide their estates equally among their children.
2. See annual statistical reports from the Council of Labor Affairs of Taiwan.

3. Taiwan has a two-year mandatory military service requirement for men, hence we choose 25 to be the critical age of college completion.

4. To increase the variation of the dependent variable, for the families that transferred assets unequally, the child with the largest share, if he or she could be identified, is chosen for certain, and the other child is selected randomly.

5. Term γ being less than 1 implies that the marginal return to education is decreasing and that some education is always rewarding.

8

The Role of the Family in Child Education

Investment in children may take several possible forms, and the most prevalent ones are investments in somatic and human capital. For the analysis of investments in somatic capital and child nutrition, researchers need the data of child calorie intake and the control of child physiological endowments. Since nutrition shortage is a problem mostly found in developing countries, previous empirical analyses have specific area foci. Yet, perhaps due to the lack of data sets in those developing countries, few studies have provided relevant evidence. China did suffer from famine and insufficient nutrition in the 1960s; but to our knowledge, there appeared to be no relevant nutrition data for empirical analysis.[1]

Our purpose in this chapter is to study parental investments in children's education in Chinese societies. Two different perspectives can be identified in previous analyses of education. First, treating incomes or earnings as the main variable to be analyzed, economists often deem education as a *means* that influences earnings. Second, for one reason or another, child education *per se* is sometimes treated as an *end* by Chinese parents. In what follows, we shall discuss the content of both perspectives.

8.1. The Role of Education: Conceptual Differences

When education is treated as a means of increasing child earnings, the key variable of interest is the marginal return of education on earnings. The problem, however, is compounded by the fact that this rate of return is also affected by child endowment or ability, which in turn is correlated with the education investment decision of the parents, i.e., parents may invest more in better-endowed (smarter) children. In the earnings equation, child ability is unobservable and is partly captured by the error term, therefore education is an explanatory variable correlated with the error term, again causing the so-called endogeneity problem in estimation. This problem can be solved either by a special data set (such as twins) which controls the endowment of children, or by econometric methods (such as the instrumental variable approach) which under some assumptions can remove the correlation between explanatory variable and disturbance. A good survey can be found in Card (1999).[2]

A comparison of the education data of siblings alone generates some interesting research. If parents are efficient investors, according to Becker (1991), they should invest in the education of their children to the point where the marginal benefit of education to each child is equal. This implies that one can use the sibling data to infer the efficiency of parental decisions. However, this is true only when parents have an interior-solution strategy. Ermisch and Francesconi (2001) took into account the possibility of a corner solution of bequest, and modified the resulting implications on education investment among children accordingly. Focusing on the difference in sibling education, Behrman et al. (1989) predicted that this difference should be negatively related to the sibship size.

If child income is what parents care about, we expect that parents should be more concerned with children's permanent income than their transitory income. However, since permanent incomes are hard to measure or to calculate, Behrman and Taubman (1985) suggested that we use education as a proxy of permanent income. If parents also take this perspective, then child education becomes an end for parents rather than a means. Another type of objective that parents expect education to help accomplish is social mobility or social stratification. Sociologists often use indices such as occupational prestige scales to capture the concept of social ladder, and education is a typical variable explaining the movements on this ladder in a society. Under this context, researchers study the association between the child's and the parents' education, which will be the focus of Chapter 9.

In fact, traditional emphasis on education in Chinese societies is so strong that the purpose of education is sometimes lost sight of. Chinese and Jewish families are known to pay more attention to child education than families from many other ethnic backgrounds.[3] Ho (1962) provided detailed evidence to illustrate why this was so for Chinese families in ancient China: Since AD 1371, the Chinese have adopted systems of civil-service exams, which resulted in the award of various official ranks according to different passing criteria. Such exams tested the candidates mainly on the moral and behavioral teachings of the Confucian tradition. The final

157

grand examination was often presided over by the emperor himself, and those who did well in the final exams were usually assured of good career prospects in the civil service. According to Ho (1962) and Chu (1991), this civil-service test system was a key to the promotion of social mobility. Poor children, as long as they were smart enough and studied hard enough, could always have a chance to pass the test and end up somewhere in officialdom. Short of revolution, this might be the only chance at mobility across social classes in ancient China.

Perhaps because of the low probability of advancement out of the plebeian status, preparing for and taking civil-service examinations became a widely shared aspiration of China's common people. An old Chinese proverb says that "bequeathing a basket of gold to sons is never as good as leaving them a legacy of ancient teachings." And "houses of gold and beauties of jade are to be found in books" is also a popular Chinese saying attributed to an emperor of the Song Dynasty. Thus, educating one's children not only was perceived as an important means by parents in ancient China, it is actually "rationalized" as an objective in the minds of many of today's parents as well. Our question in this chapter is: if child education is so important, how are parents to divide their finite resources among their children? Are the practices in Chinese societies different from those in the West?

8.2. Child Education with Gender Preferences: Evidence from Some Asian Countries

The enthusiasm for education in ancient China mentioned in the previous section in fact has persisted into modern times, despite the fact that the rate of return on a basket of gold or other physical investments may actually be higher, and that the civil-service exams had been abolished since 1905. As mentioned above, the emphasis on child education has become part of Chinese culture. In the past several centuries, million of Chinese migrated to Taiwan, the Malay Peninsula, Indonesia, and many other parts of southeast Asia, and we are able to observe the education of Chinese families in different places today. They share a very high priority given by parents to child education, and a tendency to favor the education of sons over daughters. This is consistent with the ethos of male dominance we described in Chapter 1. Below is some evidence we summarize.

Behrman and Deolalikar (1995) studied the situation in Indonesia, and found that the rates of return to schooling were different across genders in

1986. As is well known, this difference in rates of return confronted the parents with distinct objective incentives to invest in the education of their boys and girls, which would confound the analysis.

Geographically closer to China, Malaysia has more Chinese immigrants than Indonesia. Lillard and Willis (1994) studied child education in Malaysia among different ethnic groups. Dividing the education ladder into four parts, Lillard and Willis (1994) used a sequential probit model to analyze the education choices at different stages. They found that before 1970, the year when the New Economic Policy was adopted in Malaysia, children in Chinese families had an education advantage over Malays, perhaps due to the wide availability of Chinese-language schools. But this advantage has disappeared since 1970, when Malay became the official language of school instruction according to the new law. Concerning within-family competition, they used their survey data to find that competition for education resources was mainly among siblings of the same sex, in the sense that elder brothers hurt boys and younger sisters hurt girls. However, these findings with respect to all ethnic groups are not reproduced when the sample is restricted to Chinese families alone.

Greenhalgh (1985) was the first to study the gender-specific preferential treatment in child education in Taiwan. Using the panel data collected from an extensive survey of eighty families, she showed that the conventional view that economic modernization usually brings more education "opportunity" for girls was problematic. Greenhalgh showed that, constrained by limited resources, Taiwanese parents in the 1960s and 1970s often sent their girls into the labor market, with the expectation that their remittance might supplement the family budget and hence allow more boys to achieve higher education. Even if girls indeed wound up with more education, the author argued that this might still be due to parents' gender-based cost–benefit analysis which showed that girls going to school were able to remit more resources to the family, net of the education expenses spent on them. In short, she suggested that a boy's education would be much helped if he had one more elder sister in the family.

Using a different data set of Taiwan, Parish and Willis (1993) provided some echo to Greenhalgh's analysis. They reached the following three conclusions: (1) elder sisters helped the younger siblings' education, (2) siblings of the same sex usually hurt each other's education opportunity, and (3) siblings of the opposite sex were neutral. Unlike Greenhalgh, Parish and Willis had a much larger sample size (nearly 20,000), which allowed them to do more empirical analysis on the impact of sibling structure. We shall come back with more discussion later.

At the end of this section, we would like to present the average educational attainment of Taiwan and China using the PSFD survey. To convert different education tiers into years of schooling in a systematical way is not an easy task for China, since its education system experienced frequent changes from the late 1950s till the early 1980s. A shortening of the education period for certain education tiers was tried in some areas during the late 1950s. In the 1950s, most such experiments were area specific. However, in 1961 the Chinese government announced a national policy of shortening the length of elementary and secondary school education from twelve to ten years, to be implemented gradually from area to area. In 1966, Mao Zedong advocated a further shortening of schooling years and a reform of the education system. As described in Lee and Wang (2000: 119), the Chinese government experimented with different education tiers during the period of the Cultural Revolution (1966–76). The chaotic state of the education system ended some time in the early 1980s. In 1980, the length of elementary and secondary school education was readjusted to twelve years.[4]

Since the changes in the education system of China are both area and time specific, it is difficult to trace a respondent's educational experience down to fine details and recover his or her years of schooling accurately. So we calculate the years of schooling for the respondent and his or her parent according to the usual practice of China, and the ways of measurement are listed in Table 8.1 for China and Taiwan respectively. Still, it should be borne in mind that the years of schooling computed for China may be subject to measurement errors, especially for the cohort who experienced the Cultural Revolution in their schooling years.

Table 8.1. Measures for years of schooling, China and Taiwan

Years of schooling	China's education category	Taiwan's education category
0	No education	No education
3	Self-educated	Self-educated
6	Elementary school	Elementary school
9	Junior high school	Junior high school
12	Senior high school/ vocational high school/3-year vocational school	Senior high school/ vocational high school
14	2-year vocational college	5-year vocational school/ 2-year vocational college
16	University	University
18	Graduate school	Graduate school

Table 8.2. Average years of schooling in China and Taiwan (in years)

	Year of birth							
	1936–40	1941–5	1946–50	1951–5	1956–60	1961–5	1966–70	1971–5
China								
Male	6.20	7.12	6.72	6.47	7.42	8.13	7.83	8.58
Female	4.18	4.56	5.73	5.67	6.96	7.31	6.87	8.17
Taiwan								
Male	6.72	8.06	9.31	10.16	11.99	11.89	12.65	13.11
Female	3.79	4.42	7.38	8.50	10.02	11.53	12.78	13.22

Notes: The sample of Taiwan is from the first wave of the PSFD survey conducted in 1999, 2000, and 2003 respectively and the counterpart of China is from the 2004 China survey.

In Table 8.2, we calculate from the PSFD data the average education years in China and Taiwan, by gender and cohort. As one can see, the number of years of schooling is always higher for males than for females in both China and Taiwan, and the number of years of schooling is higher in Taiwan than in China for all cohorts. Many of the Chinese cohorts we interviewed grew up during the Cultural Revolution and the Great Leap Forward (1958–60) against a backdrop of widespread poverty and a society in turmoil, as we explained in the above paragraphs and Chapter 2. The corresponding parental "choice" in child education investment was in fact much distorted. Therefore caution is called for when interpreting our empirical analysis where China is concerned in this chapter.

8.3. Sibling Structure and Child Education: Hypotheses in the Literature

Following the logic in Angrist et al. (2006), we shall first distinguish between conditional and unconditional inferences of sibling structure on child education. If we directly compare the average child education achievement between families with different sibship structure, the observed achievement differences are called *unconditional* ones. If we further control (the possibly latent) idiosyncratic family factors, such as parental preferences that may simultaneously affect fertility size and child education, then the obtained achievement differences are called *conditional* ones, meaning that those idiosyncratic conditions have been controlled. The IV approach of quantity–quality analysis in Chapter 4 is a conditional one, whereas the analysis in this chapter is an unconditional one.

We shall review the literature in the West, before returning to propose our modeling of the Chinese society. In empirical analyses of sibling structure on child education, there is uniform evidence showing that a large sibship size is detrimental to a child's education achievement. Then scholars tend to pursue further, probing the possible influence of other aspects of sibling structure, namely sibling density and the sex composition of siblings, on child education. In order to compare the literature with the situation in a Chinese society, we shall provide more discussion below.

8.3.1. Sibling Density

Powell and Steelman (1990, 1993) summarized the following possible hypotheses for the effect of sibling density on education achievement.

1. *Physical/genetic hypothesis*: It states that when the density of siblings increases, so does the probability of health or genetic problems of the child in question. These may depress academic performance (Broman et al. 1975). Evidence also shows that children who are spaced closely together tend to have more health problems (Adams 1972).

2. *Confluence model*: Zajonc and Markus (1975) argue that the intellectual milieu of a child, defined to be the average of intellectual levels of family members, is a key to his or her own intelligence. Therefore the more condensed the sibship, the lower the quality of the family's intellectual environment, and the worse is their education achievement.

3. *Resource dilution*: Blake (1981) and Downey (1995) propose that sibling density may constrain the resources distributable to children. The resources in question include not only physical ones, but also parental attention, cultural opportunity, intellectual stimulation, etc.

8.3.2. Sex Composition

Arguments in the previous subsection are mostly gender neutral, in the sense that there is no presumed pattern of gender bias within the family. Some researchers argued that the influence of sibling structure is actually related to the sex composition of the siblings. Conley (2000) suggested the following hypotheses for the possible influence of the sex composition of siblings on child education.

1. *Confluence model:* Powell and Steelman (1990) argued that males are advantaged in math and females are advantaged in literature. Having a

sibling of a particular gender carries its advantage and disadvantage in the opportunity to learn from one's siblings.

2. *Resource dilution:* Given differential returns to education by sex, parents who are resource constrained may be more willing to invest in boys than in girls. Thus, brothers should be more harmful to one's education opportunity than sisters (Powell and Steelman 1993).

3. *Normative climate:* Families with more male children are likely to have male role expectations, which may benefit children's education in a society that confers psychological advantages on males. Thus, the hypothesis suggests that brothers are less harmful than sisters to sibling education (Powell and Steelman 1990). Butcher and Case (1994) suggested that the presence of a girl is harmful to girls but neutral to boys.

4. *Sex minority hypothesis:* A child of a minority gender in the sibling constellation may enjoy a special status, particularly with respect to parental attachment and expectations (Rosenberg 1965). This is especially true for the only-boy or only-girl cases.

5. *Revised sex minority:* Conley (2000) stated that same-sex siblings may stimulate a competitive, achievement-oriented environment among children, while siblings of opposite sexes may engender a less aggressive environment.

8.3.3. *Existing Empirical Findings*

Although the above hypotheses on sibling density all sound reasonable, empirical studies testing the link between sibling density and education (or intellectual performance), as shown in Broman et al. (1975), Nuttall et al. (1976), Cicirelli (1976) and Gailbraith (1982), yielded equivocal results. Powell and Steelman (1993) attributed the lack of consensus to (1) the unrepresentative samples restricted to small families or selected populations such as college students; or (2) the incomplete or over-generalized measurement of age spacing. Concerning the sex composition of siblings, Butcher and Case (1994) argued that the presence of a girl is detrimental to the education of girls, but not of boys. But Kuo and Hauser (1997) and Hauser and Kuo (1998) disputed this finding by applying the same approach to various other data sets. Controlling the sibship size, they found no effect of gender composition. The only unequivocal finding concerning sibship structure is the negative impact of sibship size (Steelman et al. 2002: 248).

The above empirical findings, regardless of their being consistent or contradictory with each other, were mainly against the background of societies of the West, where there was no general pattern of male dominance. If one takes a look at the findings of Greenhalgh (1985), Parish and Willis (1993), and Lillard and Willis (1994), where the foci were on southeast Asian countries, the general conclusion was that gender composition does matter. This seems intuitive, for otherwise the evidence would be inconsistent with the gender-specific differential treatment we found prevalent in many Asian countries. Thus, prior to a study of the empirical analysis of Chinese societies, we should preferably propose a theory concerning the role of sibling structure in societies with widespread son preferences. Only in that context will we be in a clear position to propose hypotheses that can be compared with the ones in the literature.

8.4. How Does Sibling Structure Matter in Chinese Societies?

Given that boys as well as girls carry half of the parents' genes, it is biologically natural to assume that, to a large extent, parents are indifferent to the gender of their children. If there is a sex-specific differential treatment toward boys or girls, as Becker (1991) argued, it is likely to be due to differences in gender-specific rewards and other compounded factors. For instance, if the rate of return to education is higher for men than for women, then it is "more beneficial" for parents to invest in boys. Of course, the traditional Chinese belief of lineage preservation and the default rule of assigning the family surname along the male line may also magnify the sex-specific differential treatment. But let us leave those factors aside and concentrate for the moment on the cost–benefit analysis of parents.

8.4.1. *The Case of Taiwan*

Greenhalgh (1985) correctly pointed out that an elder sister in the Chinese society of Taiwan may be encouraged or forced to enter the labor market and quit her schooling, with the expectation that she may remit her future incomes to support the family, and also help her younger brothers' education. This is a starting point for our observation. We shall call Greenhalgh's story the "helpful elder sister" (HES) hypothesis, and see whether we can say more about it in detail under a general sibship structure. Note that HES is a story with gender preferences, and our theory derived from it may be different from the previous hypotheses in the literature. Below we shall list the implications one by one.

1. If the HES hypothesis is right, then the composition of siblings certainly matters. This is a theoretical prediction different from that in Hauser and Kuo (1998). Controlling the sibship size, it is more beneficial to have elder sisters than other compositions of siblings. This implies that in later empirical analysis we should view the sibling structure of a family as composed of at least two groups, elder-sister/not-elder-sister, or even better as a four-group sex-seniority partition (elder sisters, elder brothers, younger sisters, and younger brothers). If the elder sister could augment the family income, it is also possible that the elder brother could do the same when a real need arises. Moreover, junior siblings of a female child may also become her burden and contribute to the interruption of her education. Thus, a sex-seniority division of sibling structure is necessary to identify the helping group and the helped group.

2. If the HES hypothesis is right, then the *respondents* should also be separated into males and females. A respondent having several junior siblings may or may not be disadvantaged, depending on his or her own sex. If Greenhalgh (1985) is correct, then senior *female* respondents are more disadvantaged than senior *males*.

3. If the HES hypothesis is right, it also implies the importance of sibling density. If the elder sister is only one year older than her brother, she would be too young to be of much help when her brother needs the tuition, say, to go to high school. Usually, an elder sister with an age difference of three or four years is more likely to provide help than in the case of a shorter age spacing. Conversely, if a female respondent has a younger sibling with a small (large) age difference, the latter is less (more) likely to become a burden to her. This prediction based on sibling spacing is different from those made in Powell and Steelman (1990, 1993), who suggested that close-by siblings are likely to hurt each other. The key difference, according to Chu et al. (2007), is that the family resource is assumed fixed in Powell and Steelman, whereas in Chinese families it is dependent on the elder sisters' remittance.

4. The HES hypothesis assumes a poor family income; when the financial situation of the family gradually improves with rising income, the need for help from elder sisters should decrease. Thus, the economic factors have to be controlled as we investigate the HES hypothesis.

From the above discussion, we can summarize our reasoning as follows. In the traditional Taiwanese family, sons are permanent members of their natal family and retain lifetime contractual relationships with their parents. They are expected to contribute to their parents' economic well-being throughout their adult lives. Thus, it is "rational," or in their self-interest, for parents to invest in sons because they can reap the benefits of the investment over a long period of time. In contrast, daughters are only transitory members of their natal families before their marriage, upon which they move in with and contribute to the family of their parents-in-law, though daughters are expected to contribute to their natal family before marriage. Thus, the time span during which daughters contribute to their natal family is limited. Since education, as human capital, takes time both to accrue and to yield a return, parents mobilize resources from daughters, particularly unmarried elder daughters, to augment the family budget in general, and sometimes to benefit the educational outcomes of sons in particular. The resources in question are primarily remittances from daughters' market labor but can also be household work, which frees up parents to work longer hours. In Greenhalgh's (1985: 276) words, "Put baldly, parents' *key strategy* was to take more from daughters to give more to sons and thus get more for themselves."

In the classical resource-dilution model, which assumes only downward resource flow, resources are highly constrained when children are spaced closely. Indeed, the finding of Powell and Steelman (1990, 1993) that the negative sibship size effects are most pronounced for closely spaced siblings provides strong support for the resource-dilution explanation. However, in the Taiwanese context, we may observe the negative effect of having younger brothers on an elder sister's educational attainment only if there is sufficient spacing between her and her younger brothers. That is, economic resources of elder daughters can only be diverted to help fund the education of their *much* younger brothers. Thus, contrary to the claim of Powell and Steelman (1990, 1993), we may observe a stronger effect of sibship size when spacing is *far apart* rather than when it is close.

8.4.2. *The Case of Mainland China*

We have shown in Chapter 7 that, as far as asset transfer is concerned, the parental preference for sons in China may well be as strong as in Taiwan. However, when this preference is translated into the decision on the allocation of education resources, we find one possible difference between Taiwan and China.

As we know, Taiwan had a head start over China in economic development. This, plus the fact that Taiwan is a small island, favored women's labor force participation in modern sectors in the early stages of Taiwan's development. According to Brinton et al. (1995), the percentage of women working in Taipei city began to increase as early as 1969, and 93 per cent of unmarried women aged 25–9 were employed in 1985. This implies that if a female in Taiwan was expected to help augment the family income, she would be more likely to work in the market. On the other hand, since China is large and was a latecomer in economic development, for our respondents' generation, a female had very few opportunities of market work in cities. As shown in Quan (1991), both the share of urban population and the proportion of non-agricultural labor in China began to increase only after 1979. Thus, if a girl in Mainland China is expected to work to help the family, it is likely that she may simply work in the field, or help take care of her younger siblings at home.

The above-mentioned observation implies a possible difference in sibling interactions. Since age restrictions are more rigid in market work than in non-market work, the help provided by Chinese girls to their families is unhampered by requirements of sibling spacing or seniority, as it is in Taiwan. Thus, if girls are pressured to help their family in China, they do not necessarily have to be senior girls spaced apart.

In what follows, we shall propose an empirical model with the sibling structure refined by sex, seniority, and age spacing. We also separate the respondents into male and female groups. Other explanatory variables, such as the parents' education, are kept as usual.

8.5. Empirical Analysis

We first follow the line of analysis most commonly found in the literature and analyze the effects of sibship size on educational attainment. Then we distinguish sibship size sequentially by gender, spacing, and seniority to further explore the influence of sibship structure on education. In our regressions, we use years of schooling as the dependent variable, which is calculated based on Table 8.1. The sample of Taiwan is from the first wave of the PSFD survey conducted in 1999, 2000, and 2003 respectively. And the counterpart of China is retrieved from the 2004 China survey. In the following analysis, the sibship of a family refers to the respondent and his or her siblings. Furthermore, sibling data are used in the empirical analysis of this chapter, while in Chapter 4 the subjects of analysis are confined to respondents.

Because children from the same family may be subject to unobservable family background, applying family-siblings data should take family (siblings) effect into account. In previous literature, the sibling fixed-effects model and variance-corrected ordinary least squares (OLS) model had been adopted to lessen such problems. Concerning the choice between these two models, Griliches (1979) argued that the use of the sibling fixed-effects approach controlled family characteristics, but did not account for differences in unobservable characteristics between siblings that might be correlated with child outcomes. Another potential problem with the fixed-effects approach is the presence of measurement error. In taking educational differences across siblings, the bias associated with measurement error becomes larger, since the signal-to-noise ratio decreases with the differencing process. Based on the above argument, we choose the OLS model with the Huber–White (Huber 1967, White 1980) adjustment instead of the sibling fixed-effects model. While assuming that respondents from different families are uncorrelated, the Huber–White adjustment procedure allows for correlation between siblings within the same family.[5]

In Table 8.3, we present the results of a basic model with the interaction terms of the subject's sibship size and gender controlled. The regressions (Model A and Model A') for Taiwan and China are listed in columns 2–3 and 4–5 respectively. The results for both Taiwan and China show that sibship size has a negative effect on the female's educational outcomes, but not on male ones, which is consistent with previous literature. These preliminary findings offer some evidence for our prior conjecture, that additional siblings may even provide help to males in addition to diluting the resources in the family. We will return to this topic later in this chapter.

As to other explanatory variables, one could observe from Table 8.3 that both the father's schooling and the mother's schooling have positive effects on educational achievement. The effect of the father's schooling is greater than that of the mother's, probably because the education of the father, who is the primary breadwinner, may better reflect the economic situation of the family. Relative to those subjects whose mother never worked, the ones with a working mother have lower educational attainment. There are two potential reasons for this. First, child care and work are competing for the mother's time. Even though working mothers could bring more resources to their families, the time and energy they could devote to their children would diminish. Second, the mother's work could indicate a relatively poor economic situation of a family that required her to work

Table 8.3. Estimated effects of sibship size on educational attainment, Taiwan and China

Explanatory variables	Model A: Taiwan		Model A': China	
	Coefficient	Standard error	Coefficient	Standard error
Constant	7.962***	0.475	11.480***	0.403
Male (= 1 if yes)	0.132	0.184	0.067	0.146
Father's schooling (in years)	0.284***	0.016	0.250***	0.014
Mother's schooling (in years)	0.199***	0.017	0.152***	0.017
Mother's age at birth ≥40 (= 1 if yes)	−0.199	0.246	0.174	0.133
Working mother (= 1 if yes)	−0.351***	0.110	−1.088***	0.142
Father's ethnicity (aborigine as ref. group)				
Fukienese	2.266***	0.331		
Hakka	2.691***	0.352		
Mainlander	3.069***	0.356		
Father's birthplace (other areas as ref. group)				
Shanhai			0.107	0.211
Zeijiang			−1.281***	0.170
Fujiang			−2.085***	0.172
Male × sibship size	0.034	0.043	−0.050	0.036
Female × sibship size	−0.216***	0.044	−0.299***	0.043
Joint F test for birth cohort dummies	82.01***		124.22***	
	df = (10, 2,590)		df = (19, 3,513)	
R-squared	0.453		0.276	
Number of families	2,591		3,513	
Number of observations	10,654		12,304	

Notes: The birth cohort dummies are omitted from the table for brevity. *, **, *** denote significance at 10%, 5%, 1% levels respectively.

outside the home in the first place. The dummy variable for "mother working" thus could capture this unobserved selectivity.

With respect to ethnicity dummies, relative to aborigines, samples of other ethnic backgrounds tend to have higher education in Taiwan. Among all groups, the educational attainment of Mainlanders in Taiwan is the highest due primarily to their more favorable circumstances for receiving an education (Jao and McKeever 2006). As post-war immigrants, Mainlanders are less likely to own land than early immigrants, but are more likely to live in urban areas and hold non-farming jobs. These circumstances might have meant better education opportunities and dedication to learning for the children of Mainlanders. In China, compared to those who originated from areas other than Shanghai, Zhejiang, and Fujian, the subjects from Zhejiang and Fujian had lower educational attainment, but no significant effect prevails for the Shanghai dummy. This finding is partly a result of the urbanization differences among areas. As to the reason why the immigrants achieved better educational attainment than those who had resided in Zhejiang and Fujian for generations, the above-mentioned argument proposed for Taiwan might apply also.

To analyze the effects of sibship size by the siblings' gender, we further rerun the regressions separately for brothers and sisters. The results presented in Table 8.4 (Model B) show that both brothers and sisters have detrimental effects on the female subjects' educational attainment in Taiwan, and the magnitudes of these two coefficients are similar. However, there are no corresponding effects on males. In China (Model B'), the effect is different: the negative impact is from brothers, not sisters; and the number of brothers affects both male and female subjects, although the effect on males is much smaller, both in magnitude and in significance level. Since other findings are similar to those in Table 8.3, we do not repeat the interpretation here.

Now we further divide siblings into two groups—those spaced closely and those spaced apart—and present the results in Table 8.5. From Model C of Table 8.5, we find that in Taiwan, siblings (brothers or sisters) spaced apart have negative effects on education, yet the effects of siblings spaced closely are not significant. Again, this impact is evident only for females, not for males. This surprising finding directly contradicts the conventional resource theory as formulated by Powell and Steelman (1990, 1993). In the case of China (Model C'), again we find that brothers always hurt, whether they are spaced closely or apart. This observation is consistent with our description in Section 8.4.2. As we see from Table 8.5, this detrimental effect is more serious for females than for males.

Table 8.4. Estimated effects of sibship size by gender on educational attainment, Taiwan and China

Explanatory variables	Model B: Taiwan		Model B': China	
	Coefficient	Standard error	Coefficient	Standard error
Constant	7.942***	0.477	11.589***	0.395
Male	0.166	0.185	0.018	0.144
Father's schooling	0.284***	0.016	0.247***	0.014
Mother's schooling	0.199***	]0.017	0.143***	0.017
Mother's age at birth ≥ 40	−0.197	0.246	0.203	0.134
Working mother	−0.352***	0.110	−1.113***	0.140
Father's ethnicity				
Fukienese	2.266***	0.332		
Hakka	2.686***	0.354		
Mainlander	3.067***	0.358		
Father's birthplace				
Shanhai			0.088	0.210
Zeijiang			−1.290***	0.168
Fujiang			−2.056***	0.171
Male × brothers	0.009	0.058	−0.117**	0.050
Female × brothers	−0.181***	0.058	−0.508***	0.052
Male × sisters	0.053	0.048	0.009	0.046
Female × sisters	−0.236***	0.052	−0.074	0.061
Joint F test for birth cohort	81.48***		120.20***	
dummies	df = (10, 2,590)		df = (20, 3,513)	
R-squared	0.453		0.280	
Number of families	2,591		3,513	
Number of observations	10,654		12,304	

Notes: The birth cohort dummies are omitted from the table for brevity. *, **, *** denote significance at 10%, 5%, 1% levels respectively.

Finally, to examine whether younger or elder spaced-apart siblings are detrimental to the subject's educational attainment, we further divided sibship size by seniority and presented the results in Table 8.6. The findings for Taiwan (Model D) are straightforward: we confirm that only females are influenced by siblings spaced apart, such effects being more pronounced for females with younger siblings spaced apart than for those with elder siblings spaced apart. The finding that the number of elder siblings spaced apart has a weak negative effect on females' educational attainment is unexpected. One possible interpretation is that these late-born females were unwanted by their parents, who had hoped for a boy but ended up with a girl, and as a result, their educational needs were not well attended to by their disappointed parents. This is only a conjecture and needs to be examined further in future research.

In the case of China (Model D'), again brothers always hurt females, regardless of seniority or spacing. Other than this general pattern

Table 8.5. Estimated effects of sibship size by gender and density on educational attainment, Taiwan and China

Explanatory variables	Model C: Taiwan		Model C': China	
	Coefficient	Standard error	Coefficient	Standard error
Constant	7.942***	0.477	11.589***	0.395
Male	0.166	0.185	0.018	0.144
Father's schooling	0.284***	0.016	0.247***	0.014
Mother's schooling	0.199***	0.017	0.143***	0.017
Mother's age at birth ≥ 40	−0.197	0.246	0.203	0.134
Working mother	−0.352***	0.110	−1.113***	0.140
Father's ethnicity				
Fukienese	2.266***	0.332		
Hakka	2.686***	0.354		
Mainlander	3.067***	0.358		
Father's birthplace				
Shanhai			0.088	0.210
Zeijiang			−1.290***	0.168
Fujiang			−2.056***	0.171
Male × brothers spaced closely	−0.062	0.078	−0.008	0.071
Female × brothers spaced closely	−0.024	0.072	−0.462***	0.071
Male × brothers spaced apart	0.039	0.070	−0.166***	0.056
Female × brothers spaced apart	−0.249***	0.063	−0.535***	0.059
Male × sisters spaced closely	0.033	0.065	0.085	0.065
Female × sisters spaced closely	−0.080	0.068	−0.055	0.082
Male × sisters spaced apart	0.037	0.054	−0.025	0.054
Female × sisters spaced apart	−0.307***	0.064	−0.084	0.075
Joint F test for birth cohort dummies	76.24*** df = (10, 2,590)		10.2.23*** df = (22, 3,513)	
R-squared	0.455		0.281	
Number of families	2,591		3,513	
Number of observations	10,654		12,304	

Notes: The birth cohort dummies are omitted from the table for brevity. *, **, *** denote significance at 10%, 5%, 1% levels respectively.

confirmed by previous tables, Table 8.6 also suggests that males are hurt by younger brothers spaced apart, and females are hurt by younger sisters spaced apart. This looks more like a dilution effect among siblings of the same gender, and it may be explained by a theory of resource competition, rather than gender preferences on the part of parents.

From the findings of Tables 8.2–8.6, we may conclude that sibship structure does affect males and females differently. Furthermore, the educational

Table 8.6. Estimated effects of sibship size by gender, seniority, and spacing on educational attainment, Taiwan and China

Explanatory variables	Model D: Taiwan		Model D': China	
	Coefficient	Standard error	Coefficient	Standard error
Constant	7.686***	0.479	11.254***	0.395
Male	0.423**	0.198	−0.037	0.148
Father's schooling	0.284***	0.016	0.249***	0.014
Mother's schooling	0.199***	0.017	0.149***	0.017
Mother's age at birth ≥40	−0.233	0.251	−0.119	0.143
Working mother	−0.339***	0.110	−1.089***	0.138
Father's ethnicity				
Fukienese	2.267***	0.339		
Hakka	2.678***	0.360		
Mainlander	3.073***	0.364		
Father's birth place				
Shanhai			0.043	0.209
Zeijiang			−1.263***	0.167
Fujiang			−1.964***	0.170
Male × elder brothers spaced closely	−0.116	0.085	0.060	0.081
Female × elder brothers spaced closely	−0.035	0.086	−0.507***	0.092
Male × elder brothers spaced apart	−0.017	0.075	0.032	0.063
Female × elder brothers spaced apart	−0.155**	0.078	−0.374***	0.067
Male × younger brothers spaced closely	−0.023	0.088	−0.099	0.079
Female × younger brothers spaced closely	−0.027	0.085	−0.393***	0.091
Male × younger brothers spaced apart	0.080	0.086	−0.392***	0.065
Female × younger brothers spaced apart	−0.328***	0.085	−0.810***	0.082
Male × elder sisters spaced closely	−0.007	0.076	0.258***	0.084
Female × elder sisters spaced closely	−0.028	0.076	−0.036	0.092
Male × elder sisters spaced apart	0.032	0.061	0.067	0.070
Female × elder sisters spaced apart	−0.142**	0.069	0.054	0.082
Male × younger sisters spaced closely	0.061	0.087	−0.094	0.085
Female × younger sisters spaced closely	−0.115	0.076	−0.080	0.095
Male × younger sisters spaced apart	0.046	0.080	−0.091	0.070
Female × younger sisters spaced apart	−0.492***	0.078	−0.246***	0.089
Joint F test for birth cohort dummies	52.52*** df = (10, 2,590)		90.66*** df = (34, 3,513)	
R-squared	0.457		0.289	
Number of families	2,591		3,513	
Number of observations	10,654		12,304	

Notes: The birth cohort dummies are omitted from the table for brevity. *, **, *** denote significance at 10%, 5%, 1% levels respectively.

Table 8.7. Summary for the difference of estimates between gender, Taiwan and China

Model/variables	Taiwan		China	
	$|t|$ statistic for difference between male and female	F statistic for overall difference between male and female	$|t|$ statistic for difference between male and female	F statistic for overall difference between male and female
Model A/Model A'				
Sibship size	5.00***		5.97***	
Model B/Model B'				
Brothers	2.77***	13.29***	6.99***	25.79***
Sisters	4.82***	df=(2, 2,590)	1.28	df = (2, 3,513)
Model C/Model C'				
Brothers spaced closely	0.40		5.28***	
Brothers spaced apart	3.54***	11.00***	5.55***	13.44***
Sisters spaced closely	1.33	df = (4, 2,590)	1.45	df = (4, 3,513)
Sisters spaced apart	4.65***		0.72	
Model D/Model D'				
Elder brothers spaced closely	0.71		4.99***	
Elder brothers spaced apart	1.46		5.41***	
Younger brothers spaced closely	0.00		2.65***	
Younger brothers spaced apart	3.94***	8.82***	4.86***	8.23***
Elder sisters spaced closely	0.20	df = (8, 2,590)	2.46**	df = (8, 3,513)
Elder sisters spaced apart	2.17**		0.14	
Younger sisters spaced closely	1.66*		0.10	
Younger sisters spaced apart	5.66***		1.62	

Notes: The test statistics are constructed based on the estimates of Tables 8.3–8.6. *, ** , *** denote significance at 10%, 5%, 1% levels respectively.

attainment of females is affected by the composition of sibling structure. Siblings spaced apart, regardless of gender or seniority, have negative effects on the educational attainment of females in Taiwan, whereas brothers with different spacing and seniorities have different impacts on subjects in China. To further explore whether the coefficients of individual sibship size variables are equivalent between males and females, we conducted the corresponding t tests, the results of which are presented in columns 2 and 4 of Table 8.7, for Taiwan and China respectively. An F test was also performed to examine the overall difference between genders for each model, with the results listed in columns 3 and 5 of the same table. These test statistics show that the overall difference in sibship effects between genders is significant for all models (Models A–D, A'–D').

In summary, our study explores the effects of sibship on education in the Chinese context by refining sibship configuration, and in doing so questions the conventional wisdom based on American and Western European findings. The key hypothesis we suggest is a modified resource-dilution model with son preference in the Chinese family tradition, where family resources are composed of both parental earnings and sibling remittances. The son preference culture suggests the likelihood of sacrificing the education opportunity of older girls, who help the family at an earlier age and contribute to the family income pool. In Taiwan extraction of resources from elder daughters is more likely to happen when the girl in question has more siblings who are younger and spaced apart, who constitute an additional burden on the family budget. In China, the seniority and spacing effect is smaller, but brothers (regardless of seniority and spacing) are always detrimental to the female's education. Overall, in both Chinese societies male siblings indeed dilute the parental resources, whereas sisters augment such resources by stopping schooling to help the family. The scenario revealed in our empirical analysis is complicated and can be identified only when the sibling structure is refined according to the sex-seniority-spacing dimensions.

8.6. Conclusions

In this chapter, we argue that, perhaps following a traditional norm rooted in history, Chinese parents generally pay more attention to their children's education than parents in the West. Somehow in Chinese societies child education has become an *end* in itself for parents, rather than some *means* of increasing earnings. Given this particular emphasis on education, it is particularly interesting to study how parents allocate their resources among children.

We find that for the families in our Taiwan PSFD data, the negative effects of sibship size are the strongest for girls who have younger brothers and sisters spaced apart. We interpret this unusual high-order interaction involving sibship size, gender, density, and seniority in the context of Taiwan's patriarchal culture, in which families often favor boys over girls. In the case of China, sibling structure is less important, but brothers always hurt the education opportunity of girls. While our work is motivated by Greenhalgh's (1985) insight that Chinese parents mobilize resources from elder daughters to benefit younger sons, the full story seems more complicated.

In the case of Taiwan, in families with sons born ahead of daughters, it appears that the parents did not consciously sacrifice daughters to benefit sons. It was only when daughters could help add to the family income that parents discontinued the education of the sisters and transferred their resources to benefit the family as a whole, and possibly their siblings in particular. Interestingly, it seems that sisters' education is sacrificed to benefit mostly brothers, both for Taiwan and for China. In Taiwan, while there may be gender asymmetry in terms of which elder siblings were sacrificed, there is no gender asymmetry in terms of which young siblings benefited from the intrafamily transfer. In light of these findings, Parish and Willis's (1993) interpretation is appealing: financially strapped parents may extract resources from their elder daughters under credit market imperfections. Once they have adequate resources (say remittances from elder daughters), they no longer discriminate against younger daughters. This interpretation suggests that parents' differential treatment of sons and daughters is an extreme measure under severe resource constraint. Once they have adequate resources, parents' treatment of daughters, in terms of education, is not very dissimilar to their treatment of sons. In China, however, the gender asymmetry is significant both on the receiving end and the giving end. Perhaps the part on the allocation of monetary transfers in Chapter 7 can be combined with the discussion here to give us a more comprehensive picture of Chinese gender preferences.

Notes

1. A good survey on child nutrition analysis can be found in Behrman (1992). With respect to the possible gender difference in child nutrition intake, Behrman suggested that (p. 317) the situation was more serious in South and West Asia.

2. Education is evidently not the only means through which parents can increase their child's income. If education and bequests are both available means for parents to choose, what should they do when they have several children? We have referred to this issue briefly in Chapter 7.

3. Kao and Thompson (2003) provided some explanation on why ethnic background is a factor influencing a child's education achievement.

4. A detailed discussion on the evolution of the education system of China can be found in Lee and Wang (2000).

5. In Chapter 4, when sibship size was the only exogenous variable, we were able to find an instrumental variable (IV) to do the conditional analysis. In this chapter, since the sibship structure is rather complex, we cannot find sufficient IVs, and hence have to constrain ourselves to unconditional analysis.

9

Intergenerational Mobility

Concerning intergenerational mobility between family members, researchers often try to study the mobility of incomes or earnings across generations. However, there are three difficulties associated with the study of income/earnings mobility. First, a meaningful discussion of income in the context of intergenerational mobility should refer to a person's *permanent* income. Nevertheless, what researchers observe are usually *temporary* incomes. Moreover, the relationship between permanent income and transitory income is itself a complicated one, and hence it is impractical to tie the discussion of intergenerational mobility to that of permanent/transitory income differentiation. Second, even if one wants to focus on the incomes of two generations of a particular age range (say mid-career), there are still data problems. Since age-specific incomes often cannot be recollected at the time of an interview, comparing the incomes of a father and his son at age, say, 35–40 will demand a data set with unusually long follow-up interviews of family members. To our knowledge, few survey data provide such long panels. Third, the income of a person hinges upon both ability and education. Suppose we adopt the common assumptions that people with higher innate ability often earn higher incomes, and that a child's innate ability is partly inherited from his or her parents. Then, as we run the regression using children's income as the dependent variable and their parent's income as an explanatory variable, the latter may be correlated with the error term, and some statistical complications appear.

The first and third problems mentioned above can be solved or mitigated; but since we do not have sufficient parent–child income data, the second problem becomes formidable. Many researchers therefore pay more attention to the intergenerational mobility of *education*, which has a high correlation with permanent incomes, as pointed out by Behrman and Taubman (1985: 146). Empirically, Behrman and Taubman (1985: 147) also believed that the intergenerational correlation of education provides an *upper bound* for the true correlation of income, for transfers of physical and financial assets often cause the mobility index to deteriorate. Thus, analysis of education mobility is partly what we intend to do in this chapter. The PSFD data also allow us to analyze the mobility of occupation status; however, since the economic system in China is different from the one in Taiwan, we cannot make a systematic comparison. Therefore we leave that part to possible future research.

Concerning the intergenerational mobility of education, two factors are involved: one is the macro-level environment of the society, and the other is the micro-level family background. The former specifies the regime of education opportunity faced by each family, and the latter determines the capacity of parental support that can be provided. We have explained the macro environment for China and Taiwan in Chapter 2. As to the influence of families at the micro level, the parental discretion of allocating family resources among children has been discussed in Chapter 8. So in this chapter, we focus on the mobility between parents and a *particular* child. It is especially intriguing to compare the intergenerational mobility of two societies otherwise similar in culture, one basically under capitalism (Taiwan) and the other basically under communism (Mainland China).

9.1. Various Mobility Research Approaches

In the USA and most countries in Western Europe, we observe that the level of public education provided is positively correlated with the level of economic development. The general perception may be that more public education translates into more mobility in society. This perception, however, was recently challenged by Checchi et al. (1999), who compared the education systems in the USA and Italy. They found that Italy experienced less mobility, despite its more centralized and egalitarian school system, which is supposed to reduce the cost of education for poor families. Checchi et al. showed that while the public education system does lower the cost of education, what is equally important is the marginal benefit of individual effort in the production function of human capital. If student effort is a more important factor than the provision of education, then a public education system may even create a scenario of lower social mobility, which Checchi et al. believed to be the case in Italy.

9.1.1. *The Role of Parental Background*

Conceptually, even if education is public funded, there are still reasons to justify the phenomenon of higher upward mobility for children of highly educated parents. Behrman et al. (2000: 141–3) listed nine reasons why this might be the case, and here we quote five of them, which are believed to be more relevant to the context of Chinese families.

1. Under capital market imperfections, better-educated parents are able to provide their children with more support in home tutoring, health, and nutrition, thus giving their children an advantage over those from poor families.

2. Better-educated parents may have better learning ability, which may be genetically transferred to their children, giving the latter an advantage.

3. Better-educated parents often have better social networks, which can help their children access better opportunities, including in education.

4. Better-educated parents may have some information advantage, which can help them make more informed decisions in child education in case of uncertainties.

5. Better-educated parents are usually more affluent, hence financially less constrained. This facilitates their expenditure on child education, which may be crucial for child achievements.

Note that some of the above-mentioned causes (such as genetics) are not related to parents' decisions, but they provide reasons for parents' and children's education to be positively correlated. Moreover, these factors may also have a lasting impact on parents' decision in education resource division among their children. For instance, if financially constrained parents are forced to discriminate against some of their children in education, then when the deprived children form their own families, they are likely to be poor and constrained, too. As a result, they also tend to make some discriminatory decisions as they allocate their education resources.

9.1.2. *Regression Analysis*

There are various ways in which researchers investigate intergenerational mobility. The first and the most popular one is the regression approach. One usually puts child education as the dependent variable, and parental education as the explanatory variable, controlling other socio-economic background if necessary. The education measurement may be either schooling years, or education tiers. Along this line, there has been research on the USA (see, e.g., Behrman and Taubman 1985), Malaysia (Lillard and Willis 1994), the UK (Dearden 1999), Mexico (Binder and Woodruff 2002), and many other countries. The same regression can be applied to analyze the mobility of intergenerational incomes (or earnings) and occupation status. The findings on these countries are not cited here.

In these regressions of intergenerational education, the coefficients of the parents' education usually represent the influence of parents on children. In the literature we review, these coefficients are all positive and significant. The only argument we saw for a negative influence was provided by Behrman and Rosenzweig (2002), who argued that mothers' education may facilitate their labor market devotion, which in turn reduces their time for home tutoring, and hence leads to less child education achievement. There is no consensus in the literature on the relative importance between mother's education and father's education.

Another research angle looks at the proportion of variance explained by the family background, including parental education, in these regressions; the larger this proportion is, the more important is the family background on child achievement. Behrman et al. (2000) listed the results for twelve countries in Latin America. The country with the largest proportion is Brazil, which is the only one for which the proportion is more than a quarter. Most other countries have a contribution proportion less than 20 per cent.

9.1.3. Correlation Coefficient and Mobility Indexes

The second approach is to calculate the correlation coefficients between parental education (usually the father's) and children's education directly. This approach requires little information and can be applied to many countries. Binder and Woodruff (2002) listed results for Mexico, Germany, Panama, Malaysia, and the United States; Corak (2001) focused on the situation of Canada; Dearden (1999) studied the scenario in the UK; and Checchi et al. (1999) compared the situations in Italy and the USA. For Chinese societies, of course, we are able to calculate this simple correlation for both China and Taiwan.

The correlation coefficient is the simplest index we can calculate, and some further refinement can also be easily made. As we separate the education or occupation status into N categories, the correspondence between the parent's and child's status will constitute an $N \times N$ transition matrix, from which several mobility indices can be calculated, including the trace, the determinant, the second-largest eigenvalue, etc. Checchi et al. (1999) provided some summaries of such indices and their corresponding formula.

Another kind of correlation analysis focuses on the relationship between siblings. Dahan and Gaviria (2001) argued that if there were perfect social mobility, family background would not matter, and siblings would not be more alike than two people selected at random. The logic, however, is not entirely correct, in our opinion. Because siblings carry 50 per cent of the same genes, it suggests that the correlation in sibling achievement must be more likely to be positive than that in random pairs drawn from society at large. However, it may be interesting to calculate the correlation coefficients for both parent–son and parent–daughter paired samples, and see how the two numbers differ, even though children of both sexes share a genetic similarity with their parents. In societies with a male-dominance tradition, it is believed that the parent–child mobility indices may be different for boys and girls. The questions we shall ask are how this gender-specific differential treatment may affect the upward mobility of boys and girls in the family, and how this differential treatment may disappear with economic development. The literature in this area is limited, and the best-known work is by Lillard and Willis (1994) on Malaysia.

9.2. Mobility across Education Tiers

9.2.1. Mobility Indices

We first study the mobility matrices in China and Taiwan. As a benchmark case, for the time being we do not separate our samples into rural–urban groups; we shall proceed with that analysis later.[1] The data come from our PSFD survey. The sample of Taiwan is composed of the respondents interviewed in the first-wave survey conducted in 1999, 2000, and 2003 respectively. And the sample of China is from the 2004 China survey. The child and parent in this chapter refer to the respondent and his or her parent (usually the father) in the survey. The education tiers are separated into five, namely less-than-elementary, elementary, junior high, senior high, and college-or-above. We had also tried dividing education into four categories. It turns out that our main conclusion remained the same under this setting. Since Chinese families have a male-line dominance tradition, in most of our samples, the father typically has a higher education in the parent generation. We therefore concentrate on the father–child mobility and ignore the mother-line analysis. We calculated several 5 × 5 mobility

Table 9.1. Educational transition matrices (5 × 5), China and Taiwan

China	Son					Daughter					No. of obs. father–son/ father–daughter
	Less than elem.	Elem.	Junior high	Senior high	College or above	Less than elem.	Elem.	Junior high	Senior high	College or above	
Father											
Less than elem.	0.131	0.418	0.335	0.093	0.024	0.295	0.347	0.261	0.081	0.017	1,302/844
Elementary	0.020	0.226	0.469	0.198	0.086	0.087	0.275	0.384	0.204	0.049	650/549
Junior high	0.013	0.097	0.388	0.321	0.181	0.044	0.144	0.339	0.362	0.111	237/271
Senior high	0.009	0.139	0.287	0.324	0.241	0.028	0.120	0.269	0.398	0.185	108/108
College or above	0.000	0.047	0.163	0.326	0.465	0.000	0.082	0.265	0.469	0.184	43/49
No. of observations	187	731	871	375	176	312	500	565	344	100	2,340/1,821

Taiwan	Son					Daughter					No. of obs. father–son/ father–daughter
	Less than elem.	Elem.	Junior high	Senior high	College or above	Less than elem.	Elem.	Junior high	Senior high	College or above	
Father											
Less than elem.	0.077	0.463	0.214	0.182	0.064	0.312	0.489	0.080	0.095	0.023	687/797
Elementary	0.006	0.131	0.190	0.444	0.230	0.031	0.237	0.138	0.392	0.202	732/739
Junior high	0.011	0.069	0.091	0.480	0.349	0.006	0.123	0.088	0.462	0.322	175/171
Senior high	0.000	0.024	0.095	0.325	0.556	0.015	0.069	0.099	0.374	0.443	126/131
College or above	0.000	0.000	0.000	0.227	0.773	0.000	0.071	0.048	0.524	0.357	44/42
No. of observations	59	429	314	585	377	275	598	196	516	295	1,764/1,880

matrices, for fathers–sons and fathers–daughters, and listed them in Table 9.1, for China and Taiwan, respectively.

From this table it can be seen that upward mobility seems to be higher for sons than for daughters, for both China and Taiwan. For instance, for children of a father in the lowest education tier, the son's probability distribution of moving toward various educational tiers actually *first-degree stochastically dominates*[2] that of a daughter. If we look at fathers with the highest education (college or above), we also find that they are much more unlikely to have a son move downward than a daughter. Comparing the first rows of the matrices of Taiwan and China, it appears that children of low-educated fathers in China find it more difficult, both for sons and for daughters, to move upward than in Taiwan, implying a higher mobility in Taiwan. But we will have to check it later using more sophisticated techniques.

To be comparable with Checchi et al. (1999), we construct two 2×2 matrices for Taiwan and China, respectively, in which the two education categories are specified as "college or above" and "below college." The results are listed in Table 9.2. The corresponding numbers for Italy and the USA are given in the bottom part of this table. As one can see, the father–son mobility structure in Taiwan is similar to that in the USA, and it is relatively difficult for the young generation of Italy to break out of the lower-education block. It is especially interesting to note that in China, children of a father with college-or-above degree have an extremely low probability of staying in the same educational block, compared with the numbers in Taiwan, Italy, or USA. This is conjectured to be related to the education turmoil caused by the Cultural Revolution as mentioned in Chapter 2. Finally, we find from Table 9.2 that upward mobility for girls is significantly worse than for boys, in both China and Taiwan, which is consistent with the gender bias we referred to in previous chapters.[3]

In Table 9.3 we calculate some one-dimensional mobility measures for both Taiwan and China. Checchi and Dardanoni (2002) proposed ten different measures of mobility, and here we adopt some modified versions of them. The modified formulae mainly come from Formby et al. (2004), who derived the large sample properties for these mobility measures, which facilitate the conduct of various statistical tests. From Table 9.3 we see that the mobility measures are indeed higher in Taiwan than in China for four out of five father–daughter measures, with an insignificant difference in the M_1 measure. Similarly, the mobility measures are higher for Taiwan in three out of the four significant measures for the father–son connection. Overall, we observe that the parent–child mobility in terms of education is higher in Taiwan than in China, despite the fact that in Communist China all education used to be

Table 9.2. Educational transition matrices (2 × 2), China, Taiwan, Italy, and USA

China	Son		Daughter		No. of obs. father–son/father–daughter
	Less than college	College or above	Less than college	College or above	
Father					
Less than college	0.880	0.120	0.948	0.052	2,297/1,772
College or above	0.535	0.465	0.816	0.184	43/49
No. of observations	2,164	176	1,721	100	2,340/1,821

Taiwan	Son		Daughter		No. of obs. father–son/father–daughter
	Less than college	College or above	Less than college	College or above	
Father					
Less than college	0.800	0.200	0.847	0.153	1,720/1,838
College or above	0.227	0.773	0.643	0.357	44/42
No. of observations	1,387	377	1,585	295	1,764/1,880

Italy/USA	Italy		USA	
	Less than college	College or above	Less than college	College or above
Father				
Less than college	0.927	0.071	0.792	0.208
College or above	0.349	0.651	0.389	0.611
No. of observations	1,374	131	754	283

Note: The figures of Italy and USA are from Checchi et al. (1999). Others are computed by the authors.

public and private ownership of property is not allowed, a fact that would lead one to expect a decreased influence of families. This result is similar to the comparison between the USA and Italy found by Checchi et al. (1999). As we mentioned in the previous section, Checchi et al. provided some explanation for their findings, but the scenario in China seemed to be more sensitive to the upheavals in its education system.

In Tables 9.4a and 9.4b, we further separate the father–child comparisons into two groups, by the birth year of children in Taiwan. Since Taiwan extended its mandatory education from six to nine years in 1956, as we described in Chapter 2, it provided a natural experiment to examine whether this exogenous change in mandatory education affects the inter-generational mobility of parent–child education. From the columns corresponding to Taiwan in Tables 9.4a and 9.4b, we see that the answer seems to be a clear yes, that cohorts born after 1956 do enjoy a better intergenerational mobility, both for father–son and for father–daughter. Furthermore, we see that for children born before 1956, the father–son

Table 9.3. Mobility measures for educational transition matrices (5 × 5), China and Taiwan

Measures	China		Taiwan		Difference between Taiwan and China	
	Father–son	Father–daughter	Father–son	Father–daughter	Father–son	Father–daughter
$M_1 = \dfrac{m - \sum_i p_{ii}}{m-1}$	0.86648 (0.024)	0.87716 (0.020)	0.90054 (0.020)	0.90800 (0.023)	0.03406 (0.031)	0.03084 (0.031)
$M_2 = 1 - \|\lambda_2\|$	0.66396 (0.006)	0.62370 (0.002)	0.64711 (0.003)	0.63678 (0.001)	−0.01685*** (0.006)	0.01308*** (0.002)
$M_3 = 1 - \|\det(P)\|$	0.99980 (0.000)	0.99996 (0.000)	0.99992 (0.000)	0.99999 (0.000)	0.00012*** (0.000)	0.00003*** (0.000)
$M_4 = \dfrac{m - m\sum_i \pi_i p_{ii}}{m-1}$	1.00213 (0.010)	0.87658 (0.013)	1.07993 (0.010)	0.91556 (0.013)	0.07780*** (0.014)	0.03898** (0.018)
$M_5 = \dfrac{\sum_i \sum_j \pi_i p_{ij}\|i-j\|}{m-1}$	0.31645 (0.005)	0.26400 (0.005)	0.39399 (0.006)	0.30745 (0.006)	0.07754*** (0.007)	0.04345*** (0.008)
$M_3' = 1 - \|\det(P)\|^{\frac{1}{m-1}}$	0.88133	0.92241	0.90430	0.94626	0.02297	0.02385

Notes: The top 5 measures are the same as those adopted by Formby et al. (2004). To be comparable to Checchi et al. (1999), a measure similar to M_3 is listed in the bottom row. p_{ij} is the (i, j)th cell in the transition matrix (P); m is the number of classes; $|\lambda_2|$ is the modulus of the second greatest eigenvalue; $|\det(P)|$ is the determinant of matrix P; π_i is the proportion of people in the ith class.

Standard errors are in the parentheses. In the last two columns, *, **, *** denote that the difference is significant at 10%, 5%, 1% significance levels respectively.

Table 9.4a. Mobility measures for father–son educational transition matrices (5×5) by birth cohorts, China and Taiwan

Measures	China		Taiwan		Difference between Taiwan and China	
	Son's birth year <1956	Son's birth year ≥1956	Son's birth year <1956	Son's birth year ≥1956	Son's birth year <1956	Son's birth year ≥1956
$M_1 = \dfrac{m - \sum p_{ii}}{m-1}$	0.87787 (0.041)	0.86761 (0.029)	0.84986 (0.029)	0.94173 (0.029)	-0.02801 (0.051)	0.07412* (0.041)
$M_2 = 1 - |\lambda_2|$	0.70253 (0.726)	0.61601 (0.004)	0.50163 (0.003)	0.73740 (0.017)	-0.20090 (0.726)	0.12139*** (0.018)
$M_3 = 1 - |\det(P)|$	0.99911 (0.002)	0.99998 (0.000)	0.99961 (0.000)	1.00000 (0.000)	0.00050 (0.002)	0.00002 *** (0.000)
$M_4 = \dfrac{m - m\sum_i \pi_i p_{ii}}{m-1}$	0.97453 (0.016)	1.02141 (0.012)	1.00318 (0.015)	1.16788 (0.009)	0.02865 (0.022)	0.14647*** (0.015)
$M_5 = \dfrac{\sum_i \sum_j \pi_i p_{ij}|i-j|}{m-1}$	0.30068 (0.007)	0.32747 (0.006)	0.33280 (0.008)	0.46411 (0.006)	0.03212*** (0.011)	0.13364*** (0.008)
$M_3 = 1 - |\det(P)|^{\frac{1}{m-1}}$	0.82715	0.93537	0.85986	1.00000	0.03271	0.06463

Notes: The top 5 measures are the same as those adopted by Formby et al. (2004). To be comparable to Checchi et al. (1999), a measure similar to M_3 is listed in the bottom row. p_{ij} is the (i, j)th cell in the transition matrix (P); m is the number of classes; $|\lambda_2|$ is the modulus of the second greatest eigenvalue; $|\det(P)|$ is the determinant of matrix P; π_i is the proportion of people in the ith class.

Standard errors are in the parentheses. In the last two columns, *, ** , *** denote that the difference is significant at 10%, 5%, 1% significance levels respectively.

Table 9.4b. Mobility measures for father–daughter educational transition matrices (5×5) by birth cohorts, China and Taiwan

Measures	China		Taiwan		Difference between Taiwan and China	
	Daughter's birth year <1956	Daughter's birth year ≥1956	Daughter's birth year <1956	Daughter's birth year ≥1956	Daughter's birth year <1956	Daughter's birth year ≥1956
$M_1 = \frac{m - \sum p_{ii}}{m-1}$	0.83040 (0.036)	0.90364 (0.025)	0.79079 (0.035)	1.05410 (0.027)	-0.03961 (0.050)	0.15046*** (0.037)
$M_2 = 1 - |\lambda_2|$	0.54942 (0.002)	0.68209 (0.003)	0.49813 (0.002)	0.68409 (0.002)	-0.05129*** (0.003)	0.00200 (0.004)
$M_3 = 1 - |\det(P)|$	1.00000 (0.000)	0.99998 (0.000)	0.99998 (0.000)	0.99999 (0.000)	-0.00002*** (0.000)	0.00001*** (0.000)
$M_4 = \frac{m - m\sum \pi_i p_{ii}}{m-1}$	0.75040 (0.025)	0.94140 (0.015)	0.76941 (0.018)	1.11943 (0.013)	0.01901 (0.031)	0.17803*** (0.020)
$M_5 = \frac{\sum_i \sum_j \pi_i p_{ij}|i-j|}{m-1}$	0.22087 (0.009)	0.28616 (0.006)	0.21598 (0.007)	0.43503 (0.007)	-0.00489 (0.011)	0.14887*** (0.010)
$M'_3 = 1 - |\det(P)|^{\frac{1}{m-1}}$	0.97818	0.93012	0.93607	0.95205	-0.04211	0.02193

Notes: The top 5 measures are the same as those adopted by Formby et al. (2004). To be comparable to Checchi et al. (1999), a measure similar to M_3 is listed in the bottom row. p_{ij} is the (i, j)th cell in the transition matrix (P); m is the number of classes; $|\lambda_2|$ is the modulus of the second greatest eigenvalue; $|\det(P)|$ is the determinant of matrix P; π_i is the proportion of people in the ith class.
Standard errors are in the parentheses. In the last two columns, *, **, *** denote that the difference is significant at 10%, 5%, 1% significance levels respectively.

and father–daughter mobility differences between China and Taiwan do not look very large statistically. Most of the distinction appears for cohorts born after 1956, when a capitalist society changes its system to move further toward public (mandatory) education, as shown by the significant changes in all five mobility indices for sons and four out of five indices for daughters. This is a phenomenon that deserves further investigation in the future.

Area-wise, we calculate the mobility indices separately for rural and urban samples. We found that the China–Taiwan difference is more evident for father–son in rural areas, and not so evident or consistent for father–daughter. Intuitively, in Chinese societies sons are blessed and are expected by parents to achieve higher education. The poor economic condition in rural China makes the parental wishes for their sons unrealizable, hence resulting in lower mobility measures relative to Taiwan. However, a comparison of the same mobility index for daughters does not show a consistent pattern. We are not sure whether this is caused by the inconsistency of indices *per se*, or the insignificant patterns for daughters. Perhaps a longer panel in the future can help us solve the puzzle.

9.2.2. Ordered Probit Analysis

In Table 9.5 we present the ordered probit estimation results for both genders in China and Taiwan. For each model, the dependent variable is the educational attainment of the respondent, with five education categories being distinguished as we described. The explanatory variables include father's education tiers, respondent's birth year, mother's working status, respondent's area of residence when young, and respondent's number of siblings. The μ values in each column of Table 9.5 are estimates of constant terms for the five-category ordered probit models. It can be seen from Table 9.5 that most explanatory variables have signs consistent with previous studies: father with higher education, children born later, urban residence all contribute to the education of both sons and daughters, whereas a larger number of competing siblings impedes the education for daughters only, not for sons.[4] As to the working status of mothers, we find that children with non-working mothers achieve better education than the ones with working mothers. This is probably due to the job market and home tutoring competing for the mother's time, a finding consistent with the argument of Behrman and Rosenzweig (2002).

Table 9.5. Ordered probit models for respondent's education (5-category), China and Taiwan

Explanatory variables	China		Taiwan	
	Son	Daughter	Son	Daughter
Father's education ("less than elem." as ref. group)				
Elementary	0.597***	0.570***	0.719***	0.986***
	(0.054)	(0.061)	(0.065)	(0.066)
Junior high	0.930***	0.873***	1.082***	1.455***
	(0.082)	(0.081)	(0.100)	(0.103)
Senior high	1.054***	1.197***	1.536***	1.652***
	(0.112)	(0.115)	(0.119)	(0.116)
College or above	1.594***	1.244***	2.502***	1.915***
	(0.179)	(0.163)	(0.217)	(0.185)
Respondent's birth year ("≤ 1945" as ref. group)				
1946–1955	−0.097	0.286***	0.539***	1.022***
	(0.074)	(0.103)	(0.076)	(0.076)
1956–1965	0.404***	0.823***	1.022***	1.532***
	(0.074)	(0.101)	(0.086)	(0.086)
≥ 1966	0.439***	0.885***	1.337***	2.171***
	(0.078)	(0.105)	(0.090)	(0.096)
Mother non-working (= 1 if yes)	0.052	0.324***	0.217***	0.226***
	(0.064)	(0.068)	(0.054)	(0.053)
Respondent living in urban area before age 16 (= 1 if yes)	0.872***	1.017***	0.290***	0.436***
	(0.066)	(0.068)	(0.066	(0.064)
Number of siblings	−0.023	−0.140***	−0.013	−0.048***
	(0.016)	(0.018)	(0.017)	(0.015)
Birth order	0.024	0.078***	0.020	0.026
	(0.019)	(0.020)	(0.018)	(0.018)
μ_1	−0.966***	−0.164	−1.047***	0.079
	(0.077)	(0.106)	(0.099)	(0.077)
μ_2	0.359***	0.894***	0.644***	1.743***
	(0.075)	(0.108)	(0.092)	(0.090)
μ_3	1.576***	2.016***	1.354***	2.235***
	(0.079)	(0.113)	(0.096)	(0.094)
μ_4	2.458***	3.192***	2.553***	3.543***
	(0.086)	(0.124)	(0.102)	(0.104)
Pseudo R^2	0.117	0.159	0.178	0.269
Log likelihood	−2,930.463	−2,279.593	−2,064.989	−2,052.825
Number of observations	2,335	1,816	1,728	1,841

Notes: *, **, *** denote significance at 10%, 5%, 1% levels respectively. Standard errors are in parentheses.

To explore further the relationship of the education levels between generations, we derive the marginal effects of the father's education on the respondent's education based on the results of Table 9.5.[5] In Table 9.6, we present the marginal effects of father's education on the respondent's education based on the results of Table 9.5, with the reference group for the father's education tier being "less than elementary." It can be seen that,

Table 9.6. Marginal effects of father's education on respondent's education, China and Taiwan

China	Son					Daughter				
	Less than elem.	Elem.	Junior high	Senior high	College or above	Less than elem.	Elem.	Junior high	Senior high	College or above
Father										
Elementary	-0.064	-0.160	0.067	0.108	0.049	-0.120	-0.104	0.092	0.112	0.020
Junior high	-0.079	-0.243	0.045	0.172	0.105	-0.155	-0.174	0.098	0.187	0.045
Senior high	-0.082	-0.270	0.027	0.193	0.132	-0.177	-0.244	0.066	0.266	0.089
College or above	-0.089	-0.352	-0.096	0.245	0.292	-0.180	-0.253	0.059	0.277	0.097

Taiwan	Son					Daughter				
	Less than elem.	Elem.	Junior high	Senior high	College or above	Less than elem.	Elem.	Junior high	Senior high	College or above
Father										
Elementary	-0.022	-0.212	-0.047	0.153	0.127	-0.111	-0.266	0.046	0.253	0.080
Junior high	-0.024	-0.283	-0.103	0.173	0.236	-0.124	-0.401	0.010	0.333	0.181
Senior high	-0.025	-0.335	-0.174	0.128	0.406	-0.126	-0.445	-0.011	0.343	0.239
College or above	-0.025	-0.368	-0.259	-0.102	0.754	-0.127	-0.492	-0.042	0.332	0.329

Notes: The figures are computed based on the results of Table 9.5.
The reference group for father's education is "less than elementary."

other factors being controlled, the respondents with fathers being "college or above" are more likely to stay in the same education tier than those whose fathers are low-educated. And the pattern is more evident in Taiwan than in China, for both males and females. This result is consistent with our previous analysis of the 2×2 mobility matrix in Table 9.2.

9.3. Regression for Years of Schooling

To compare the mobility situation of China and Taiwan with another strand of literature, we transform different education tiers into years of schooling, and make some analysis in parallel to the previous subsection.[6] Correlation coefficients between years of schooling of two generations, as mentioned in past studies, could be used to measure the degree of intergenerational mobility. In Table 9.7, the correlation coefficients for Mexico, Germany, Malaysia, and the USA are retrieved from Binder and Woodruff (2002: Table 3). And the figures for China and Taiwan are computed from the PSFD data sets. It can be seen from Table 9.7 that the correlation coefficients for Taiwan and Mexico are higher than those for China and the USA, which are in turn higher than the estimates for Germany and Malaysia. And Table 9.7 also shows that the correlation coefficient in rural areas is higher than that in urban areas, and the difference is especially

Table 9.7. Correlation coefficients between father's and child's years of schooling for various societies

	Year	Father–son	Father–daughter	Age of child
Mexico	1994	0.498 (7,189)	0.528 (8,588)	23–69
Germany	1984	0.237 (384)	0.016 (245)	19–26
Malaysia	1988	0.194 (2,435)	0.226 (2,359)	8–50
United States	1984	0.418 (1,139)	0.402 (1,209)	20–30
China				
Urban	2004	0.332 (400)	0.379 (420)	25–68
Rural	2004	0.405 (1,940)	0.397 (1,401)	25–68
Taiwan				
Urban	1999	0.537 (382)	0.523 (432)	25–65
	2000			
	2003			
Rural	1999	0.539 (1,382)	0.598 (1,448)	25–65
	2000			
	2003			

Notes: Numbers of observations are in parentheses.
  Figures of China and Taiwan are from the PSFD survey. Other figures are retrieved from Binder and Woodruff (2002: Table 3).

Table 9.8. Regression models for respondent's years of schooling, China and Taiwan

Explanatory variables	China		Taiwan	
	Son	Daughter	Son	Daughter
Model 1: simple regression				
Father's years of schooling	0.391***	0.440***	0.509***	0.699***
	(0.016)	(0.020)	(0.019)	(0.022)
Constant	6.893***	5.606***	8.045***	5.544***
	(0.088)	(0.125)	(0.120)	(0.132)
R^2	0.201	0.206	0.299	0.364
Number of observations	2,335	1,816	1,728	1,841
Model 2: multiple regression				
Father's years of schooling	0.295***	0.298***	0.382***	0.439***
	(0.017)	(0.020)	(0.019)	(0.020)
Respondent's birth year ("$\leq$1945" as ref. group)				
1946–1955	−0.237	1.008***	1.588***	3.193***
	(0.210)	(0.310)	(0.204)	(0.201)
1956–1965	1.150***	2.640***	2.923***	4.825***
	(0.209)	(0.303)	(0.224)	(0.227)
$\geq$1966	1.273***	2.980***	3.614***	6.565***
	(0.220)	(0.314)	(0.227)	(0.236)
Mother non-working (= 1 if yes)	0.173	0.965***	0.526***	0.616***
	(0.182)	(0.212)	(0.147)	(0.149)
Respondent living in urban area before age 16 (= 1 if yes)	2.291***	3.028***	0.817***	1.220***
	(0.184)	(0.207)	(0.177)	(0.179)
Number of siblings	−0.051	−0.404***	−0.032	−0.114***
	(0.045)	(0.055)	(0.046)	(0.041)
Birth order	0.067	0.245***	0.053	0.061
	(0.054)	(0.062)	(0.049)	(0.050)
Constant	6.156***	3.900***	6.145***	2.955***
	(0.206)	(0.313)	(0.237)	(0.209)
R^2	0.277	0.368	0.420	0.581
Number of observations	2,335	1,816	1,728	1,841

Notes: *, **, *** denote significance at 10%, 5%, 1% levels respectively. Standard errors are in parentheses.

significant for the father–son pair in China. This reveals the mobility disadvantage of children in rural areas in a large country such as China, a fact we have already mentioned.

To better understand the contribution of the father's education to the child's education, we regress the respondent's education on his or her father's education and present the results in Table 9.8. From Model 1 of Table 9.8, we can see that the father's education alone explains about 20 per cent of the variation in education in the China sample, regardless of males or females. As to the case of Taiwan, about 30 per cent of the variation is explained by the father's education for the sample of sons and 36 per cent for daughters. Compared to the findings of Thomas (1996) on Asians in South Africa, where the variation explained in his samples is about one-third, the figure in Taiwan is a close match. However, compared with the prevalent evidence of less than 20 per cent found in Latin America by Behrman et al. (2000), the number for Taiwan and those quoted in Thomas are very high indeed.

In addition to the simple regression models (Model 1), the results for multiple regressions are presented in Model 2 of Table 9.8. To be comparable to the findings of the ordered probit models listed in Table 9.5, all explanatory variables, except for the father's education (which is now measured by schooling years), are the same. It can be clearly seen from Table 9.8 that all explanatory variables have the same signs and significance levels as appeared in Table 9.5. Thus the interpretations will not be repeated here. What is worth noting is the magnitude of the estimates for father's education. Model 2 of Table 9.8 shows that, as the father's schooling increases by one year, his son's (daughter's) schooling would increase by 0.295 (0.298) year for the sample of China. And concerning the sample of Taiwan, the magnitudes for father–son and father–daughter pairs are 0.382 and 0.439 years, respectively. This suggests that the marginal effect of the father's schooling on the child's schooling is greater in Taiwan than in China. With respect to gender, the marginal effect is greater on the daughter's side than on the son's side, especially in Taiwan.

9.4. Conclusions

In this chapter we study the intergeneration mobility in Chinese families. We modify the mobility indexes in Checchi et al. (1999) and adopt the revised formulae provided by Formby et al. (2004), which facilitate our testing of the differences between Taiwan and China.

Dividing the education regimes by college, we find that the 2 × 2 transition matrix of Taiwan is similar to that of the USA. The probability for the son to remain in the high-education status, given that his father is high school or upper degree, is extremely low in China. This is believed to be due to the disturbance of the Cultural Revolution.

As far as the more refined 5 × 5 transition matrix is concerned, we find that the intergenerational mobility for Taiwan is better than that in China. This is particularly so for cohorts born after 1956, whose mandatory education has been extended from six to nine years in Taiwan. The Taiwan–China mobility difference is more evident in rural areas, which is reasonable, since the large area and inconvenient transportation of rural China are particularly detrimental to the education opportunities of the poor. We also calculate the marginal effect of the father's education on child education achievement. It turns out that the coefficient is larger in Taiwan relative to China. All such evidence suggests that the intergenerational mobility in Taiwan is higher relative to China.

Notes

1. Whether a respondent comes from a rural or urban area is decided by the answer to a retrospective question. Suppose the respondent answers that he or she resided in an urban area at the age of 16, they are assigned to the urban group. Otherwise, they are assigned to the rural group.
2. A random variable X first-degree stochastically dominates Y means that the cumulative distribution function of X is everywhere lower than that of Y.
3. Because the sample size is small for the father generation having a college degree, both in Taiwan and China, we also calculated the transition matrices using high school as a threshold. Since it is difficult for us to compare the result with the case of the USA or Italy, the results are not presented here.
4. See Binder and Woodruff (2002) and Mayer and Lopoo (2005) as well as our Chapter 8 for relevant references.
5. This approach has been adopted by Di Pietro and Urwin (2003) and some other scholars.
6. The different education tiers are transformed into years of schooling based on Table 8.1. However, the years of schooling may not be a precise measure of educational attainment in China, especially for those who experienced the Cultural Revolution in their schooling years. See Chapters 2 and 8 for further discussion.

10

Family Reciprocal Supports

In the literature there have been many articles studying the practices of family transfers. Such transfers may be intra-household, such as in the form of parents' investments in children's education or financial subsidies to unmarried children, or inter-household, such as the *inter vivos* or *post mortem* asset transfers between parents and children. In Western societies, most family transfers are downward, from parents to children. What children usually do in return is to pay some visits to their parents. Existing literature studying the Western world usually has a focus abstracted from the above background.

In Chinese societies, however, the scenario between parents and adult children is drastically different. We shall discuss in Chapter 11 some features of parental transfers and child feedback, including a large proportion of parents who transfer all their assets *inter vivos* (which is deemed strategically irrational from some Western researchers' point of view), the negative correlation between the parental exhaustion of assets and the frequency of their children's visits, and the possible influence of the kinship network on child feedbacks. In this chapter, we are going to discuss more about the inter-family resource support. Let us start with an overview of the changes in the old-age security systems of China and Taiwan.

10.1. Institutional Background of China and Taiwan

10.1.1. *The China Scenario*

As noticed by Sheng and Settles (2006), Wang (2006), and some other scholars, the old-age security policies in China have changed dramatically over the past few decades. Early in the era of Mao Zedong, the government introduced comprehensive social welfare coverage for employees in urban areas. In addition to the lifelong employment policy, the government guaranteed pensions, housing, and health insurance after retirement for employees in the state-owned enterprises and work units. Under the employment-based security system, most urban retirees were financially independent and did not need to rely on monetary support from their children.

Since China's market-oriented reform in the late 1970s, the employment-based social security system has been dismantled. The emergence of private enterprises and the abolition of the lifelong employment policy in state-owned enterprises in the mid-1980s changed the relationship between enterprises and employees. As cited by Sheng and Settles (2006: 298), between 1978 and 2000, the number of workers in state-owned units remained roughly the same, while those employed by private enterprises increased from zero to 1.268 million. Within the same period, the proportion of contract workers increased twenty-eight times, from 1.8 per cent in 1984 to 40.9 per cent in 1996, and by 2000 almost all workers had become contract workers. To accommodate these changes, the government of China has taken steps to reform the pension system, which included experimentation with personal accounts and the introduction of social insurance. Based on the statistics from the China Urban and Rural Elderly Survey in 2000, 70.7 per cent of urban elderly inhabitants aged 60 or above received employment-based pensions and 12.1 per cent relied on social insurance. Nevertheless, the huge deficits of the accounts cast doubt on the future of the social security system.

In contrast to the urban areas, the coverage of pensions in the rural areas of China is much lower. In Mao's time, land and other basic means of production were collectively owned in the rural communes. Rural workers were entitled to a share of the agricultural output through participating in the collective production activities. Childless or disabled elderly people were guaranteed food, clothing, medical care, housing, and burial expenses by the collectives, while other elderly people were cared for by their own family.

The introduction of the household responsibility contract system in the late 1970s led to a collapse of the collective-based social security system in the rural areas of China. The basic guarantees that used to be provided by the collectives now became the peasants' own responsibilities. Since 1986, China has tried to establish an old-age social insurance system for the rural elderly, but the huge size of the ageing population and the overall poverty in the rural areas have hindered the progress of the scheme. According to the 2000 China Urban and Rural Elderly Survey, only 6.9 per cent of the rural elderly aged 60 and above received pension benefits or social insurance, whereas 85.0 per cent relied on family support.[1]

197

10.1.2. *The Taiwan Scenario*

As in the urban areas of China, the old-age security system in Taiwan is employment based. Employees of government agencies and well-established corporations are covered by their respective insurance programs. However, small-scale businesses are reluctant to provide such support. According to Lin (2002), government employees (who account for about 6 per cent of Taiwan's labor force) could choose between a lump-sum retirement benefit and a monthly pension. By contrast, most private-sector employees are eligible for a lump-sum retirement benefit only. In addition to old-age income security, most programs also provide health insurance to employees.

To establish a more comprehensive social security system, the government of Taiwan has made several reforms since the latter half of the 1980s. These included the introduction of farmers' health insurance in 1985 and universal health insurance in 1995.[2] Along with the above schemes, starting from the early 1990s some local governments have provided monthly subsidies to elderly residents, excluding government retirees and the very rich. However, the amount and duration of these old-age benefits vary according to the financial situation of the local governments. According to the Elderly Survey conducted in 2005, 14.2 per cent of the elderly (aged 65 or above) reported that they relied on pensions as their main source of retirement income, 33.3 per cent relied on government benefits or subsidies, and 53.4 per cent relied on support from children or the spouses of children.[3]

10.1.3. *Legal Responsibilities of the Young*

The above discussion illustrates that, for either China or Taiwan, a comprehensive old-age security system has not been established yet. To meet the increasing demands of old-age support, both China and Taiwan have legislated against neglect of the elderly by their families. In China, the Criminal Law and the Marriage Law impose responsibilities on adult children to support their aged family members. In addition, the Law for the Elderly specifies the responsibility of married couples to support their parents and parents-in-law (Sheng and Settles 2006: 308). As to Taiwan, the Civil Law stipulates that adult children are obligated to care for their parents and other elderly relatives. The Criminal Law of Taiwan further provides that those who do not care for their parents could be sentenced up to seven years in prison. The Senior Citizens Welfare Law revised in 2007 imposes a pecuniary penalty on adult children who abandon their parents.

Nevertheless, these legal obligations on the family to care for the elderly may produce only mild effects, since the state is usually unwilling to step into the family domain, except in cases of outrageous neglect. See Leung (1997) and Sheng and Settles (2006) for further discussion about related issues.

10.2. Special Features of Chinese Family Transfers

As was already mentioned, Western family transfer flows discussed in the literature are predominantly downward, from parents to children, but the situation is very different in Taiwan and China. Based on the information collected from married respondents of the PSFD survey, we see from Table 10.1 that in Taiwan, among the married couples who had at least one parent alive on the husband's side during the survey time, 33.55 per cent of them responded that they had provided *upward* transfer flows *to* the husband's parents in the past year, and only 2.59 per cent received *downward* transfers *from* their parents. And the corresponding figures for China are 23.76 per cent and 9.91 per cent respectively, with the former lower than Taiwan, the latter higher. The difference between China and Taiwan probably reflects the institutional factors mentioned in the previous section. Basically, the socialist government of China assumes more responsibility for the care of the elderly, so that the necessity of upward transfers from children is reduced. As a result, these parents with stable subsidies also have more capability to provide downward transfers to their children.

On the wife's side, as shown in Table 10.2, the figures are only slightly different: in Taiwan, 29.81 per cent provided *upward* transfers to the wife's parents, and only 1.46 per cent received transfers from parents. The situation in China is similar, with the numbers being 23.35 per cent and 10.17 per cent respectively. The one-child policy in China has resulted in many only-daughter families, and this should increase some wives' obligation of upward transfers. In short, the general practice of transfers in both Chinese societies is upward, consistent with the Chinese tradition of filial piety.

It is somewhat surprising to observe from Tables 10.1 and 10.2 that the co-existence of upward and downward transfers is rarely observed in Taiwan, but it is more common in China. This indicates some degree of

Table 10.1. Cross-tabulation of two-way transfers between the couples and the husband's parent(s)

	Taiwan			China		
	Any upward transfers to husband's parent(s)			Any upward transfers to husband's parent(s)		
	No	Yes	Sum	No	Yes	Sum
Any downward transfers from husband's parent(s)						
No	64.73	32.67	97.41	71.15	18.94	90.09
	(1,474)	(744)	(2,218)	(1,551)	(413)	(1,964)
Yes	1.71	0.88	2.59	5.09	4.82	9.91
	(39)	(20)	(59)	(111)	(105)	(216)
Sum	66.45	33.55	100.00	76.24	23.76	100.00
	(1,513)	(764)	(2,277)	(1,662)	(518)	(2,180)

Notes: The sample is confined to couples with the husband's parent(s) alive.
The figures in each cell are the proportion in percentage, and the corresponding number of observations (in parentheses).

Table 10.2. Cross-tabulation of two-way transfers between the couples and the wife's parent(s)

	Taiwan			China		
	Any upward transfers to wife's parent(s)			Any upward transfers to wife's parent(s)		
	No	Yes	Sum	No	Yes	Sum
Any downward transfers from wife's parent(s)						
No	69.22	29.32	98.54	71.82	18.01	89.83
	(1,570)	(665)	(2,235)	(1,815)	(455)	(2,270)
Yes	0.97	0.49	1.46	4.83	5.34	10.17
	(22)	(11)	(33)	(122)	(135)	(257)
Sum	70.19	29.81	100.00	76.65	23.35	100.00
	(1,592)	(676)	(2,268)	(1,937)	(590)	(2,527)

Notes: The sample is confined to couples with the wife's parent(s) alive.
The figures in each cell are the proportion in percentage, and the corresponding number of observations (in parentheses).

reciprocity between parents and children, somewhat akin to the tendency of *prestation* mentioned in the anthropology literature of Mauss (1954). Although the proportion of two-way transfers is small, it indicates that more than material support is associated with these transfers; such inefficient two-way transfers could not otherwise be explained.

Table 10.3. Cross-tabulation of upward transfers toward husband's parent(s) and wife's parent(s)

	Taiwan			China		
	Any upward transfers to wife's parent(s)			Any upward transfers to wife's parent(s)		
	No	Yes	Sum	No	Yes	Sum
Any upward transfers to husband's parent(s)						
No	57.39	8.70	66.09	71.39	3.54	74.94
	(990)	(150)	(1,140)	(1,148)	(57)	(1,205)
Yes	13.16	20.75	33.91	3.92	21.14	25.06
	(227)	(358)	(585)	(63)	(340)	(403)
Sum	70.55	29.45	100.00	75.31	24.69	100.00
	(1,217)	(508)	(1,725)	(1,211)	(397)	(1,608)

Notes: The sample is confined to couples with the husband's parent(s) and the wife's parent(s) alive.
The figures in each cell are the proportion in percentage, and the corresponding number of observations (in parentheses).

For those with both husband's and wife's parents alive, it can be seen from Table 10.3 that about one-fifth of the couples provided transfers to the husband's and wife's parents simultaneously. The pattern prevalent in Taiwan and China shows that it is a common practice for married couples to support both sides' parents in Chinese societies.

In Table 10.4, we present some information about financial or in-kind transfers that the couples received in the past or currently. During the couples' lifetime, downward transfers from either the husband's parents or the wife's parents might take various forms, including providing free housing at the present time or at the time of marriage, offering financial support on housing mortgages or business loans, helping taking care of grandchildren, or doing household chores. There might be some interest payment or compensation associated with these transfers, but the mere fact of such financing or transfers between family members suggests that the family provides a better deal than the market, otherwise the recipients might as well deal with the market.

Table 10.4 demonstrates that the interaction between generations in Chinese families is much more complicated than that observed in Western society. Evidently, the existence of financial interactions among family members in the past may blur the meaning of current transfer flows. Specifically, a transfer made at a given period may be related to some past events, and hence the multiplicity of possible interpretations. Note that in Table 10.4, we have not included parental subsidies of children's college tuition or living expenses; if we counted those as early subsidies as well, the

Table 10.4. Proportions of married couples who received in-kind or monetary transfers from husband's or wife's parent(s) (%)

Transfer item	Taiwan	China
Support from husband's parent(s)		
- Whether resided in house of husband's parents or in house bought by the husband's parents after marriage	51.12	56.46
- Whether received financial assistance (on business, home-buying, or others) from the husband's parents in the past 10 years	16.77	10.41
- Whether any of the couple's children was taken care of by the husband's parents before age 3	18.95	17.50
- Whether the husband's parents helped with housework at the time of the survey	21.38	34.07
- Whether resided in a place owned by or bought by the husband's parents at the time of the survey	17.64	15.06
Support from wife's parent(s)		
- Whether resided in house of wife's parents or in house bought by the wife's parents after marriage	9.73	10.54
- Whether received financial assistance (on business, home-buying, or others) from the wife's parents in the past 10 years	9.48	10.48
- Whether any of the couple's children was taken care of by the wife's parents before age 3	10.47	6.90
- Whether the wife's parents helped with housework at the time of the survey	4.86	12.92
- Whether resided in place owned by or bought by the wife's parents at the time of the survey	2.93	3.58

Notes: Sample is confined to couples with both the husband's parent(s) and the wife's parent(s) alive. The number of observations for Taiwan and China are 1,604 and 1,594 respectively.

transfer scenarios would be even more complex. Concerning the prevalence and importance of complex Chinese family transfers, we shall elaborate our point in the next section by reviewing the literature.

10.3. Reviewing Some Models in the Literature

There is a wealth of articles in the literature about family transfers, and we shall only use several classic ones to illustrate our point. The child's income in period t is denoted y_{ct}, and the parent's income in period t is y_{pt}.

The first model of family altruism we review was proposed by Cox (1987). The author presented a nested structure of parental altruism and compared the implications of two scenarios, altruism and exchange. The child has the option of whether or not to participate in the transfer-feedback game proposed by the parents. In the exchange (altruism) case, the child's participation constraint would (would not) be binding; this relationship allows Cox to derive testable implications for empirical analysis.

The second model of family altruism was due to Altonji et al. (1992). They showed that when the parent and the child are altruistically linked in the sense of income pooling, the child's optimal consumption in period t, denoted c_{ct}, should have a zero coefficient with respect to y_{ct}, controlling for the combined income of the parent and the child $(y_{ct} + y_{pt})$. The third classic approach to family transfers concerns the practice of family risk-sharing. Hayashi et al. (1996) defined family risk-sharing in terms of the ability of family members to absorb contingencies. If income contingencies can be faced and absorbed by family members jointly, then Hayashi et al. showed that a family member's marginal utility of consumption should have a particular factor structure: those contingencies that cannot be insured by families will be isolated from the remaining ones. The fourth model of family altruism and transfers was also proposed by Altonji et al. (1997). They argued that if intra-family transfers occur when the child's income is below a certain critical level, then there is some generic non-linearity in the transfer equation, which requires a more sophisticated estimation technique.

Finally, there are also some pure empirical analyses of family transfers, such as Cox and Rank (1992) and Cox et al. (2004). The main focus of this strand of studies was the "transfer derivative," which measures the responsiveness of the amount of transfers to household incomes or resources. It turns out that the estimate in the USA was small, in general less than 20 per cent, and the estimates of developing countries such as the Philippines were larger.

A common feature of the above-mentioned literature was the specification of the agent's utility only as a function of current consumption flows. It is clear when one looks at the child as an example, however, that the following characteristics of Chinese families cannot be captured by previous models.

1. Suppose period 1 indicates the child's young adult period. A child's early career is usually characterized by financial constraint for the child. When the child contemplates the purchase of an apartment or condo in period 1, given the imperfect capital market, subsidy or financing support from parents (or parents-in-law) will make a big difference in easing the child's financial constraint in this period. For instance, the financially constrained young couple may be forced by onerous mortgage obligations to cut down on their dining out, travel, and transportation expenses. However, they do not have to face such constraints if their parents provide some support. In general, the utility function of the child in period t should be written as $u_t(c_{ct}; H_t)$, where H_t is an index indicating whether the parent provides financial support at t. In return, the dutiful child may want to "pay back" some of their income to their parents in some later periods, such as $s > t$.

As one can see from Table 10.4, parental subsidizing of married children's housing and business is not uncommon in Taiwan and China. When a historical event H_t enters the flow utility function of the child, conceptually it is difficult to distinguish between altruism, exchange, and risk sharing. Parents' willingness to support their financially constrained children certainly reveals some kind of altruism (Becker and Murphy 1988: 3). The child's later upward transfers may not be made in the proper sense of relieving the parents' budget, but rather show a pattern of reciprocity, an exchange in return for parents' earlier support. If we have in mind some kind of "transfer derivative," it should reflect the response of *current* transfers to *past* generous subsidies from the parent, instead of *current* income of the child. Furthermore, the parents' support with a view to easing the child's financial constraint is certainly a form of intergenerational risk sharing. In short, the above discussion shows that the Chinese practices cannot be used to confirm or reject any particular hypothesis proposed in the Western literature.

2. According to the PSFD data of Taiwan, nearly 20 per cent of married couples had their children cared for by the husband's or the wife's parents before they reached the age of 3, and the percentage for China is similar in magnitude (21.38 per cent). In this case, if there are some transfers from a couple to either spouse's parents, it is difficult to identify the meaning of such transfers. Again, parents may take care of the couple's kids out of altruism; but they may also do it because they believe they offer a more efficient alternative to market day care. This also implies that the couple's parents can help avoid some risks (child abuse, inadequate care) inherent in market day care, indicating some form of family support. And married couples' possible payments to their parents may also be a token of compensation in return for the latter's contribution to child care. This is again a particular form of exchange.

3. Suppose the parents undertake babysitting duties and the respondent and his or her spouse provides some reciprocal transfers as mentioned above, the causal relationship between incomes and transfers may be different from what is normally expected. In the West, it is expected that when the income of a couple decreases, the transfers to their parents should also decrease. However, in Chinese societies it may be the case that only relatively poor couples who cannot afford market day care services would enlist the help of their parents. If these young couples provide some transfers to their parents, we may observe a pattern wherein poor (instead of rich) respondents tend to provide transfers to their parents, contrary to the

usual expectation. Thus, without taking account of the older generation's babysitting contribution in the background, the correlation between household income and upward transfers may be quite misleading.

From the preceding discussion one can draw some important inferences. First, the prevalent upward transfers found in Chinese societies are usually associated with some historical events (previous downward transfers) in the early period of one's life; and looking at contemporary income and transfer data is simply not enough. More specifically, none of the tests in the literature can help us confirm or refute a hypothesis that involves reciprocal transfers that occur in different time periods. Furthermore, since there are many kinds of events in the child's past that can trigger his or her later transfer, and since a child may experience multiple events, it is difficult to derive an orthodox micro-economic model. In the next section, we do try to suggest some testable hypotheses for our empirical analysis.

10.4. Some Hypotheses on Reciprocal Family Support

We try to formalize the risk-sharing scenario in a Chinese society as follows. We consider an overlapping generations framework, and separate the lifetime of a person after childhood into three periods: young adult (roughly aged 30–50), mature adult (aged 50–70), and retired old (aged more than 70). A general structure of overlapping generations should involve multiple lines of transfers between individuals of different generations, and at different stages of their respective lives. To simplify our analysis, however, we shall concentrate on the interaction of two generations only: the parent and the adult child (see Figure 10.1); the young adults' investments in their children have been discussed in our other chapters on education. To facilitate the

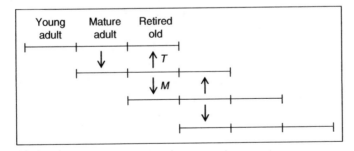

Figure 10.1 Dynamic transfers in an overlapping generation structure

discussion, we assume that the parent's mature adulthood (indexed period 1) corresponds to the child's young adulthood, and the parent's retired old age (indexed period 2) corresponds to the child's mature adulthood.

10.4.1. A Simple Overlapping Generations Model

For $t = 1, 2$, let the child's period-t income be y_{ct}, her period-t consumption be c_{ct}, where the subscript c indicates child. Similarly, for the parent with a subscript p, her income and consumption at period t are y_{pt} and c_{pt}, respectively. The child's utility function in these two periods is $u_1(c_{c1}) + u_2(c_{c2})$ and that of the parent is $v_1(c_{p1}) + v_2(c_{p2})$.

Following the general observation of the life cycle hypothesis, we assume that the mature adult's income (y_{c2} or y_{p1}) is relatively high and stable, whereas the net incomes of young adults and retired olds may be relatively low and unstable. In particular, the young adults may have a large mortgage payment, and may face more job insecurity in their early career as they enter the job market. The retired olds may have unexpected health problems, and may spend more on related medical expenses. Thus, if some mechanism can help reduce such risks during young adulthood and retired old age, it can certainly improve family efficiency.

Let M be the subsidy from a parent at her mature adulthood to her child at young adulthood, and T be the transfer from the child at her mature adulthood to her parent at her retired old age, as shown in Figure 10.1. We use M and T to indicate the meaning of these transfers, for *mortgage* subsidy and for *transfer*, respectively. The utility of the child and parent can now be rewritten respectively as follows:

$$Eu_1(y_{c1} + M) + Eu_2(y_{c2} - T),$$
$$Ev_1(y_{p1} - M) + Ev_2(y_{p2} + T),$$

where E indicates an expectation operator. Without resorting to any particular pattern of family altruism, we follow Chiappori (1992) and assume that family members try to maximize the following problem of efficient frontier, or a weighted average of the parent's and the child's utility functions.

Now let us study the reciprocal support schemes that may be implied from the above maximization problem. We first study the question of when a subsidy or transfer will occur. Consider the simplest case, in which there are two possible realizations of y_{at}, where $a = c, p$ and $t = 1, 2$. Suppose that the marginal utility is high for very low consumptions. One can easily see that, if the down side of $y_{c1}(y_{p2})$ is very low, then it is efficient for family members to design a positive $M(T)$ in their intergenerational support contract, once $y_{c1}(y_{p2})$ does turn out low. If $y_{c1}(y_{p2})$ turns out to be reasonably high, then, as we shall explain below, parent–child transfers may not be necessary.

10.4.2. Incomplete Insurance

Note that the family support scheme discussed above is not the same as those insurance schemes studied in the literature, where the insurance is implicitly an income pooling between family members. A complete insurance means that many family members pool their incomes together, and absorb all contingencies. The usual problem with a complete insurance, even between family members, is moral hazard, of which a particular form is Samaritan's dilemma. Despite the close ties of family members and relatively low monitoring costs, a complete pooling of income is likely to generate an agency problem. We do not expect such a complete income pooling between the parent and the child to happen; rather, we expect that transfers are made only if the young adults or the retired old receive a sufficiently low income, which creates an incentive for the mature adults to fill the gap of marginal utility of different family members. Compared with complete income pooling, this kind of partial support (on occasions needed) seems to be more prevalent in reality.

Since there is rarely any written contract between family members, a family support scheme such as we describe above is usually enforced by social norms. Under the norm of filial piety, a child is supposed to support his or her old parents, especially if the latter have frail health. The norm would suggest an even stronger force of feedback if the child has received a generous subsidy M from the parent at a young age.

In summary, this discussion suggests the following implications: (1) A family should ask members with higher and more stable income to absorb some contingencies of other members; in other words, mutual support among family members is not symmetric, not to mention income pooling. (2) Such absorption of contingencies should not be complete, as long as there is a concern of moral hazard. (3) The usual inverted-U pattern of life cycle incomes suggests that the transfer is likely from mature adults to young adults and to retired olds. (4) If a person has received generous subsidies from his or her parents in period 1, the usual assumption of reciprocity (Mauss 1954) would suggest that the period-2 transfer T may be different.

10.4.3. *Some Implications*

Now we take a more detailed look at period 2. In period 2, the parent is retired, and, for simplicity, we assume that y_{p2} is a constant instead of a stochastic variable. The adult child in her mature age, with the welfare of her parent at heart, has the following weighted average objective function:

$$u_2(y_{c2} - T) + \lambda(M)v_2(y_{p2} + T) \equiv \Omega.$$

In the above expression, we write the weight λ as a function of mortgage subsidy, with the assumption that $\lambda'(.) > 0$, which characterizes the notion of reciprocity of Mauss, or the Chinese notion of reciprocity. It can be shown through simple calculus that children's upward transfer T should increase if (1) child incomes y_{c2} increase, (2) previous parental subsidies M increase, and (3) parents' incomes y_{p2} decrease.

In our empirical analysis, we do not have the income data of the parents. So we use their age, education, and occupation as proxies. Older parents are believed to have lower disposable income, because of reduced savings or increased medical expenses. This is likely to be the case in societies where pensions or medical insurance are not prevalent. Higher-educated parents have more human capital, thus are more likely to have accumulated more assets when they were younger. Parents who worked for government or state enterprises, as mentioned in Section 10.1, are more likely to be covered by old-age pensions in Taiwan and China.

10.4.4. *The Role of Gender*

The above analysis did not take into account the role of an individual's gender. When we consider intergenerational transfers between married couples and both spouses' parents, the scenario is more complicated. It can be seen from Table 10.4 that, for most categories of downward transfers, married couples are more likely to receive transfers from the husband's parents than from the wife's parents. And Tables 10.1–10.3 also reveal that couples are more likely to make upward transfers to the husband's parents than to the wife's parents. These findings imply that transfers between spouses and their parents are asymmetric with respect to the husband's and the wife's line.

Previous theories usually assume that family members have divergent preferences, and the intrafamily allocations are decided through some collective decision process (Manser and Brown 1980, McElroy and Horney 1981, Lundberg and Pollak 1996, Lundberg et al. 1997, Chiappori 1992), so that spousal incomes may have different effects on upward transfers. The work of Blood and Wolfe (1960) also discusses how relative resources of family members might affect family decisions. In general, empirical studies have rejected the hypothesis that men's and women's resources have equivalent effects.[4] Relative to men, researchers also found that women tend to spend more on goods that benefit their children (Dwyer and Bruce 1988, Pahl 1990, Schmeer 2005). Married women's resources were found to be positively related to expenditures on children's clothing (Lundberg et al. 1997, Phipps and Burton 1998), children's schooling (Kusago and Barham 2001, Quisumbing and Maluccio 2003), child care (Phipps and Burton 1998), and children's nutrition intake (Engle 1993, Thomas 1990, Schmeer 2005). Nevertheless, none of these studies attempted an analysis to determine whether men's and women's resources make a difference with respect to upward transfers.

When we analyze transfers between married couples and their parents in male-dominant societies such as China or Taiwan, it is important to distinguish between upward transfers to husbands' parents and to wives' parents, and to examine whether husbands' and wives' resources affect upward transfers differently. A reasonable conjecture is that the resources of husbands are more critical than those of wives in determining the amount of transfers toward their parents or their parents-in-law.

10.5. Empirical Analysis on Reciprocal Transfers

In the remainder of this chapter, therefore, we follow Cox et al. (2004) and analyze transfers of China and Taiwan empirically. Other than estimating the "transfer derivative" as in the literature, we take advantage of the detailed information contained in the PSFD data set, and take into account several historical events. We shall combine the information of the married respondent and his or her spouse and use the couples' data to investigate whether previous downward transfers from parents of either side affect the amount of upward transfers later. If there is a positive effect, then it implies some kind of reciprocity to previous downward transfers by parents, indicating the existence of a reciprocal family support scheme.

10.5.1. Cross-sectional Evidence

We first use one-period data of Taiwan and China to analyze upward transfers toward parents and parents-in-law. The sample of Taiwan is from the first-wave PSFD survey data collected in years 1999, 2000, and 2003 respectively. And the sample of China is from the 2004 survey. To analyze upward transfers toward husband's parents and wife's parents jointly, we confine our samples to the married couples with at least one parent alive on both the husband's side and the wife's side. The deletion of observations with missing values left 1,383 and 1,010 married couples for Taiwan and China respectively. Within the sample of Taiwan, about 36 per cent (52 per cent) of the couples did not provide any upward transfers to husbands' parents (wives' parents). And the corresponding ratio for China is 73 per cent (75 per cent).

For the ith couple, the regressions of upward transfers with respect to husband's parents (T_{wi}) and wife's parents (T_{wi}) are specified as follows:

$$T_{hi} = \beta_{y,h} y_{hi} + \beta_{y,h} y_{wi} + M'_{hi} \beta_{M,h} + Z'_{hi} \beta_{Z,h} + u_{hi},$$
$$T_{wi} = \beta_{y,w} y_{wi} + \beta_{y,w} y_{wi} + M'_{wi} \beta_{M,w} + Z'_{wi} \beta_{Z,w} + u_{wi},$$

where y_{hi} and y_{wi} denote husband's and wife's incomes, M_{hi} and M_{wi} represent vectors of past transfers from husband's and wife's parents, including a dummy indicating whether the couple ever received any financial assistance (on housing, business, etc.) in the past ten years, and a dummy indicating if any child of the couple was taken care of by the parents before age 3. Terms Z_{hi} and Z_{wi} are vectors of other controlled variables, which include spousal education, number of the spouses' own children, a dummy indicating the existence of siblings on the spouse's side, parental education, parental widowhood status, parents' age, and a dummy indicating whether parents worked in the government or were state enterprise employees. In addition, ethnicity dummies and regional dummies were controlled in Taiwan and China separately. Selected means and standard deviations of some variables are listed in Tables 10.5 and 10.6. To take into account the censoring of dependent variables and the possible correlation between the error terms (u_{hi} and u_{wi}), we adopt the bivariate Tobit model to estimate the above regressions.

The results of the bivariate Tobit model are presented in Table 10.7. It can be seen from the bottom of the table that the correlation coefficients (ρ) of Taiwan and China are both positively significant, indicating the necessity of estimating the two regressions jointly. As to the effects of the spouses' income, the findings of the two areas are coherent in the sense that the husband's income has positively significant effects on transfers to either spouse's parents (at 1 per cent significance level), but the wife's income turns out to be insignificant under a 10 per cent level. This is consistent

Table 10.5. Means and standard deviations of selected variables by transfer status, Taiwan

	Positive transfers to husband's parent(s) and positive transfers to wife's parent(s)	Positive transfers to husband's parent(s) and zero transfers to wife's parent(s)	Zero transfers to husband's parent(s) and positive transfers to wife's parent(s)	Zero transfers to husband's parent(s) and zero transfers to wife's parent(s)
Transfers to husband's parent(s) (in thousand local dollars)	9.086 (16.371)	10.448 (38.709)	0.000 (0.000)	0.000 (0.000)
Transfers to wife's parent(s) (in thousand local dollars)	5.356 (11.192)	0.000 (0.000)	5.002 (5.649)	0.000 (0.000)
Husband's income (in million local dollars)	0.053 (0.042)	0.052 (0.268)	0.058 (0.057)	0.042 (0.037)
Wife's income (in million local dollars)	0.026 (0.049)	0.023 (0.063)	0.025 (0.041)	0.016 (0.020)
Financial help from husband's parents in the past ten years (= 1 if yes)	0.220 (0.415)	0.171 (0.377)	0.226 (0.423)	0.096 (0.295)
Financial help from wife'sparents in the past ten years (= 1 if yes)	0.140 (0.347)	0.116 (0.321)	0.132 (0.342)	0.043 (0.202)
Child caring for kids under age 3 by husband's parents (= 1 if yes)	0.209 (0.407)	0.229 (0.421)	0.113 (0.320)	0.159 (0.366)
Child caring for kids under age 3 by wife's parents (= 1 if yes)	0.131 (0.338)	0.076 (0.266)	0.170 (0.379)	0.085 (0.279)
Number of observations	609	275	53	446

Notes: Sample is confined to couples with both the husband's parent(s) and the wife's parent(s) alive.
Standard deviations are in parentheses.

with our patrilineal conjecture that married men's resources are more dominant than their spouses' resources in the determination of upward transfers.

In a patrilineal society, downward transfers to sons are natural and typical, and so are male adults' upward support of their parents. Thus for male samples, the effect of previous subsidies is not significant. However, if *unusual* downward support has been provided to the wife, then it is more likely to see feedback from the recipient. Similarly, a positive coefficient of previous child care on current transfers may indicate a favor to be returned in the society in question. This background may be worth bearing in mind.

As we can see from Table 10.7, previous downward transfers show slightly different effects in Taiwan and China. In the case of Taiwan, financial and child

Table 10.6. Means and standard deviations of selected variables by transfer status, China

	Positive transfers to husband's parent(s) and positive transfers to wife's parent(s)	Positive transfers to husband's parent(s) and zero transfers to wife's parent(s)	Zero transfers to husband's parent(s) and positive transfers to wife's parent(s)	Zero transfers to husband's parent(s) and zero transfers to wife's parent(s)
Transfers to husband's parent(s) (in thousand local dollars)	1.672 (7.492)	3.680 (14.712)	0.000 (0.000)	0.000 (0.000)
Transfers to wife's parent(s) (in thousand local dollars)	0.945 (1.410)	0.000 (0.000)	1.046 (2.320)	0.000 (0.000)
Husband's income (in million local dollars)	2.013 (4.673)	1.129 (0.864)	1.149 (1.119)	1.201 (1.328)
Wife's income (in million local dollars)	0.956 (1.653)	0.838 (0.696)	0.562 (0.327)	0.770 (0.852)
Financial help from husband's parents in the past ten years (= 1 if yes)	0.202 (0.402)	0.061 (0.242)	0.206 (0.410)	0.061 (0.240)
Financial help from wife's parents in the past ten years (= 1 if yes)	0.188 (0.392)	0.082 (0.277)	0.147 (0.359)	0.075 (0.264)
Child caring for kids under age 3 by husband's parents (= 1 if yes)	0.224 (0.418)	0.265 (0.446)	0.265 (0.448)	0.196 (0.397)
Child caring for kids under age 3 by wife's parents (= 1 if yes)	0.063 (0.243)	0.102 (0.306)	0.059 (0.239)	0.074 (0.262)
Number of observations	223	49	34	704

Notes: Sample is confined to couples with both the husband's parent(s) and the wife's parent(s) alive. Standard deviations are in parentheses.

care support received by the couple has positive effects on both the wife's and the husband's sides, but the effects on the latter are relatively minor. In the case of China, financial support from parents has positive effects on the wife's side only, while child care support has positive effects on the husband's side only. These divergent findings between Taiwan and China probably reveal differences in social backgrounds between the two societies.

Another finding worth mentioning in Table 10.7 is the effect of parental age dummies. For Taiwan, parents aged between 61 and 80 received more

Table 10.7. Bivariate Tobit models for upward transfers from married couples to husband's and wife's parent(s)

	Taiwan		China	
	Upward transfers to husband's parent(s) (1)	Upward transfers to wife's parent(s) (2)	Upward transfers to husband's parent(s) (3)	Upward transfers to wife's parent(s) (4)
Husband's/wife's education (elementary or below as ref.)				
Junior high	2.481	0.305	−0.339	0.211
	(2.912)	(1.190)	(1.134)	(0.193)
Senior high	6.614**	0.525	1.820	0.414
	(2.732)	(1.038)	(1.363)	(0.263)
College or above	4.620	1.584	−0.643	0.882**
	(2.968)	(1.233)	(1.798)	(0.356)
Husband's income (million local dollars)	54.256***	15.743**	0.846***	0.176***
	(17.235)	(7.386)	(0.168)	(0.030)
Wife's income (million local dollars)	19.176	8.305	0.626	0.078
	(17.728)	(7.593)	(0.440)	(0.080)
Number of kids	−0.262	0.050	−0.356	0.029
	(0.909)	(0.393)	(0.719)	(0.128)
Husband/wife without sibling (= 1 if yes)	0.730	1.435	−3.209	−0.488
	(2.395)	(1.192)	(2.441)	(0.349)
Only husband's/wife's mother alive (= 1 if yes)	−0.182	−0.357	−0.423	−0.140
	(1.652)	(0.729)	(1.192)	(0.257)
Age of living parents (aged more than 80 as ref.)				
Aged 60 or below	2.188	0.434	0.115	0.224
	(2.713)	(1.057)	(1.487)	(0.249)
Aged 61–70	4.084*	2.712***	1.173	−0.026
	(2.278)	(0.925)	(1.283)	(0.236)
Aged 71–80	6.588***	1.448	−1.052	−0.042
	(2.209)	(0.958)	(1.287)	(0.234)
Husband's/wife's father's education (elementary or below as ref.)				
Junior high	0.139	0.071	1.380	0.283
	(2.565)	(1.120)	(1.327)	(0.225)
Senior high or above	1.423	0.034	0.075	−0.060
	(2.422)	(0.994)	(1.770)	(0.271)
Husband's/wife's parent(s)' worked in government or state enterprise (= 1 if yes)	−1.071	0.040	−1.514	0.232
	(2.175)	(0.973)	(1.316)	(0.230)
Residential region (Shanghai as ref.)				
Zhejiang	—	—	2.313	0.862**
			(1.945)	(0.341)
Fujian	—	—	7.145***	1.784***
			(1.980)	(0.352)
Ethnicity (aborigine as ref.)				
Mainlander	−7.071	−1.475	—	—
	(9.750)	(3.522)		

(Continued)

Table 10.7. (*Continued*)

	Taiwan		China	
	Upward transfers to husband's parent(s) (1)	Upward transfers to wife's parent(s) (2)	Upward transfers to husband's parent(s) (3)	Upward transfers to wife's parent(s) (4)
Fukienese	−5.641	−1.811	—	—
	(9.472)	(3.374)		
Hakka	−4.034	−0.333	—	—
	(9.706)	(3.479)		
Financial help from husband's/wife's parents in the past ten years (= 1 if yes)	1.330 (1.937)	2.654** (0.999)	2.069 (1.299)	0.454** (0.232)
Child-caring for kids under age 3 by husband's/wife's parents (= 1 if yes)	3.222* (1.854)	3.400*** (1.014)	3.702*** (1.029)	0.346 (0.302)
Constant	−8.402 (10.017)	−3.333 (3.652)	−17.104*** (2.610)	−3.511*** (0.457)
ρ	0.496*** (0.024)		0.674*** (0.029)	
Log-likelihood	−6349.639		−1601.683	
Number of observations	1,383		1,010	

Notes: Standard errors are in parentheses. *, **, and *** denote 10%, 5%, and 1% significance levels respectively. Sample is confined to couples with both the husband's parent(s) and the wife's parent(s) alive. The dependent variables are measured in thousand local dollars.

transfers from their children than the younger (aged 60 or below) and older (aged above 80) counterparts. This is probably because older parents incur more medical or other care expenses, but the very old (aged above 80) are more likely to be constrained by their health condition and incapable of spending much money anyway. Concerning the regional effect in China, it can be seen from the same table that Zhejiang and Fujian have higher upward transfers than Shanghai. One possible explanation is that Zhejiang and Fujian are less urbanized than Shanghai, thus are more likely to preserve the traditional value of filial piety. Furthermore, Shanghai city is also more open to market forces, has more prevalent pension support (see Section 10.1), and hence the necessity of within-family support is relatively weaker.

To obtain the results presented in Table 10.7, our sample included couples co-residing with either husbands' parents or wives' parents. Since the amount of intergenerational transfers might not be calculated precisely for the co-residing sample, for robustness check we delete such co-residing samples and rerun the regressions. Of course, we understand that by deleting

Table 10.8. Bivariate Tobit models for upward transfers from married couples to husband's and wife's parent(s): co-resident sample excluded

	Taiwan		China	
	Upward transfers to husband's parent(s) (1)´	Upward transfers to wife's parent(s) (2)´	Upward transfers to husband's parent(s) (3)´	Upward transfers to wife's parent(s) (4)´
Husband's/wife's education (elementary or below as ref.)				
Junior high	1.763	0.050	1.003	0.636**
	(4.400)	(1.742)	(1.371)	(0.289)
Senior high	6.309	−0.371	4.647***	0.717*
	(4.042)	(1.498)	(1.603)	(0.411)
College or above	3.187	0.056	0.788	1.333***
	(4.382)	(1.778)	(2.168)	(0.508)
Husband's income (million local dollars)	59.115**	18.334*	0.627**	0.172***
	(24.902)	(10.540)	(0.302)	(0.067)
Wife's income (million local dollars)	12.762	6.036	0.558	0.102
	(21.344)	(8.937)	(0.496)	(0.111)
Number of kids	−0.920	−0.155	−0.367	0.142
	(1.428)	(0.596)	(0.936)	(0.210)
Husband/wife without sibling (= 1 if yes)	−0.655	0.920	−4.621	−0.691
	(3.714)	(1.656)	(3.325)	(0.509)
Only husband's/wife's mother alive (= 1 if yes)	−0.563	−0.721	−0.080	−0.267
	(2.583)	(1.058)	(1.474)	(0.367)
Age of living parents (aged more than 80 as ref.)				
Aged 60 or below	5.517	0.775	1.166	0.563
	(4.256)	(1.614)	(1.828)	(0.374)
Aged 61–70	6.321*	3.597***	1.469	0.090
	(3.385)	(1.355)	(1.487)	(0.342)
Aged 71–80	9.012***	1.847	−0.705	−0.130
	(3.319)	(1.408)	(1.539)	(0.331)
Husband's/wife's father's education (elementary or below as ref.)				
Junior high	0.669	0.243	1.901	0.297
	(3.870)	(1.657)	(1.483)	(0.344)
Senior high or above	0.708	−0.200	−0.631	−0.202
	(3.523)	(1.397)	(2.227)	(0.396)
Husband's/wife's parent(s)' worked in government or state enterprise (= 1 if yes)	−0.218	0.674	−2.554*	0.270
	(3.068)	(1.347)	(1.508)	(0.323)
Residential region (Shanghai as ref.)				
Zhejiang	—	—	1.580	0.972**
			(2.243)	(0.482)

(Continued)

Table 10.8. (*Continued*)

	Taiwan		China	
	Upward transfers to husband's parent(s) (1)´	Upward transfers to wife's parent(s) (2)´	Upward transfers to husband's parent(s) (3)´	Upward transfers to wife's parent(s) (4)´
Fujian	—	—	5.458** (2.347)	1.786*** (0.508)
Ethnicity (aborigine as ref.)				
Mainlander	−7.671 (12.760)	0.617 (4.912)	—	—
Fukienese	−5.153 (12.347)	0.073 (4.716)	—	—
Hakka	−4.321 (12.689)	2.460 (4.875)	—	—
Financial help from husband's/wife's parents in the past ten years (= 1 if yes)	1.514 (2.707)	2.125 (1.351)	2.423 (1.540)	0.470 (0.355)
Child-caring for kids under age 3 by husband's/wife's parents (= 1 if yes)	1.817 (2.891)	3.870*** (1.404)	3.497*** (1.343)	0.445 (0.459)
Constant	−8.626 (13.578)	−4.565 (5.270)	−16.631*** (3.186)	−4.347*** (0.687)
ρ		0.490*** (0.031)		0.703*** (0.036)
Log-likelihood		−4047.245		−970.658
Number of observations		831		632

Notes: Standard errors are in parentheses. *, **, and *** denote 10%, 5%, and 1% significance levels respectively. Sample is confined to couples with both side's parent(s) alive yet non-co-resident with either parent. The dependent variables are measured in thousand local dollars.

co-residing samples we are also deleting observations with closer family ties, and some sample selection problems may occur as a result. From Table 10.8 it can be seen that our main findings remain largely intact after the deletion, except that the effect of previous downward financial help on current upward transfers is only marginally significant. Besides the bivariate Tobit model, we also try to ignore the correlation between husband's and wife's sides and use the univariate Tobit approach to re-estimate the regressions. It turns out that the results are very similar to those obtained for the bivariate Tobit model. To save space, these univariate Tobit results are not listed here.

10.5.2. *Panel-Data Evidence of Taiwan*

To examine whether the findings of the preceding section hold dynamically, we construct a set of panel data (from the first wave till the 2005 survey) for Taiwan. We use a random-effects Tobit model to capture the possible heterogeneity across the observed couples. Since the preceding section shows that the results for the univariate Tobit and the bivariate Tobit models are very similar under the cross-sectional setting, we adopt, for simplicity, the univariate approach in our panel analysis. As indicated in the bottom rows of Table 10.9, the total number of couples in our panel sample is 1,422, and the corresponding number of observations is 4,268. For comparison with the analysis based on one-period data, the meaning of the variables of Table 10.9 is the same as the ones used in Tables 10.7 and 10.8.

Under the setting of Table 10.9, the time-variant variables include upward transfers, husband's income, wife's income, number of kids, widowhood status of parents, and parental age dummies. Other variables, including previous transfers from husband's or wife's parents, are retrieved from the first-wave survey and thus are invariant with respect to time. To allow for possible effect of birth cohorts and survey waves, we take advantage of the information of our panel data, and add some variables in the regression, including a set of dummies denoting the year of the first interview, and a dummy indicating whether the observation belongs to the first two waves of the interview. The interaction terms of the wave dummy and previous transfers from parents are added in the equations to examine whether the recipient couples tend to feed back earlier than later, after they received parental supports.

Columns 2–3 of Table 10.9 (equations (1)″ and (2)″) show that the husband's current income still exhibits positive effects on upward transfers, for either the husband's side or the wife's side. But the wife's current income has a significantly positive effect on transfers to the wife's parents, which is slightly different from the insignificant coefficients of one-period data. However, if we replace current income by the income lagged one period, it can be seen from columns 4–5 of Table 10.9 (equations (1)‴ and (2)‴) that only the husband's lagged income shows significant effects, which is consistent with the findings of Tables 10.7 and 10.8.

With regard to previous transfers from parents, even if parents' financial help in the past ten years (which was asked in the first-wave survey) does not have significant effects on children's upward transfers, the interaction terms with wave dummy reveal a different pattern. The significantly positive coefficients corresponding to the interaction terms indicate that, if the

Table 10.9. Random-effects Tobit models for upward transfers from married couples to husband's and wife's parent(s), Taiwan's panel data

	Current income controlled		Lagged income controlled	
	Upward transfers to husband's parent(s) (1)″	Upward transfers to wife's parent(s) (2)″	Upward transfers to husband's parent(s) (1)‴	Upward transfers to wife's parent(s) (2)‴
Husband's/wife's education				
Junior high	0.862	−0.718	1.141	−0.554
	(1.089)	(0.526)	(1.114)	(0.458)
Senior high	4.097***	0.390	4.507***	0.789*
	(0.990)	(0.468)	(1.006)	(0.404)
College or above	5.023***	2.385***	5.951***	2.760***
	(1.093)	(0.553)	(1.102)	(0.471)
Husband's current income	22.585***	11.102***	—	—
	(4.551)	(2.119)		
Husband's lagged income	—	—	7.339*	4.139***
			(3.788)	(1.368)
Wife's current income	6.122	7.280**	—	—
	(7.649)	(3.572)		
Wife's lagged income	—	—	4.102	0.815
			(5.669)	(2.233)
Number of kids	−0.640*	−0.057	−0.804**	−0.086
	(0.339)	(0.172)	(0.346)	(0.146)
Husband/wife without sibling	−1.047	−0.644	−1.117	−1.094**
	(1.006)	(0.583)	(1.096)	(0.529)
Only husband's/wife's mother alive	0.358	−0.104	0.331	0.041
	(0.631)	(0.325)	(0.645)	(0.277)
Age of living parents				
Aged 60 or below	−2.245	0.256	−2.501*	0.138
	(1.414)	(0.582)	(1.423)	(0.492)
Aged 61–70	1.492*	1.141***	1.221	0.869**
	(0.890)	(0.420)	(0.927)	(0.361)
Aged 71–80	1.222*	1.065***	0.962	0.950***
	(0.719)	(0.370)	(0.731)	(0.311)
Husband's/wife's father's education				
Junior high	1.288	0.883*	1.467	0.712
	(1.015)	(0.519)	(1.038)	(0.443)
Senior high or above	0.571	0.500	0.636	0.630
	(0.951)	(0.479)	(0.960)	(0.410)
Husband's/wife's parent(s)' worked in government or state enterprise (=1 if yes)	−0.362	0.216	−0.541	0.125
	(0.855)	(0.446)	(0.875)	(0.384)
Ethnicity				
Mainlander	−0.175	−0.660	0.671	−0.430
	(3.188)	(1.365)	(3.285)	(1.182)
Fukienese	0.839	−0.593	1.292	−0.665
	(3.048)	(1.265)	(3.137)	(1.096)
Hakka	2.140	−0.131	2.122	−0.327
	(3.156)	(1.330)	(3.247)	(1.151)

Year of first interview (year 2003 as ref.)				
Year 1999	1.875**	1.365***	2.153**	1.246***
	(0.882)	(0.432)	(1.039)	(0.409)
Year 2000	1.717*	0.882*	2.124**	1.068**
	(0.972)	(0.493)	(0.983)	(0.417)s
First two waves of interview	−0.407	−0.747**	0.028	−0.474*
(= 1 if yes)	(0.673)	(0.294)	(0.773)	(0.269)
Previous transfers from husband's/wife's parents				
Financial help in past ten years	−1.620	−0.834	−1.657	−0.739
	(1.038)	(0.677)	(1.025)	(0.559)
Child-caring for kids	2.756***	0.477	2.738***	0.569
	(1.035)	(0.654)	(1.016)	(0.536)
Previous transfers from husband's/wife's parents × wave dummy				
Financial help in past ten years × first two waves of interview	2.722**	2.686***	2.401	2.374***
	(1.380)	(0.844)	(1.528)	(0.779)
Child-caring for kidsfirst two waves of interview	0.017	2.674***	−0.095	1.811***
	(1.349)	(0.800)	(1.430)	(0.691)
Constant	−4.949	−2.791*	−4.905	−1.881
	(3.323)	(1.433)	(3.428)	(1.241)
Log-likelihood	−13602.83	−9408.86	−12254.61	−7978.93
Number of observations	4,268	4,268	3,854	3,854
Number of subjects	1,422	1,422	1,394	1,394

Notes: Standard errors are in parentheses. *, **, and *** denote 10%, 5%, and 1% significance levels respectively. Sample is confined to couples with both the husband's parent(s) and the wife's parent(s) alive. The dependent variables are measured in thousand local dollars.

interviewed respondents stated that they had received financial support from their parents (or parents-in-law) in the first-wave survey, they are more likely to make upward transfers in the same period or the subsequent period than in later periods.[5] This means that the memory of "debt" and the drive to pay back are stronger in periods closer to the time point of the downward transfers.

As to child care provided by parents, the interaction terms with wave dummy also show the same pattern in the equations of the wife's side (equations (2)″ and (2)‴ in Table 10.9). On the husband's side, even though the interaction terms of child care and wave dummy are not significant, it can be seen from Table 10.9 that the overall effects of child care are positively significant. Other findings are similar to Tables 10.7 and 10.8, and we shall not repeat them here.

10.6. Conclusions

In this chapter, we studied the role of reciprocal family support in Chinese families. We first reviewed the institutional background of social security provided by the government, and then considered the supplementary role played by family members. Basically, the government of China and Taiwan provided limited social security support for their elderly, and within-family transfers of various forms are prevalent in these two places, in contrast to Western societies.

Since family support often involves more than intragenerational monetary transfers, we considered a model of reciprocity which fits better the pattern of transfers in Chinese societies. We conjectured that the present flow of upward transfers from adult children to their parents depends not only on children's current incomes, but also on the existence of previous support or help from parents in the form of babysitting. This dynamic framework of transfers between family members at different stages of their life cycle indicates the function of family support, and the interpretation of reciprocal transfers is also different from the traditional ones (altruism and exchange).

Using the PSFD data, we were able to estimate the transfer equation empirically. We found that the income derivative is most significant with respect to the husband's income, consistent with the patrilineal practices in Chinese societies. Furthermore, previous subsidies and child care support from parents also increase adult children's current feedback transfers. The coefficients of previous subsidies are more significant for females than for males, perhaps because downward support offered to female family members is relatively unusual in a patrilineal society and hence is something that should be repaid afterwards. We also found that in Taiwan the upward transfer derivatives with respect to previous downward subsidies tend to decrease with time.

Notes

1. For the changes in the old-age security system of China, interested readers could see Feldstein (1998), Sheng and Settles (2006), and Wang (2006) for further discussion.
2. For a detailed discussion of the reforms of the social security system in Taiwan, see Hu et al. (2000) and Lin (2002).

3. The website http://www.moi.gov.tw/english contains detailed information about the survey and relevant statistics.
4. See, for example, Lundberg et al. (1997) for a thorough review.
5. The only insignificant interaction term appears in the "lagged-income" setting (equation (1)$'''$). But the corresponding t value of 1.58 is very close to the critical t value of 10% significant level (= 1.64).

11

Parental Transfers and Child Feedbacks

Concerning parent–child interactions, the orthodox view in the mainstream literature is quite "strategic." One notes that parents often control more economic resources, and that they often like to receive visits from their children. Given such observations, it was postulated that parents may want to keep more bequeathable assets as lure, in order to attract more visits from their children. The well-known hypothesis was proposed by Bernheim, Shleifer, and Summers (hereafter BSS, 1985).[1] According to their hypothesis, once the parents have transferred all their assets, they lose their leverage, and hence children no longer have the incentive to behave obediently. Thus, rational parents should not exhaust their assets when they are still alive. This is what is called "the strategic bequest hypothesis" in the literature. Related discussion on intergenerational transfers can be found in Cox and Stark (1993), Cox (1987, 1990), and Laitner (1997). In Cox and Stark (1993), the parents "teach" their children what they should do. Discussion concerning the practices in the Philippines can be found in Davies and Zhang (1995).

The question we raise in this chapter is simple: Are the practices in Chinese societies different from what was described above? If they are different, in what ways are they different? And can we explain such differences? How is the value placed on filial piety by Chinese societies related to the possibly different practices in child visits?

11.1. Special Features in Chinese Societies

First we look at the data. The PSFD survey conducted in Taiwan and China provides evidence of *inter vivos* transfers and child visits that would seem to

222

Table 11.1. Distribution of asset-transfers status by parental widowhood, Taiwan and China (%)

Area/parental widowhood	All transferred	Partly transferred	Not yet transferred	Nothing to be transferred	All sample
	Sub-samples by asset-transfers status				
Taiwan					
All	24.34	5.97	35.08	34.61	100.00 (1,676)
With father alive only	26.03	5.02	32.88	36.07	100.00 (219)
With mother alive only	36.25	4.44	18.91	40.40	100.00 (698)
With both parents alive	12.91	7.64	50.59	28.85	100.00 (759)
China					
All	34.62	6.39	23.79	35.20	100.00 (1,534)
With father alive only	33.33	6.01	21.86	38.80	100.00 (183)
With mother alive only	37.35	5.50	17.96	39.19	100.00 (763)
With both parents alive	31.46	7.65	31.97	28.91	100.00 (588)

Notes: For both Taiwan and China, the sample is confined to the respondents who were born between 1935 and 1964, and who had at least one parent alive at the time of survey. Numbers in parentheses are the sample size.

contradict the practice in the West described in existing literature. Among the 1,676 Taiwanese adult children (aged 36–65) interviewed in 1999 and 2000,[2] 24.34 per cent of them responded that their living parents had already divided and transferred *all* their assets. As one can see from Table 11.1, although the ratio of parents who have done so is slightly higher for the sample with only one living parent, the ratios in all family types are significantly greater than zero.[3] The evidence for China is shown in the bottom panel of Table 11.1. To be consistent with the counterpart of Taiwan, the sample of China is confined to respondents of the same birth year as Taiwan (born between 1935 and 1964). As one can see from this table, it reveals a similar pattern, with the proportion of families transferring all assets in China close to one third of all samples, even higher than that in Taiwan.

Evidently, the practice in Chinese societies is quite different from that in the West, in particular the US scenario posited in BSS (1985). What are the reasons behind the parents' apparent lack of worry about the possible alienation of their children in China and Taiwan after they exhaust all their assets? And what are the factors that prevented the children from neglecting parents who have no assets left? In this chapter, we measure child feedbacks by the frequency of visits (denoted by v) to their parents. Since the answers to the question regarding the frequency of visits are not the same between the Taiwan and China surveys, we adapt the responses of Taiwan to the counterpart of China. In Taiwan, the respondents were asked to recall the number of days they visited their parents last year. As to China, the answers to the corresponding question are categorical in nature. We group the responses in China into five categories: (1)$v = 1$, 0–2 visits last year, (2) $v = 2$, visiting every 2–3 months, (3) $v = 3$, 1–3 visits per month, (4) $v = 4$, 1–2 visits per week, (5)$v = 5$, visiting almost every day. And the responses of Taiwan are manipulated in a similar way.

In terms of the relationship between parental transfers and child feedbacks, the evidence disclosed in Table 11.2 is even more surprising. It shows that the frequency of visits is *highest* for families in which parents have transferred all their assets before their death ($D_1 = 1$). We conjecture that there may be factors which *facilitate* the children's visits after their parents have exhausted all their assets. Moreover, these factors may be stronger in Taiwan than in China. This observation motivates us to search for theoretical explanations that offer an alternative to the BSS hypothesis.

We separate our later discussion into two parts: First, we propose that the theory of *kinship pressure* may help explain why children maintain, or even increase, the frequency of visits to their parents after the latter give up their

Table 11.2. Measurement and basic statistics of visits and distance variables, Taiwan and China

Variable	All	All transferred ($D_1 = 1$)	Nothing to be transferred ($D_2 = 1$)	Partly or not yet transferred ($D_3 = 1$)
Taiwan				
Visits per year ($v = 1, \ldots, 5$), measured	2.888	3.038	2.683	2.984
by ordered categorical items	(1.295)	(1.344)	(1.306)	(1.237)
Distance of residence btw respondent	4.082	3.672	4.326	4.119
and parent ($l = 1, \ldots, 7$)	(2.204)	(2.135)	(2.185)	(2.229)
Number of observations	1,676	408	580	688
China				
Visits per year ($v = 1, \ldots, 5$), measured	3.671	3.904	3.497	3.608
by ordered categorical items	(1.302)	(1.278)	(1.346)	(1.241)
Distance of residence btw respondent	3.355	3.032	3.580	3.462
and parent ($l = 1, \ldots, 7$)	(1.732)	(1.517)	(1.864)	(1.750)
Number of observations	1,534	531	540	463

Notes: Standard errors are in parentheses. The means and standard deviations of "visits per year (v)" are computed based on the non-co-residing sample.

leverage of bequeathable assets. Second, we study empirically whether the data support our hypothesis. We argue that in a Chinese society where filial piety is a tradition, besides bequeathable assets, kinship pressure is a major factor influencing children's behavior. In Section 11.2 of this chapter we introduce a theoretical model along the lines of Bott (1968) and Kandel and Lazear (1992), and explore the interactions between adult children's visits, parental assets status, and the kinship network.

Intuitively, within a tight-knit kinship network, if parents are to complain about being neglected by their children *after* the transfer of all their assets, these children would certainly be shamed for their lack of filial devotion either by their siblings and relatives, or by friends and neighbors within the relevant network. By contrast, children whose parents have not transferred all their assets or who are surrounded by a loose network would not face such pressure. Thus, the assets status can actually trigger the network pressure on children's behavior toward their parents. Note that if kinship pressure is a complementary force that sustains the parent–child interactions, then intergenerational support will not necessarily disappear with economic development, as opposed to what one often observes in some Western countries. Thus, our analysis supports the observation found in Lee et al. (1994), who showed that intergenerational altruism in Chinese societies may not go away along with the process of modernization.

We conjecture that the kinship network may be tighter in Taiwan than in China, mainly due to the fact that a major target of China's Cultural Revolution was indeed the traditional lineage network and family value. We figure that the norm of filial piety may not have been seriously affected by the Cultural Revolution, but the tightness of the lineal structure could have been diluted. This may influence the strength of the lineage network in China. We shall come back to this question in the section of empirical analysis.

11.2. A Model of Filial Attention

11.2.1. *The Benchmark Case*

To study the interaction between child visits and bequeathable assets, we first start with the benchmark model that is compatible with the framework of BSS (1985) and then introduce the concern of bequests. Suppose there are n siblings in a family who all care about their parents. The n siblings' care inputs are denoted by the vector $(v_1, \ldots, v_n) = V$. We denote these inputs by v_i because in our later analysis v_i will refer to the number of "visits" by individual i. The parents' total satisfaction (S) is assumed to be a function of V: $S = f(v_1, \ldots, v_n)$. Parents may prefer more visits from a particular child; but adding concerns like this only creates some *ad hoc* complexities with no effects on our argument. Thus, we assume that parents care about the total visits received, and hence for child $i >$ the f function can be written as $S = f(v_i + \sum_{j \neq i} v_j)$.

For an altruistic child i, his or her target is to maximize

$$f\left(v_i + \sum_{j \neq i} v_j\right) - c(v_i), \quad i = 1, \ldots, n, \tag{11.1}$$

where $c(.)$ is the cost function of visits by i. To avoid unnecessary complications, we assume that f and c are not individual specific so that there is no subscript i associated with them in equation (11.1). We also adopt the usual technical assumptions associated with $f(.)$ and $c(.)$.

Following the line of reasoning in Kandel and Lazear (1992), we know that in any equilibrium, $v_i = v$ for all i must hold. Given the result of a symmetric solution, one can show through standard economic analysis that in a family with more siblings (larger n) the optimal per-child visits are less. This is the free-riding effect among siblings mentioned in the literature.

11.2.2. The Case with Bequeathable Assets

Now we consider the case where children care about not only their parents' satisfaction f, but also what they expect to receive from their parents, an idea that is consistent with the one considered in BSS (1985). Given $(v_1, \ldots, v_n >$, suppose the share of bequest child i expects to receive is $s(v_i/\sum_{j \neq i} v_j)$. Then child i's objective function may be revised as

$$f\left(v_i + \sum_{j \neq i} v_j\right) - c(v_i) + A \cdot s\left(v_i/\sum_{j \neq i} v_j\right), \quad i = 1, \ldots, n,$$

where A is the size of the parent's bequeathable assets. The corresponding analysis under a symmetrical Nash equilibrium leads to the prediction that child visits will increase when parents hold more bequeathable assets A.

11.2.3. The Case with Kinship Pressure for Conformity to Filial Piety

In a society emphasizing filial piety, regular visits to parents are considered part of the duties of children. A child failing to carry out this filial duty may incur criticism or a norm discipline from the social network. Lee et al.

(1994: 1016) argued that the greatest shame of all for Chinese children is to abandon one's parents. This is a value often reinforced by school textbooks and by society at large.

Indeed, as Bott (1968: 193) pointed out, it is the norm that dictates people's ideas as to what is customary and which kind of behavior is right and proper. The forces that drive children to visit their parents more often may come from neighbors, peer groups, and/or relatives, and these forces may have nothing to do with, and are possibly more powerful than, the strategic lure of possible inheritance. Bott (1968: 102–3, 122, 194) and Wellman (1990) suggested that the influence of such norms is stronger for groups which are homogeneous and small, share a similar social status, have strong economic ties, and are spatially accessible. Bott (1968: 202, 206) also pointed out that most spontaneous expressions of norms take the form of gossip spread by friends, neighbors, and relatives, and that "gossip is one of the chief means by which norms are stated and reaffirmed." Evidently, visits and gossip both influence the utility of the child, and we hypothesize that a child who tends to avoid *ex post* gossip would devote more *ex ante* visits to their parents.

The particular gossip in our context is caused by the status of bequeathable assets of parents. For instance, after the parents transfer more and more of their assets to children, if the parent–child relationship becomes alienated, as between King Lear and his daughters, then such alienation will be subject to greater opprobrium. Thus, let A_0 be the parent's initial asset size, and $T = A_0 - A$ be the amount of transferred assets, we expect that gossip is an increasing function of T. Notice that the gossip scenario described here only applies to the case where the parents do transfer some of their assets.

The pressure felt by a child depends upon the intensity and quality of gossip she or he hears. The stronger the parents' social network, the more disciplinary pressure the child may feel. On one hand, a child facing a tighter kinship network is more likely to *receive* complaints concerning his or her alienation. On the other hand, parents facing a closer network of neighbors and friends have more opportunities to *voice* their complaints. The neighbors and friends are not kinsmen, but they usually pass such gossip to the child (or to relatives of the child). From now on we shall use the term *kinship pressure* to describe the above two gossip-spread scenarios.

The above-mentioned kinship network is particularly important in Taiwan and China. In a traditional Chinese society, the relationship between generations is guided by a set of widely agreed-upon and culturally stressed obligations, according to which parents have the duty to help their children in their education, job searching, or even marriage matching. In return, children have the obligation of supporting their parents in their old age (Greenhalgh 1984: 533). As we showed in Chapter 3, Taiwan and China have just started to witness a shift in family structure from extended families to nuclear ones. Although the average family size gradually shrinks along with this family transition, the financial interactions, communications, and festival gatherings are largely unchanged.

Based on the above discussion, we let $N{\cdot}g(v_i, T)$ be the total gossip cost faced by child i, where N is a variable characterizing the intensity of network pressure. Here we use the simplest multiplicative form to capture the "broadcasting" impact of the kinship network. We assume that (1) a higher frequency of visits implies less gossip pressure; (2) the kinship pressure increases when parents have transferred more to children; and (3) the marginal pressure cost of negligence (fewer visits) increases if the size of transferred assets increases. Technically, the first two assumptions say that the derivative of g with respect to v (T) is negative (positive). The last assumption is consistent with the "shame effect" mentioned in Kandel and Lazear (1992: 806).

As such, the child i's objective is to choose v_i to maximize

$$f\left(v_i + \sum_{j \neq i} v_j\right) - c(v_i) + (A_0 - T){\cdot}s\left(v_i / \sum_{j \neq i} v_j\right) - N{\cdot}g(v_i, T), \quad i = 1, \ldots, n.$$

From the above setting we can derive the following two predictions: (1) child visits are more frequent in families with a strong kinship network, and (2) the impact of transfers on visiting frequency is not known, for there are two conflicting forces at work: when T increases, the bequest-lure effect is negative but the kinship pressure effect is positive. If the kinship pressure is strong enough, which will be the case when the kinship network N is large, the latter effect may dominate. This prediction is a departure from the previous bequest-lure hypotheses on parent–child interactions. We shall let the empirical evidence in the next section tell us whether the bequest-lure effect or the kinship pressure effect would dominate.

To sum up, we have highlighted several important hypotheses in the prior discussion. First, the sibship size should have a negative effect on children's visits. Second, the kinship network N should have a positive effect. Third, the effect of asset transfers may be positive or negative, depending on the interaction of the kinship network; when N is large, it is more likely to be positive.

11.3. Empirical Setup

11.3.1. *Variable Definitions*

Our purpose is to estimate the effect of asset transfers and kinship network on child-to-parent visits. A problem with the co-residing samples is that the frequency of visits in question is not observable. However, it does not mean that we should discard these observations altogether, because co-residence *per se* does contain some useful information. We will return to this question in the next section as we consider the statistical settings.

Parents' assets status is classified into three types: those who have transferred all their bequeathable assets ($D_1 = 1$), those who have no bequeathable assets ($D_2 = 1$) to begin with, and those who have assets but have not yet transferred all of them ($D_3 = 1$). It can be easily seen from Table 11.2 that, for both Taiwan and China, children in $D_1 = 1$ families on average visit their parents more often than children in the $D_2 = 1$ or $D_3 = 1$ families. The measurement of the visit variable (v) is described in Section 11.1. As we mentioned earlier, for either China or Taiwan, the visit variable is treated as an ordered categorical variable.

The measurement of the residence distance variable (l) in Taiwan and China refers to the following question in the questionnaire: "In terms of traveling time, how far is your parents' residence from yours?" Possible answers to this question include: (1) $l = 1$, co-residing, (2) $l = 2$, next door or in the same building, (3) $l = 3$, within 10 minutes, (4) $l = 4$, 10–30 minutes, (5) $l = 5$, 30–60 minutes, (6) $l = 6$, 60–120 minutes, and (7) $l = 7$, more than 2 hours. The classification is so designed because Taiwan is a small island and most populated areas can be reached within a short time, while the strict regulation on migration in China constrains the residential distance between generations for most families.[4] This "distance of residence" is therefore coded as an ordered categorical variable with discrete values ranging from 1 to 7. For those respondents who choose (1), we call them "co-residing samples."

A tightness measure of the kinship network (N) is the frequency of attendance at relatives' wedding parties, with 1 being "frequent" and 0 otherwise. Note that N is used to capture the intensity of gossip pressure on an alienated child. When a child has more intensive interaction with his or her relatives, she or he may *hear* more gossip. We had tried another measure for kinship network, which is defined by whether the parents interact with their neighbors daily.[5] The rationale behind this variable is that parents who have active interactions with their friends and neighbors have more opportunities to spread gossip. Since our main findings remain intact under either setting, the results for the latter case are omitted for brevity.

As to the other explanatory variables, our data set provides abundant information on both the child and the parents. These variables include the child's age, gender, education, income, marital status, family structure, living area, kinship relation, and some information about his or her siblings; and the parents' ethnicity, health condition, living status, and social network. For ease of comparison, most of the regressors are the same between the relevant models of Taiwan and China. The only exception is that we use a Mainlander (those who migrated to the island after the Second World War) ethnicity dummy in the case of Taiwan. The respondents of China are defined as "new migrants" if their current residence is different from that of their father's birthplace. The ethnicity dummy (Taiwan) and the migrant dummy (China) are used to capture a possible behavioral difference between recent immigrants versus early ones and aborigines.

Except for the ethnicity and migrant dummies, the explanatory variables used in our models are the same as those adopted by Perozek (1998). Among these explanatory variables, the child's income, number of siblings, and parental education deserve some special attention. As noted by Perozek (1998), the above-mentioned variables can help clarify the relationship between child visits and parental bequeathable wealth, and lessen the omitted-variable bias. If the respondent has only one living parent, then the parental education refers to this parent's education level. If there are two living parents, the usual meaning of average applies.

11.3.2. *Imputed Cost of Time for Children*

As noted by Cox and Rank (1992), children's cost of time is important in determining their parental visits, which is also what the $c(.)$ function in (11.1) tries to capture. To impute the cost of time, one approach is to use the wage rate as a proxy. Since 29 per cent and 27 per cent of our Taiwan and China respondents are not employed and hence do not have observable market wages, we have to apply some statistical method to impute wage rates for these samples. Alternatively, because one's wage rate is correlated with one's education and income, another option is to rely on variables such as education and income to capture the influence of children's time cost. In this analysis, we adopt both approaches, and the results are qualitatively the same. For brevity, we only present the results when an imputed wage rate is used to measure time cost, and skip the counterpart when the wage rate variable is replaced by a proxy variable. In Appendix 11.1, we briefly explain how we obtain the imputed wage rate.

11.3.3. The Empirical Setup

A usual dependent variable measuring the attention provided by children to their parents is the number of child-to-parent visits (per year), denoted by v^*. However, to take into account the prevalence of extended families in Chinese societies, we must consider the many observations of respondents who live with their parents (25.32 per cent and 20.21 per cent for Taiwan and China respectively). For these co-residing samples, child-to-parent visits are not observable, but we can use the co-residence information to help our estimation. For such a purpose, the visit frequency (v^*) and residence distance (l^*) are considered jointly.

Intuitively, a child who intends to visit his or her parents frequently is more likely to choose a residence closer to the parental home. Thus, the distance of a child's residence from the parents' is theoretically negatively correlated with v^*.[6] Knowing that v^* and l^* are related variables, it is natural to consider the following two-equation system:

$$v_i^* = X_i\alpha_1 + \beta_{11}N_i + \beta_{12}D_{1i} + \beta_{13}D_{2i}$$
$$+ \beta_{14}(D_{1i} \times N_i) + \beta_{15}(D_{2i} \times N_i) + \varepsilon_{1i}, \tag{11.2}$$

$$l_i^* = X_i\alpha_2 + \beta_{21}N_i + \beta_{22}D_{1i} + \beta_{23}D_{2i}$$
$$+ \beta_{24}(D_{1i} \times N_i) + \beta_{25}(D_{2i} \times N_i) + \varepsilon_{2i}, \tag{11.3}$$

where the error terms ε_{1i} and ε_{2i} are allowed to be correlated. In the above two equations, term X_i is a vector of demographic and family background variables for observation i, N_i is a dummy variable measuring the tightness of the kinship network, and $D_{ki}(k = 1, 2)$ is a dummy variable characterizing the parent's assets status, as indicated in Table 11.2.

Other than the effects of N_i and D_{ki} on (v_i^*, l_i^*), we also consider the influence of the interaction term $D_{ki} \times N_i(k = 1, 2)$ in view of the fact that, as stated in Section 11.2, network pressure is particularly likely to be in effect if parents have transferred all their assets to their offspring. Specifically, if parents have not transferred and exhausted their assets (generously given up their final say), the child's feedback attitude could not become a potentially negative gossip topic among relatives that may form a pressure on this child. And if the kinship network is not tight, the gossip could not be serious enough to give the child a real pressure. We conjecture that there will be an impact on the child's behavior only if *both* these factors are operative.

11.3.4. *The Estimation Method*

As explained earlier, the answers to the question "how far away is your parents' residence from yours?" range from 1 to 7 as the interviewees' transportation time increases. The relationship between the observed l_i and the latent l_i^* is assumed to be as follows:

$$l_i = \begin{cases} 1, & \text{if } l_i^* \leq c_1, \\ m, & \text{if } c_{m-1} < l_i^* \leq c_m, \quad m = 2, \ldots, 6, \\ 7, & \text{if } c_6 < l_i^* < \infty, \end{cases} \tag{11.4}$$

where $c_1, \ldots, c_6$ are parameters to be estimated. For those who live with their parents, their "visits" are not observable. Thus, for the non-co-residing samples ($l_i \neq 1$), the observed visit (v_i) is an ordered categorical variable, and the relationship between the observed v_i and the latent v_i^* is assumed as:

$$v_i = \begin{cases} 1, & \text{if } v_i^* \leq d_1, \\ k, & \text{if } d_{k-1} < v_i^* \leq d_k, k = 2, 3, 4 \\ 5, & \text{if } d_4 < v_i^* < \infty, \end{cases} \tag{11.5}$$

where $d_1, \ldots d_4$ are parameters to be estimated.

We assume that the error terms (ε_1, ε_2) are bivariate normally distributed with mean zero and covariance σ_{jk} ($j, k = 1, 2$). To help identify the system, we normalize $\sigma_{11} = \sigma_{22} = 1$. Thus, the correlation coefficient between ε_1 and ε_2 (namely ρ_{12}) is simply σ_{12}. Our empirical model consists of equations (11.2) to (11.5) for Taiwan and China. Given the assumption of a bivariate normal distribution for (ε_1, ε_2), the likelihood function can be derived, and hence the maximum likelihood estimation (MLE) method is applied to estimate the model.

As we specify the status of asset transfers as an explanatory variable of child visits, an implicit assumption is that such a transfer is a pre-determined event when the decision of child visit is made. To judge whether this is a reasonable assumption, we should have some knowledge of the ordering of events. In Appendix 11.2, we provide some background information about this.

11.4. Empirical Results

We present the results in Tables 11.3 and 11.4 for Taiwan and China respectively. In Model B of Tables 11.3 and 11.4, two asset transfers dummies (D_1 and D_2) are controlled in addition to other demographic variables. And in Model A of both tables, kinship network (N) and its interaction with the asset

Table 11.3. MLE estimates for visits and distance equations, Taiwan

	Model A		Model B	
	Visits	Distance	Visits	Distance
Respondent's information				
Age (in years)	−0.007	0.002	−0.003	−0.002
	(0.005)	(0.004)	(0.005)	(0.004)
Male (1 = yes)	0.720***	−0.747***	0.713***	−0.742***
	(0.062)	(0.057)	(0.062)	(0.057)
Years of schooling	0.021***	0.013*	0.021***	0.013*
	(0.008)	(0.008)	(0.008)	(0.008)
Imputed hourly wage rate (in	−0.468	−0.053	−0.048	−0.057
thousand local currency)	(0.087)	(0.079)	(0.085)	(0.077)
Family yearly income (in	−0.000	0.001***	0.000	0.001***
thousand local currency)	(0.000)	(0.000)	(0.000)	(0.000)
Married (1 = yes)	−0.315***	0.357***	−0.253***	0.303***
	(0.096)	(0.088)	(0.096)	(0.087)
Having any kid (1 = yes)	−0.161	0.502***	−0.161	0.499***
	(0.148)	(0.126)	(0.147)	(0.126)
Number of siblings	−0.021	0.038***	−0.017	0.034**
	(0.015)	(0.014)	(0.015)	(0.014)
Living in rural area (1 = yes)	0.126*	−0.096	0.157**	−0.121
	(0.070)	(0.065)	(0.069)	(0.065)
Parental information				
Both parents alive (1 = yes)	−0.042	0.050	−0.063	0.066
	(0.062)	(0.058)	(0.062)	(0.058)
Father being a Mainlander	−0.076	−0.088	−0.052	−0.098
(1 = yes)	(0.105)	(0.098)	(0.104)	(0.098)
Parents' average education being	0.074	−0.019	0.067	−0.018
junior high or above (1 = yes)	(0.087)	(0.082)	(0.087)	(0.082)
Living parent(s) in very poor	0.013	−0.233	0.040	−0.247
health condition (1 = yes)	(0.169)	(0.153)	(0.168)	(0.152)
N (= 1 if respondent attended relatives'	0.108	−0.109		
wedding parties frequently)	(0.092)	(0.087)		
D_1 (= 1 if all assets were transferred)	−0.113	0.037	0.146*	−0.217***
	(0.133)	(0.125)	(0.079)	(0.074)
D_2 (= 1 if nothing to be transferred)	−0.368***	0.221**	−0.143**	0.080
	(0.113)	(0.107)	(0.069)	(0.065)
$D_1 \times N$	0.413***	−0.388***		
	(0.156)	(0.146)		
$D_2 \times N$	0.365***	−0.232*		
	(0.137)	(0.129)		
ρ_{12}	−0.724***		−0.730***	
	(0.019)		(0.019)	
Number of observations	1,676		1,676	
Log likelihood	−4,475.2		−4,496.8	

Notes: The constant terms are omitted from the table for brevity. Standard errors are in parentheses. *, **, and *** denote 10%, 5%, and 1% significance levels respectively.

Table 11.4. MLE estimates for visits and distance equations, China

	Model A		Model B	
	Visits	Distance	Visits	Distance
Respondent's information				
Age (in years)	−0.014***	0.012**	−0.014***	0.012**
	(0.005)	(0.005)	(0.005)	(0.005)
Male (1 = yes)	0.935***	−0.886***	0.935***	−0.886***
	(0.060)	(0.057)	(0.060)	(0.057)
Years of schooling (in years)	−0.004	0.011	−0.004	0.011
	(0.008)	(0.007)	(0.008)	(0.007)
Imputed hourly wage rate (in	−0.473*	0.185	−0.470*	0.192
thousand local currency)	(0.246)	(0.238)	(0.244)	(0.237)
Family yearly income (in	0.001	0.005	0.000	0.004
thousand local currency)	(0.010)	(0.010)	(0.010)	(0.010)
Married (1 = yes)	−0.340***	0.387***	−0.338***	0.386***
	(0.117)	(0.106)	(0.117)	(0.105)
Having any kid (1 = yes)	−0.420*	0.317	−0.421*	0.314
	(0.231)	(0.196)	(0.231)	(0.196)
Number of siblings	−0.037**	0.050***	−0.036**	0.051***
	(0.017)	(0.015)	(0.017)	(0.015)
Living in rural area (1 = yes)	0.106	−0.262***	0.108	−0.262***
	(0.069)	(0.065)	(0.069)	(0.083)
Parental information				
Both parents alive (1 = yes)	−0.081	0.118**	−0.082	0.117**
	(0.062)	(0.058)	(0.062)	(0.058)
Father born in different	−0.092	0.226***	−0.089	0.226***
province (1 = yes)	(0.088)	(0.084)	(0.088)	(0.084)
Parents' average education being	−0.022	0.107	−0.025	0.106
junior high or above (1 = yes)	(0.082)	(0.076)	(0.082)	(0.076)
Living parent(s) in very poor	0.440**	−0.281*	0.441**	−0.278*
health condition (1 = yes)	(0.182)	(0.157)	(0.182)	(0.157)
N (= 1 if respondent attended relatives'	−0.067	−0.013		
wedding parties frequently)	(0.116)	(0.108)		
D_1 (= 1 if all assets were transferred)	0.032	−0.023	0.078	−0.078
	(0.149)	(0.136)	(0.077)	(0.071)
D_2 (= 1 if nothing to be transferred)	−0.161	0.059	−0.081	0.100
	(0.134)	(0.123)	(0.072)	(0.068)
$D_1 \times N$	0.065	−0.067		
	(0.169)	(0.155)		
$D_2 \times N$	0.111	0.060		
	(0.158)	(0.146)		
ρ_{12}	−0.829***		−0.828***	
	(0.013)		(0.013)	
Number of observations	1,534		1,534	
Log likelihood	−3900.9		−3902.7	

Notes: The constant terms are omitted from the table for brevity. Standard errors are in parentheses. *, **, and *** denote 10%, 5%, and 1% significance levels respectively.

transfers dummies are further controlled. To simplify our presentation, the estimation results for parameters $c_1 - c_6$, $d_1 - d_4$, and constant terms are omitted from the tables. We note here that the estimated correlation coefficients (ρ_{12} values) in Tables 11.3 and 11.4 are all significantly negative, implying the necessity of estimating (11.2) and (11.3) together. This is rather intuitive indeed, suggesting that the child's residence distance and visit frequency are negatively correlated. In the subsequent analysis, we first discuss the general findings and leave the crucial discussion on asset transfers and kinship network to Section 11.4.2.

11.4.1. General Findings

RESULTS FOR TAIWAN

From Models A and B of Table 11.3, we see that all significant variables have the expected signs, and the general findings in these two models are qualitatively the same. As to the variables concerning the child, it is noted that children with children of their own tend to live further away. This implies that even though an adult child with children of his or her own may take advantage of grandparents for help with child care (Perozek 1998), she or he tends to live at a greater distance from the parents, probably due to the concerns of the school district or the neighborhood environment in which to raise children. Children with more siblings also tend to reside further away from their parents, which may reveal the free-rider psychology among siblings (Konrad et al. 2002).

The findings that male and single respondents tend to live closer by and visit their parents more frequently correspond to the perceived role of responsibility of a male child to look after his parents, and of a married child to care for his or her own family after marriage. These results are consistent with those in Chen (1996), but are opposite to the US scenario described in Perozek (1998), possibly revealing a cultural difference. Table 11.3 also shows that children with more education tend to make more visits but live further away from their parents. This may be because children with higher education feel a greater obligation to pay back toward their parents (Anderberg and Balestrino 2003), but tend to reside further away for their own concerns. In comparison to children who resided in urban areas, those who lived in rural areas tended to pay more visits to their parents, probably in a reflection of a norm difference between urban and rural areas. As to the variables on the parent's side, none of them is significant.

RESULTS FOR CHINA

The results for China (Table 11.4) are largely consistent with the findings for Taiwan. One exception is the child's age. It can be seen from the table that for the older respondents, their visits tend to be less frequent, and the traveling time tends to be longer. This indicates some kind of cohort effect in China. For instance, older cohorts might not have been able to catch the train of China's economic reform, and hence have less economic capacity to travel and visit. And unlike the case of Taiwan, imputed wage rates prove to have a significant effect (at 10 per cent), which implies that the cost of time is a contributing factor in determining the child's visits in China.

Contrary to the findings of Taiwan, some parental variables turn out to be significant in China. The findings of China indicate that, for parents in very poor health condition, their children tend to visit more frequently and live closer, revealing the fact that in a less developed economy such as China, children's responsibilities in taking care of their parents' health cannot be replaced by market options (healthcare institutions), as is the case in more developed economies such as Taiwan. And the above reasoning is also applicable to the finding that a widowed parent tends to live closer to his or her children. Finally, if father's birthplace and child's current residence are in different provinces, the child would live further away from the parents.

11.4.2. *Asset Transfers and Kinship Networks*

RESULTS FOR TAIWAN

In Model B of Table 11.3, the positively significant coefficient of visits with respect to D_1 (all assets transferred) is consistent with the simple statistics shown in Table 11.2, but inconsistent with the proto-type bequest-as-lure intuition in BSS (1985). Furthermore, children of parents with no assets to begin with ($D_2 = 1$) visit their parents less than those of the reference group ($D_3 = 1$), which comprises families with some bequeathable assets.

The coefficient associated with D_1 in Model B may look puzzling at first, but may be explained by the interactions between kinship network and assets status in Model A of the same table. Here the kinship network variable (N), as described earlier, is a dummy indicating the frequency of attending relatives' wedding parties; $N = 1$ if the answer is "frequent," and $N = 0$ otherwise. As we explained, the frequency of attending wedding parties captures the receiving end of gossip.

In Model A of Table 11.3 where the network dummy (N) and interaction terms ($D_1 \times N$ and $D_2 \times N$) are added, the D_1 variable itself is not significant any more, but the impact of D_1 on child visits or residential distance becomes apparent when it interacts with the child's kinship network ($D_1 \times N$). This demonstrates that the kinship network has a greater impact when the parents have transferred all their bequeathable assets. This is also consistent with our theoretical conjecture that assets status may trigger gossip among relatives when the child's post-transfer behavior displays signs of alienation toward his or her parents.

Concerning the no-asset group, D_2 still shows a negative effect in the visits equation, while the interaction term with kinship network ($D_1 \times N$) has a positive coefficient in the same equation; the opposite sign prevails in the distance equation. The coefficients associated with the interaction terms indicate that the kinship pressure brought on by a child's alienation affects not only families with all assets transferred ($D_1 = 1$), but also those with no assets to begin with ($D_2 = 1$). The latter no-assets status *per se* also has a negative (positive) effect on child visits (distance) due to the lack of lure. It is the combined effect of D_2 and $D_1 \times N$ in Model A that makes the joint impact of D_2 in Model B.

RESULTS FOR CHINA

The results for China reveal a different scenario. From Model B of Table 11.4, it can be seen that none of the asset-transfer dummies is significant in the regressions of China. When the kinship network variable and the interaction terms are introduced (Model A of Table 11.4), the asset-transfer dummy remains insignificant, and the kinship network variable and the interaction terms are not significant, either. These results show that, in families in China, the children's feedback toward parents is not affected by the parental asset-transfer status. And for parents who had transferred all their assets, a tighter kinship network would not help them receive more visits from their children.

POSSIBLE EXPLANATIONS FOR THE DIFFERENCE

The above-mentioned discrepancies between the findings of Taiwan and China deserve some discussion. To gain insight into this problem, we briefly review the institutional changes of the two societies in the past few decades. Whyte et al. (2003) pointed out that Taiwan and China share the same Confucian family tradition and the common beliefs about filial obligations. But the dramatic changes in China and Taiwan over the last forty to fifty years have made family attitudes and behavior divergent between these two societies (Whyte et al. 2003: 226).

As suggested by Hermalin et al. (2003), some distinctive measures adopted by post-Communist China (until the late 1970s), such as the pension provided by the work unit and the absence of family-owned enterprises and property ownership, have weakened intergenerational relations in China. Even though Taiwan has experienced a higher level of economic development in the same period, both Hermalin et al. (2003) and Cornman et al. (2003) suggested that Taiwan is more "traditional" with regard to family attitudes or family behavior. Yang (1965) also claimed that the institutional changes in China not only affected the authority of the traditional family, but also shook the structure of the clan. Since the clan network is based upon age hierarchy and proximity of kinship (Yang 1965: 192), the violent class struggle in the Communist land reform and the Cultural Revolution had both contributed to the dilution of the network.

Given this background, we may have a clue to the different findings for China and Taiwan. In a society with strong intergenerational relations, the children have the obligation to take care of their parents after the latter have transferred all the assets, and a tight clan network would help enforce such an agreement. The kinship network in Taiwan remains strong, therefore we observe positively significant effects of D_1 and $D_1 \times N$ on child visits (also for $D_2 \times N$), whereas the network is not strong enough in China to sustain a similar effect. However, the norm of filial piety is still existent in China, and hence children would not reduce their contact frequency even if their parents transferred all their assets. The positive association between asset-transfer status and visits we observe from Table 11.2 may in fact be due to other features of the parents. For instance, parents who transferred all their assets might be those who had bad health and were forced to make such transfers. Thus the more frequent child visits we observe in China may simply reveal children's care about the poor health of their parents, instead of the asset-transfer status *per se*; this is perhaps why we observe significantly positive coefficients associated with parental health in Table 11.4. After the parental health variable is controlled, the asset status is no longer crucial.

Since the coefficients with regard to asset-transfer status are significant only in Taiwan, we confine our analysis to the case of Taiwan in the following sections.

11.4.3. *The Co-residence Arrangement*

So far we have not specified the detailed content of the assets transferred. A natural question one may raise is the following: is it possible that the parents transfer their houses to the children in exchange for the latter's acceptance of co-residence? Here we provide some evidence concerning the behavior of the non co-residing group. First, if the respondents' parents had transferred (part of or all of) their assets, respondents were asked about the items transferred in the 2004 Taiwan follow-up survey. The major answers to this question (multiple choices) include land and houses (321 counts), stock or financial assets (53), small business stores or shops (11), and 1 count of miscellaneous. It shows that houses and land are the most typical items of bequests. Second, concerning the question about the main sources of living for parents after they transferred all their assets, the answers include: their own earnings (5.08 per cent), their pension savings or retirement savings (14.07 per cent), support from a son (48.44 per cent), government subsidy or pension for senior citizens (23.44 per cent), support from daughters (5.47 per cent), and rents (1.95 per cent). It shows that the support from sons accounts for roughly half of the parental financial support categories.

Does the above evidence rebut our story of child feedbacks found in Taiwan? Among our 414 observations that have $D_1 = 1$ (parents transferred all assets), only 29.5 per cent are co-residing with their parents. Thus, a co-residence contract, which states something like "P transfers P's house to C in exchange for C's accepting P as a co-residence member," cannot capture the full picture. Our main purpose of discussion is to explain why children of parents who have transferred all their assets ($D_1 = 1$) would pay "more" visits to their parents than the children whose parents have not done so ($D_1 = 0$). As an extra precaution, we have also estimated the same model (11.2)–(11.5) after deleting the sample who had parents co-residing with them. Our conclusion of network effect turns out to be qualitatively unchanged. The evidence shows that, for parents who have transferred all their assets and who are *not* co-residing with the respondent child, the latter still pays more visits to the former. We understand that this sample deletion may cause self-selection bias; but our purpose is simply to show the robustness of our analysis with respect to the "transfer in exchange for co-residence arrangement" challenge mentioned above.

11.5. The Possible Endogeneity of Asset Transfers

As mentioned in the previous discussion, parents might have a strategic motive to transfer their assets to their offspring in the hope that the transfer may trigger the network effect and make their children more obedient. If this is the case, then there exists some correlation between D_1 and the error term (ε_{1i}, ε_{2i}) in (11.2)–(11.3). An alternative interpretation of this possible correlation is the following: if some families are more close-knit than others, then for these families, parents are more willing to transfer their assets and children are also more willing to visit their parents. When D_1 is correlated with (ε_{1i}, ε_{2i}), the maximum likelihood estimators of coefficients in (11.2)–(11.3) will not be consistent. We deal with this endogeneity problem in this section both by the instrumental variable method, and by a two-stage estimation procedure.

11.5.1. *Instrumental Variable Approach*

In the 2004 Taiwan follow-up survey, we asked the respondents to give the main reasons why their parents transferred their assets (multiple choices). Their major answers include: (1) father passed away (31.93 per cent); (2) father was very old or had poor health (17.17 per cent); (3) siblings needed some funds to start their own business (10.24 per cent); (4) siblings got married (7.83 per cent); (5) mother was old or had poor health (6.33 per cent); (6) tax concerns (6.33 per cent); (7) mother passed away (4.52 per cent); (8) siblings requested so (4.52 per cent); and (9) father retired (3.01 per cent). All other answers are less than 2.11 per cent.

As one can see, most of the reasons given seem to be exogenous events; but of course, parents may still make their endogenous decisions as these exogenous incidences happen. To allow for such a possibility, we perform tests for the endogeneity of the asset-transfer variable using the procedure suggested by Rivers and Vuong (1988) and Vella (1993). For ease of demonstration, we only present the endogeneity test as in the case where $D_1 = 1$ is treated as one group and $D_1 = 0$ as the other.

To help perform the test and estimation, we introduce an instrumental variable (IV), which is likely to be correlated with asset transfers but is expected to be uncorrelated with the error terms (ε_{1i}, ε_{2i}). The IV we choose is the father's lifetime occupation. If the father is a farmer, the IV is coded 1, otherwise 0. Since Taiwan has had a well-known land reform program (1949–53), most farmers are not tenants and have their own land. The reason we choose the farmer's occupation as an IV is as follows. On the one hand, there is no a priori reason to believe that children of farmers are more attached to their parents and tend to pay visits more frequently as they grow up. On the other hand, the transfer of land is more likely to take place before the father's death because: (1) land division among children often involves advantaged and disadvantaged sides; the parents do not

Table 11.5. Exogeneity test with generalized residuals from probit model, Taiwan

	Visits and distance equations		Asset-transfers equation
	Visits	Distance	(D_1 = 1 or not)
Respondent's information			
Age	−0.015*	0.005	0.034***
	(0.008)	(0.007)	(0.006)
Male	0.699***	−0.736***	0.131*
	(0.064)	(0.059)	(0.076)
Years of schooling	0.023***	0.012	0.009
	(0.008)	(0.008)	(0.011)
Imputed hourly wage rate	−0.008	−0.070	−0.266*
	(0.088)	(0.082)	(0.153)
Family yearly income	0.000*	0.001***	0.000
	(0.000)	(0.000)	(0.000)
Married	−0.279***	0.330***	−0.120
	(0.098)	(0.090)	(0.116)
Having any child	−0.238**	0.546***	0.363**
	(0.153)	(0.132)	(0.183)
Number of siblings	−0.022	0.038***	0.003
	(0.015)	(0.014)	(0.018)
Living in rural area	0.104	−0.084	0.100
	(0.073)	(0.068)	(0.090)
Parental information			
Both parents alive	0.067	−0.007	−0.556***
	(0.103)	(0.096)	(0.078)
Father being a Mainlander	−0.043	−0.094	−0.294*
	(0.113)	(0.105)	(0.151)
Parents' average education being junior high or above	0.094	−0.033	−0.076
	(0.088)	(0.083)	(0.123)
Living parent(s) in very poor health condition	−0.033	−0.201	0.183
	(0.170)	(0.154)	(0.188)
Father being a farmer (1 = yes)			0.215***
			(0.079)
N (= 1 if respondent attended relatives' wedding parties frequently)	0.332***	−0.280***	−0.003
	(0.062)	(0.058)	(0.079)
D_1 (= 1 if all assets were transferred)	0.875	−0.594	
	(0.560)	(0.518)	
$\hat{u}$	−0.378	0.193	
	(0.327)	(0.303)	
ρ'_{12}		−0.727***	
		(0.019)	
Number of observations		1,676	1,676
Log likelihood		−4,482.3	−832.2
Wald statistic for exog. test (df = 2)		1.35	

Notes: The constant terms are omitted from the table for brevity. $\hat{u}$ values are estimated generalized residuals from asset-transfers probit model. ρ'_{12} is the estimated correlation coefficient between the visits and distance equations. Standard errors are in parentheses. *, **, and *** denote 10%, 5%, and 1% significance.

want to risk causing legal quarrels among children, and hence they want to make the transfer before their death to guarantee the smoothness of the process; (2) unlike financial assets, farm land management and cultivation are usually beyond the capability of an old father; transferring land earlier reduces the cost of management.

The testing procedures are composed of two stages. In the first stage, a probit model is used to estimate the asset-transfer status equation (Table 11.5, column 4). It can be seen that "father being a farmer" is positively significant in the asset-transfer status equation, which implies that "father being a farmer" could not be a weak IV. The generalized residuals from the probit model ($\hat{u}$) are then obtained and used as an additional explanatory variable in the maximum likelihood estimation of equations (11.2)–(11.5). Then, a Wald test is conducted to examine whether the coefficients of the residual terms $\hat{u}$ in equations (11.2) and (11.3) are jointly zero (Table 11.5, columns 2–3). Since the individual coefficient of $\hat{u}$ and the Wald statistic listed in the bottom row are all insignificant, we can conclude that "father being a farmer" is a legitimate IV in our setting. Also, it is worth mentioning that even though D_1 is not significant under 10 per cent in the visits equation, its t value of 1.56 is very near the critical value of 10 per cent significance ($= 1.64$).

As to the evidence presented above, our findings are consistent with the prediction in Sung (1974). Sung (p. 1) argued that the practice and *timing* of asset transfers in Taiwan is very much dominated by custom, and is more likely to take place when the family head (usually father) dies, or when the children grow up and need financial support for career development or family use. Nevertheless, we must caution that the IV approach has its limitation and an alternative solution to the endogeneity problem exists (Heckman 1978, 1997).

11.5.2. Two-Stage Estimation

To be cautious, we apply a two-stage estimation method to account for the possible endogeneity problem in Taiwan. The first stage of the estimation procedure is the same as that for the endogeneity test. In the second stage, we use the estimated $\hat{D}_{1i}$ values obtained from the first stage to replace the D_{1i} values in (11.2)–(11.3) and rerun the MLE. The corresponding results are listed in Table 11.6.

If there is a scenario that causes the spurious correlation in the population, it also suggests a correlation between error terms in (11.2)–(11.3) and in the equation of D_{1i}. A two-stage estimation can generate a consistent estimator even if the problem of spurious correlation exists. Table 11.6 confirms that

Table 11.6. MLE with fitted asset-transfers probabilities, Taiwan

	Visits	Distance
Respondent's information		
Age	−0.017*	0.006
	(0.009)	(0.009)
Male	0.694***	−0.737***
	(0.067)	(0.062)
Years of schooling	0.023***	0.013
	(0.008)	(0.008)
Imputed hourly wage rate	−0.001	−0.071
	(0.090)	(0.083)
Family yearly income	0.000*	0.001***
	(0.000)	(0.000)
Married	−0.288***	0.345***
	(0.100)	(0.092)
Having any child	−0.229*	0.520***
	(0.158)	(0.138)
Number of siblings	−0.023	0.038***
	(0.015)	(0.014)
Living in rural area	0.104	−0.089
	(0.073)	(0.069)
Parental information		
Both parents alive	0.091	−0.005
	(0.128)	(0.118)
Father being a Mainlander	−0.018	−0.103
	(0.119)	(0.110)
Parents' average education being	0.088	−0.022
junior high or above	(0.090)	(0.084)
Living parent(s) in very poor	−0.039	−0.202
health condition	(0.071)	(0.155)
N (= 1 if respondent attended relatives'	0.085	−0.032
wedding parties frequently)	(0.115)	(0.108)
$\hat{D}_1$ (fitted probability from	0.267	0.187
asset-transfers equation)	(0.804)	(0.744)
$\hat{D}_1 \times N$	1.092**	−1.089***
	(0.435)	(0.403)
ρ_{12}		−0.729
		(0.019)
Number of observations		1,676
Log likelihood		−4,486.7

Notes: The constant terms are omitted from the table for brevity. Standard errors are in parentheses. *, **, and *** denote 10%, 5%, and 1% significance.

our main findings remain unchanged qualitatively, which implies that our results are robust even if the endogeneity problem is taken into account.

11.6. Conclusions

An analysis of the PSFD data set in Taiwan and China shows that a high proportion of parents have divided and transferred to their offspring all their assets *inter vivos*. Moreover, compared with other respondents, children whose parents have transferred all their assets tend to visit their parents more frequently and reside closer to their parents. We propose that the theory of social networks may be able to explain the filial devotion of these children and we examine this theory empirically by analyzing the PSFD data sets. Our empirical results using the Taiwan sample show that, for children in tighter kinship networks, their frequency of visits (residence distance from parents) tends to be greater (shorter). Furthermore, relative to the parents who have some bequeathable assets, the influence of the kinship network will be stronger for parents who have transferred all their assets. However, the asset transfers and kinship dummies as well as their interaction terms are insignificant in the case of China. A possible explanation is that the kinship structure has become weakened in China in the past few decades, thus no significant pattern prevails for our China sample. Nevertheless, the results for Taiwan are consistent with our theoretical argument that assets status may trigger talk among relatives if the child's post-transfer filial behavior is seen to be less than satisfactory.

Considering the possibility that the asset-transfer decision may be a strategic move on the part of the parents, we explore the causes of asset transfers as well as the solution to the endogeneity of the asset transfers by applying the IV method on the Taiwan sample. Our results show that our main findings remain largely intact under the IV approach. To be cautious, we exercise a two-stage estimation procedure. The two-stage estimation results are qualitatively the same as before. We also tried different measures of kinship networks. Results from all these alternative settings turn out to be similar qualitatively. This implies that our results are robust and that, at least in Taiwan, the theory of kinship pressure can stand as a possible explanation for child–parent interactions after the parents transfer all their assets.

APPENDIX 11.1 DERIVING THE IMPUTED WAGES RATES

We basically follow the traditional approach (such as Mitchell and Butler 1986) and apply Heckman's two-stage procedure (Heckman 1974). In the first stage, we estimate the labor force participation equation. And in the second stage, we use the inverse Mills ratio obtained from the first stage to estimate the log wage-rate equation. For the unemployed respondents, their wage rate is imputed from these estimated equations. As to the employed, the wage variable refers to their observed wage rates. The explanatory variables used in the labor force participation equation include gender, marital status, education and its squared term, experience and its squared term, area unemployment rates, etc. In the log wage-rate equation, in addition to the variables listed above, urbanization dummies are included to help identify the system. The signs of the estimated coefficients are very much consistent with what is found in the literature, and therefore the detailed estimation results are not presented here.

APPENDIX 11.2 THE ORDER OF EVENTS

The child–parent visiting frequency is obtained from the survey question on the visits made to parents *last year*. Obviously the time period of visits refers to the year closest to the interview time.

Concerning the time of asset transfers, a question contained in the Taiwan 2004 follow-up survey could help lessen the worry about the simultaneity of time. In the 2004 Taiwan survey, the respondents were asked, "which year was it when the *largest proportion* of your parents' assets was transferred?" Among those who responded to this question, 2.79 per cent answered that the transfer was made one year before the interview, 4.53 per cent said that it was two years before, 84.32 per cent said it was more than three years before; and only 8.36 per cent said that it was within the same year as the interview. The average duration from the time of transfer to the time of survey is 12.88 years. Therefore, aside from a few exceptions, most of our samples have a clear order of events consistent with our regression specification in (11.2)–(11.3).

Notes

1. The BBS model may not be a representative model for intergenerational transfers in the West, since it is not consistent with the almost-universal pattern of equal bequest. However, it dominates the discussion of some professional journals. For more evidence, see footnote 1 of Chapter 7.
2. The sample of Taiwan used in this chapter is confined to the respondents from the 1999 and 2000 surveys, with the 2003 respondents being excluded. The primary reason is that the questions designed for key variables are slightly different between the 2003 survey and earlier ones.
3. Parents who do not have transferable assets may still have a regular job, or they may still live on their non-transferable assets such as pensions. In China and Taiwan, pension insurance is available to all government and some public enterprise employees. See our discussion in Chapter 10.
4. Concerning China's restriction on migration, see Whyte et al. (2003: 234–5) for more discussion. Within our China sample, only 7% of the respondents reported that the traveling time to their parents' residence is more than 2 hours.
5. This variable is not available from the China survey. Hence the estimation using this variable is confined to the Taiwan sample.
6. Theoretically, variable I^* is a decision variable, and should be determined jointly with the optimal visits v^* (Konrad et al. 2002). However, the decision of residence involves many other dimensions (such as parental employment and child

education) which are not appropriate to be included in the discussion of filial visits in this chapter. Here, we use the I^* variable only to help solve the unobservability problem of the visit variable for the co-residing sample. See also the discussion in Weinstein et al. (1994), and Freeman et al. (1994) for more details of the visit–residence choice correlation.

12

Changing Gender Preferences in Taiwan

We mentioned in previous discussion a well-known prediction by Goode (1982) that along with the demographic transition and economic development, most of the "traditional" family features would gradually retreat. In particular, the inferior human rights and social roles for women should improve gradually in modern societies. In this chapter we study the question of how the pattern of educational resource allocation among children has changed across generations. The focus of this chapter will be mainly on Taiwan for two reasons: first, as we explained in Chapter 2, the dramatic changes in the education system in China during the Cultural Revolution led to inconsistencies in parental decisions over time, especially for the younger generation. Second, the one-child policy has obscured traditional gender preferences, making it harder for us to identify gender bias in the young generation. Thus, for China it is difficult to construct an intergenerational connection of changes in gender attitude.

Our analysis tackles both macro and micro aspects of the problem. For the macro perspective, we explore whether a particular pattern of within-family disadvantaged treatment (e.g., against girls) has weakened or disappeared in the young generation. At the micro level, we investigate whether a parent's differential treatment toward his or her children has any lasting impact when the children go on to form their own families and have their own children.

12.1. The Literature and Conceptual Ideas

The focus of this chapter is related to the intergenerational transmission of sex-based differential treatment. A handful of researchers have done similar

248

analysis in the past. Thornton et al. (1983) used consecutive cross-sectional surveys to examine the changes in Taiwanese sex-role attitudes between parents and children. The "attitude" in their analysis was measured by respondents' subjective scale of whether they agree with a statement of a particular gender-specific mindset. Fernandez et al. (2004) showed that the wife of a man brought up in a family in which the mother worked tends to participate in the labor market. In another paper, Fernandez and Fogli (2005) suggested that the cultural background of parents (with respect to perceptions of female labor market participation and fertility rate) affects the work and fertility decisions of their children.

In this chapter, we study the changes in intergenerational gender attitudes, similar to Thornton et al. (1983). However, despite the inclusion in our survey of attitude-related questions, we focus on the objective education resource allocation revealed by parental decisions, rather than the subjective attitude reflected in parents' answers. We hope that this can, to some extent, lessen the bias of the respondents, who may be tempted to avoid appearing to violate the social norm of gender equality during interviews. Taking advantage of our unique data set, in this chapter we also propose a statistical method of identifying the attitude change, distinct from the methods adopted by Thornton et al. multiple indicator multiple cause (MIMIC) and by Fernandez et al. (instrumental variable, IV). More details will be given as we proceed.

Our main question can be posed as follows. Suppose we have a set of sibling data of generation t, and are able to identify the effect of birth order, sibship size, and in particular child gender on siblings' education achievement. Suppose further that children of particular characteristics in some families were preferentially or poorly treated in education investment in generation t. When these individuals of generation t grew up and had their own children, i.e. generation $(t + 1)$, we explore how the pattern of unequal education resource allocation has changed among children of generation $(t + 1)$.

Intuitively, there are two different factors that may cause a change in the pattern of resource allocation among children of generation $(t + 1)$. On the one hand, because differential treatments among children are usually due to resource constraints or the traditional conceptions of parents, the pattern of differential treatment should moderate when such constraints or conceptions have weakened along with economic development. On the other hand, as predicted by theories of psychology, a child being differentially treated in childhood may form a stereotypical idea about gender roles, and pass on this attitude to his or her own children.[1] Our goal then is to study whether the sex-based differential treatment in education typical of an earlier generation may be transmitted, either in a macro or in a micro sense, to the next generation.

249

In order to study empirically the problem posed above, a comprehensive data set is indispensable. In particular, we need at least *two generations* of *sibling* data in order to identify the possible sex-based differential treatment across generations; and only with such a good data set will we be able to test whether the experience of siblings of generation t may carry over to those of generation $t + 1$. Furthermore, if we are to control for the parental education background of generation $t - 1$ so as to improve the estimation efficiency of the behavioral relationship in generation t, the data requirement is even more restrictive: we need the education data of three generations to accomplish the estimation and test. The lack of comprehensive data sets described above is perhaps a major reason why there has been no study focusing on such an important issue in the literature. Fortunately, the PSFD data of Taiwan enable us to perform this study.

To eliminate the disturbance of other possible explanations, we implement a sensitivity analysis by considering contraposition arguments, subsamples of different cohorts and sexes, the possible endogeneity of the sibship size, and other measures of education achievement. The results are all the same qualitatively. Finally, we also study what factors have caused parents to change their sex-specific attitude toward their children. We find that parents' education contributes to the elimination of sex-based differential treatments.

12.2. Changing Pattern of Sex Preferences: A Macro Analysis

There are several approaches to estimating and testing the intergenerational transmission of sex-based differential treatments. We start with a macro analysis that shows the difference in education between male and female children even after adjusting for effects of various explanatory variables and allowing for a change in mandatory education in Taiwan. This section also examines in detail the effects of various variables on education in Taiwan across generations and between genders.

12.2.1. *Gender-Specific Differences in Education*

Let the subscript *tij* refer to the *j*th child of family (actually lineage) i in generation t, and let Y be the schooling years of the child, a the family fixed or random effect parameter, S the sex indicator of the child in question, Z a vector of lineage-specific variables, X a vector of other explanatory variables, and ε the error term satisfying all regular assumptions, especially being independent of S. The first statistical model we employ is

$$Y_{tij} = \alpha_{ti} + \gamma_0 S_{tij} + \gamma_1 (I_t \times S_{tij}) + \beta_t X_{tij} + \eta Z_{ti} + \varepsilon_{tij}, t = y, o, \quad (12.1)$$

where I_t is a generational dummy variable with $I_t = 1$ if $t = y$ (young) and $I_t = 0$ if $t = o$ (old). In equation (12.1), we use various interaction terms to allow possibly different influences of variables across generations. In particular, γ_0 captures the possible existence of parents' gender preferences, and γ_1 characterizes the weakening or strengthening of this gender effect for the young generation relative to the old generation.

Following the common practice in the literature, the explanatory variable X should include the (sex- and seniority-specific) sibship size, the ethnicity background, the education levels of the parents, and other relevant variables. From our discussion in Chapter 8, we know that in some Taiwanese families, elder sisters may be compelled to quit schooling and enter the labor market in their teens; they then remit part of their earnings to help with their younger siblings' (particularly brothers') education expenses. In order to capture this possible scenario, we separate the siblings into sex-seniority (2×2) groups. The exogenous variables adopted in our regression are by and large compatible with those in Parish and Willis (1993), Lillard and Willis (1994), and Ermisch and Francesconi (2001). The possible endogeneity of the sibship-size variable will be taken into account later.

Our PSFD Taiwan sample is retrieved from the first-wave surveys conducted in 1999, 2000, and 2003 respectively, consisting of nearly 4,000 interviewees born between 1935 and 1976. Most of these interviewees and their siblings have finished their education by the time of the interview. However, since our goal is to estimate family resource allocations across generations, we can employ only interviewees that are old enough to have some children who have completed their education. Thus, interviewees who do not have children older than 25 years of age are deleted. This reduces the effective sample families to roughly 1,500. In addition, after the deletion of observations with missing information such as father's birth year, we end up with the data of 1,329 families that we used in the estimation of equation (12.1). In the empirical analysis, the old and young generations refer to the respondent (and his or her siblings) and the respondent's adult children respectively. These two sets of sibling data are used either jointly or separately in the following analysis, depending on the research purpose.

In equation (12.1), because of the existence of a common family effect, the errors ε_{tij} are not independent for sample from the same lineage. Any least squares estimation failing to take into account the correlation across observations will result in estimation inefficiency. The problem here is the same as that in Chapter 8, and hence we refer for the details to our previous discussion. Again, we follow Parish and Willis (1993) and Sanbonmatsu et al. (2006), and adopt the Huber–White approach to adjust the standard errors of the least square estimates; see Huber (1967), White (1980), and Newey and West (1987) for details.

The goal of our macro-analysis is to test whether there is any generational change in sex-specific differential treatment against a female child, i.e. to test the hypothesis $\gamma_1 = 0$ in equation (12.1). To this end, we first combine the old and young generation sample to examine whether the difference in education between male and female children is significant in Taiwan; see Models 1–3 in Table 12.1.

In Table 12.1, the numbers of younger or elder siblings refer to the subject in question, but the birth cohort dummies refer to that of the subject's father. The reference group for the father's birth cohort is "father born before 1920."[2] The regressors in Model 2 include the same variables as those of Model 1 and also the dummy variable "born after 1956," which signifies Taiwan's structural change of mandatory education from six to nine years as mentioned in Chapter 2. Comparing Models 1 and 2, we see that allowing for the change in mandatory education does not alter significantly the impacts of other variables on the years of schooling. The fourth column (Model 3) of Table 12.1 adds the interaction terms between certain explanatory variables and the generation dummy, in order to capture the coefficient change associated with the young generation.

12.2.2. Changing Pattern across Generations

From Table 12.1, we observe that the coefficients of gender are always negatively significant, indicating a clear pattern of education achievement unfavorable to the females. Thus, the data support the general belief that female children received fewer years of schooling in Chinese society on Taiwan. However, from Model 3 of Table 12.1, this gender difference is most pronounced in the old generation, but it is significantly lessened in the young generation. Indeed, as one can see from the coefficient of the product term of generation and gender (gender × generation), the net effect is

Table 12.1. Effects of gender on years of schooling (old and young generation combined)

	Model 1	Model 2	Model 3
Father's birth cohort (1930–9 being ref. group)			
Before 1920	−2.159***	−1.317***	−1.825***
	(0.204)	(0.248)	(0.314)
1920–9	−1.152***	−0.593***	−1.194***
	(0.221)	(0.225)	(0.284)
After 1940	0.306**	0.228	0.435***
	(0.148)	(0.147)	(0.148)
Born after 1956 (1 = yes)		1.015***	1.046***
		(0.196)	(0.211)
Gender (1 = female)	−1.106***	−1.134***	−1.959***
	(0.089)	(0.089)	(0.132)
Gender			1.848***
× Generation (1 = young)			(0.176)
Number of elder brothers	0.099	0.074	0.093
	(0.065)	(0.065)	(0.077)
Number of elder brothers			−0.172
× generation			(0.117)
Number of elder sisters	0.178***	0.137***	0.193***
	(0.053)	(0.053)	(0.070)
Number of elder sisters × generation			−0.227**
			(0.097)
Number of younger brothers	−0.280***	−0.247***	−0.276***
	(0.060)	(0.060)	(0.067)
Number of younger brothers			0.101
× generation			(0.124)
Number of younger sisters	−0.258***	−0.233***	−0.249***
	(0.054)	(0.054)	(0.066)
Number of younger sisters			0.048
× generation			(0.089)
Father's education	0.270***	0.271***	0.301***
	(0.020)	(0.020)	(0.033)
Father's education			−0.108***
× generation			(0.039)
Mother's education	0.243***	0.241***	0.283***
	(0.022)	(0.022)	(0.037)
Mother's education			−0.068
× generation			(0.044)
Father's occupation	0.070***	0.065***	0.180***
	(0.022)	(0.022)	(0.058)
Father's occupation			−0.135**
× generation			(0.060)
Father's ethnicity (Fukienese being ref. group)			
Aborigine	−1.848***	−1.897***	−2.036***
	(0.349)	(0.350)	(0.345)
Hakka	0.508***	0.503***	0.541***
	(0.179)	(0.178)	(0.183)
Mainlander	1.050***	0.928***	0.996***
	(0.290)	(0.296)	(0.288)
Number of observations	6,881	6,881	6,881
Number of families	1,329	1,329	1,329

Notes: Standard errors are in parentheses. *, **, and *** denote 10%, 5%, and 1% significance levels respectively. The constant term is omitted for brevity.

only slightly negative ($1.959 - 1.848 = 0.111$), albeit statistically insignificant, for the young-generation females.

As to the effect of the numbers of siblings of different sexes and seniorities, we find that *elder* sisters always have a positive effect on a child's education. This positive effect is particularly significant for elder sisters, a result consistent with the finding in Greenhalgh (1985) and in Chapter 8 of this monograph. On the other hand, a larger number of *younger* sisters or brothers always has a negative effect on the education of a child, revealing the crowding (i.e., resource-dilution) effect of younger siblings. This is consistent with the evidence found in most previous literature, e.g. Parish and Willis (1993). However, the positive effect of elder sisters decreases substantially in the young generation, as one can see from the negatively significant coefficient of the product term of the generation dummy with elder sisters in Model 3. This phenomenon is consistent with the general gender-equalization trend across generations. Although the coefficients of the product term of younger sibship size and the generation dummy also have reverse signs (indicating a weakening of the crowding effect), they are not statistically significant.

In Taiwan's early development period with general pro-boy perceptions, parents tended to ask female elder children to join the labor market early so that their incomes could support the education of younger children, especially younger boys. As the family income increases along with economic development, parental budget constraints ease; as a result, the original dependence of younger children's education on elder siblings' incomes is reduced. Of course, parents of the young generation may have a more unbiased attitude toward their children, which may also help explain the phenomenon. In summary, the macro pattern shows that, although girls were treated less favorably than boys by the old generation, there is little disadvantage for female children of the young generation. But from the macro evidence we are unable to infer whether it is the attitude change or the income increase that contributes to the weakening of female disadvantage. Later we shall investigate in greater detail the *micro* changes behind such a macro pattern.

Table 12.1 shows that parents' education has a positive effect on that of their children, a result consistent with the general perception. This positive effect is weakened in the young generation, perhaps as a result of the expansion of educational opportunity, which lessens the importance of parental background.[3] Fathers having professional occupations are generally better off and tend to provide better educational opportunity and support for their children; this is revealed in the positive coefficient of the father's occupation variable.[4] Again, the impact of the father's occupation on children's education is significantly reduced in the young generation. The reference group of ethnicity in Table 12.1 is Fukienese; the positively significant coefficients for the two other migrant groups (Hakka and Mainlander) and the negative coefficient for the aborigines indeed show the relative difference in educational achievement among distinct ethnic groups. We shall come back to this discussion later.

Finally, since we use sibling data to analyze education achievement, one may wonder whether families with a large sibship have been given more weight in the regression than families with a small sibship. As a sensitivity analysis, we rerun the regression using an alternative set of samples. In this alternative set, for families which have more than two children, we randomly choose two of them. It turns out that females are still disadvantaged relative to males, and again this disadvantage decreases in the young generation. We also refit the models in Table 12.1 using data from families that have at most five children, which reduces the number of observations. We find that all results are qualitatively the same. In particular, estimates of the key variables "gender" and "gender × generation" have the same sign as before and remain statistically significant. The results show clearly that the unfavorable treatment of female children is pronounced in the old generation, but weakened or nearly vanished in the young generation. Details will not be repeated here.

12.2.3. *Regressions for Separate Generations and Genders*

To gain insight into the changing pattern in educational achievement between different generations and genders, we rerun the basic regression models in equation (12.1) separately for the old and young generations, and for children of different sexes. The reference group of father's birth cohort is "father born before 1920" for the old generation, and "father born before 1930" for the young generation. Since there are only fifty-seven observations with fathers born during 1920–9, it is not surprising that the corresponding coefficient is insignificant. As we can see from Table 12.2, for the young generation, the negative (crowding) effect of younger siblings remains the same, whereas the originally positive effect of elder siblings (on younger ones' education) disappears or reverses, a result consistent with the finding in Table 12.1. For instance, the impact of elder brothers and sisters on a subject's education changes from positive to negative or is insignificantly different from zero across generations. This suggests that the original *supporting* effect of elder siblings has become a *crowding* (resource-dilution) effect on junior children in the young generation. Notice that whenever we find significant crowding sibling effects of younger siblings for the old generation in Table 12.2, a female subject always receives a larger impact (in absolute value) than a male one. This remains true for several other variables of the young generation, indicating that gender-specific preferential treatment may still exist in the young generation. We shall return to this point in Section 12.3. Table 12.2 also confirms that the importance of parental education and occupation has decreased in the

Table 12.2. Effects of sibling and parental education on years of schooling, by generation and gender

	Old generation		Young generation	
	Male	Female	Male	Female
Father's birth cohort				
Before 1920	−0.691	−1.461***		
	(0.444)	(0.474)		
1920–9	−0.305	−0.311		−1.346**
	(0.443)	(0.462)		(0.577)
After 1940			0.068	0.465**
			(0.185)	(0.219)
Born after 1956	0.976***	0.751***		
	(0.292)	(0.290)		
Number of elder brothers	0.153*	0.216*	−0.127	−0.454***
	(0.092)	(0.114)	(0.115)	(0.143)
Number of elder sisters	0.251***	0.304***	−0.208**	−0.033
	(0.098)	(0.090)	(0.090)	(0.090)
Number of younger brothers	−0.114	−0.334***	−0.279*	−0.457***
	(0.086)	(0.089)	(0.156)	(0.136)
Number of younger sisters	−0.151*	−0.238***	−0.203**	−0.403***
	(0.091)	(0.079)	(0.095)	(0.086)
Father's education	0.296***	0.284***	0.211***	0.154***
	(0.038)	(0.042)	(0.025)	(0.030)
Mother's education	0.234***	0.319***	0.214***	0.200***
	(0.043)	(0.047)	(0.029)	(0.032)
Father's occupation	0.228***	0.220***	−0.017	0.070**
	(0.072)	(0.075)	(0.025)	(0.031)
Father's ethnicity				
Aborigine	−1.656**	−2.410***	−1.541***	−2.021***
	(0.693)	(0.709)	(0.527)	(0.433)
Hakka	0.809**	0.631**	0.010	0.607**
	(0.322)	(0.307)	(0.313)	(0.276)
Mainlander	2.615***	1.578***	−0.192	0.791
	(0.614)	(0.513)	(0.353)	(0.493)
Constant	6.459***	5.505***	10.305***	10.065***
	(0.589)	(0.560)	(0.344)	(0.414)
Number of observations	1,863	1,898	1,653	1,467

Notes: Standard errors are in parentheses. *, **, and *** denote 10%, 5%, and 1% significance levels respectively.

young generation, again indicating the increasing importance of public education and the declining role of family background.

Among the three groups of new migrants, it is observed from Table 12.2 that, for the old generation, the groups of Mainlanders and Hakka, who migrated to Taiwan later than Fukienese, achieve higher education. But for the young generation, the differences tend to narrow, especially between Fukienese and Mainlanders. This finding indicates that the superiority of Mainlanders in educational achievement disappears in the young generation. This is indeed intuitively appealing. The more recent migrants, most of whom fled the chaotic environment of Mainland China during the Chinese Civil War in the 1940s, fully realized that "portable capital goods" were not physical assets, but human resources. Thus, they might tend to invest more in their children's education. As time passes and as memory of the chaotic past gradually fades in the young generation, they tend to behave like earlier migrants and decrease their educational investment in children. Finally, we also note that aborigines are still disadvantaged (relative to more recent migrants) in schooling even for the young generation.

To examine whether there are significant differences between generations shown in Table 12.2, we perform some Wald tests. First, tests are performed to see whether the baseline levels of education are significantly different between males and females within generations. The results show that the difference of intercept terms (baseline levels of education) is highly significant for the old generation, while it is not significant for the young generation (the corresponding chi-squared statistics are 31.79 and 0.20 respectively). A second set of tests is performed to examine whether the sibship structure behaves differently between generations of the same gender. The overall tests for the four sibship size variables show that significant differences prevail between the old and young generations, for both males and females. As to the tests for the individual sibship size variable, only elder siblings exhibit significant differences between generations. As to the joint test for four sibling size variables across generations, the chi-squared statistics are 16.65 and 24.58 for the male and the female sample, which are both significant at the 1 per cent significance level. And within the male (female) sample, the corresponding test statistics for elder brothers and elder sisters are 3.61 and 11.92 (13.45 and 7.05), which are both significant at the 10 per cent significance levels. The above findings justify the necessity of differentiating females from males, and young siblings from old ones.

12.3. Changing Pattern of Sex Preferences: A Micro Analysis

In Table 12.1, the fact that the coefficient of gender × generation is positively significant only signifies that parents' gender-specific treatment against girls is weaker for the young generation. Further analysis from Table 12.2 tells us that, as far as the crowding effect is concerned, female children of both generations seem to be affected more acutely. The goal of this section is to study the differential treatment against females within each family lineage and investigate possible reasons behind the observed phenomenon. We consider four most likely explanations for the changes. They are (1) the concept of gender equality taking hold in society, (2) an easing of budget constraints in the contemporary economic environment, (3) a change in gender cost, and (4) a change in gender wages. Our analysis shows that the reasons (2), (3), and (4) cannot explain fully the observed improvement in education of female children in the young generation. The maturing concept of gender equality thus plays a role in the change.

We employ a two-step procedure to establish the validity of our conjecture that the mature concept of gender equality plays a role in the change. First, we employ a statistical model to show the existence and direction of intergenerational carry-over effect concerning differential treatment against girls in the data. Second, we divide the data of the young generation into two sub-samples based on parents' (i.e., the interviewees') gender. The difference between the results obtained from the subgroups lends support to our conjecture via contraposition, because the data division based on parents' gender should have no impact on the carry-over effect if the effect is indeed caused by reason (2), (3), and (4).

12.3.1. *Existence of Carry-Over Effect*

Suppose a member in generation o has experienced unfair treatment against girls in educational opportunity. We would like to know how this experience affects the education resource allocation toward his or her own children in generation y. In this subsection, we propose two ways to characterize and test the existence and direction of such a micro intergenerational carry-over effect.

Consider a modified version of equation (12.1) as follows:

$$Y_{sij} = \alpha_{si} + \gamma_{si}S_{sij} + \beta_s X_{sij} + \eta Z_{si} + \varepsilon_{sij}, \quad s = y, o, \quad (12.2)$$

where γ_{si} is the sex-bias parameter of family i in generation s. The major difference between equations (12.1) and (12.2) is that the gender effect (γ) is allowed to vary across families (actually lineages) indexed by various subscript i values in (12.2). The possible cases of interest are then as follows.

1. **Compensation:** It suggests that parents who experienced unfavorable treatment of girls when they were young tend to treat their own daughters better.

2. **Habitus:** It implies that parents who experienced unfavorable treatment of girls when they were young tend to treat their own children in a similar, albeit attenuated, fashion.

3. **Reinforcement:** It suggests that parents' similar preferences against females are strengthened in the young generation.

Intuitively, one would imagine that (1) the stereotypical idea of gender would be difficult to reverse, and hence a compensation effect would be unlikely to appear; and (2) the process of modernization would weaken the gender bias, and hence neither is a reinforcement effect likely. We therefore hypothesize a habitus effect, which we shall test using empirical data. Although equation (12.2) for the old generation is easy to understand conceptually, it involves estimation of hundreds of sex-bias parameters $\hat{\gamma}_{oi}$.

One way to test the possible existence of a lagged effect of sex-based unfair resource allocation is the following. We run equation (12.2) separately for generations y and o, and obtain a set of paired gender effect parameters $(\hat{\gamma}_{oi}, \hat{\gamma}_{yi})$ for all the families with sufficient data points. If the sex-based unfair allocation of resources has a habitus (compensation) effect from generation o to generation y, then we should observe a positively (negatively) significant correlation between these two estimates. A simple test of correlation coefficients can then be exercised to see if the lagged effect exists. While this approach is intuitively appealing, it treats the estimates $(\hat{\gamma}_{oi}, \hat{\gamma}_{yi})$ as a *paired sample* in testing the correlation coefficient. This approach uses a two-step procedure to make inference; it is indirect but can help analyze the source of sex-preference changes, which we shall explain in the next section.

The second way to test the possible existence of a carry-over effect of sex-based unfair allocation is to run equation (12.2) first for the old generation to obtain an estimate $\hat{\gamma}_{oi}$, and then run the following equation for young generation (y):

$$Y_{yij} = \alpha_{yi} + \delta(\hat{\gamma}_{oi} \times S_{yij}) + \beta_y X_{yij} + \eta Z_{yi} + \varepsilon_{yij}. \qquad (12.3)$$

We then test the significance of δ according to the various hypotheses listed above. Specifically, when $0 < \delta < 1$, it suggests that the habitus hypothesis applies. Evidently, this second approach uses the lineage-specific information of sex preferences in an earlier generation to infer the possible influence on individuals of the latter generation in the same lineage.

The estimation results of equations (12.2) and (12.3) are presented in Table 12.3.[5] As we can see from the table, coefficients of most variables are the same as those in Table 12.2: (1) the number of elder sisters has a supporting effect on the juniors' education in generation o, but has a crowding effect (i.e. resource dilution) in generation y; (2) the number of junior siblings has a crowding effect in both generation o and generation y; (3) the influence of parents' education and occupation on child education decreases, either in magnitude or in significance, in the y generation; (4) the influence of ethnic background (among new migrants) on child education decreases in the y generation, but the difference between new migrants and aborigines persists.

The main focus of Table 12.3 is the coefficient of "previous generation's family-specific gender effects $\times$ gender" (i.e. δ) in equation (12.3). The result shows that the habitus hypothesis cannot be rejected at the 10 per cent level, and the effect is small in absolute value. This result can be compared with what is found in Table 12.1 to gain insight into the intergenerational effect. Combining the coefficients of "gender $\times$ generation" and "gender" in Table 12.1, we see that there is essentially no macro gender effect in the young generation. Table 12.3, on the other hand, shows that the sex-based differential treatment persists within many micro lineages into the young generation, even though the average habitus coefficient is fairly small in magnitude.

A possible improvement to Table 12.3 is to fit equation (12.3) only using data from families in which there were *significant* gender distortions in the old generation; i.e., when their corresponding $\hat{\gamma}_{oi}$ values are significant. To do this, we modify equation (12.3) as

$$Y_{yij} = \alpha_{yi} + \delta(\hat{\gamma}_{oi}^* \times S_{yij}) + \beta_y X_{yij} + \eta Z_{yi} + \varepsilon_{yij}, \qquad (12.4)$$

where $\hat{\gamma}_{oi}^* = \hat{\gamma}_{oi}$ if $\hat{\gamma}_{oi}$ is significant at the 1 per cent level, and $\hat{\gamma}_{oi}^* = 0$ otherwise. Equation (12.4) assumes that the intergenerational carry-over effect exists only in families where the old generation did have a significant gender distortion. Results show that this improvement has a minor impact only, and hence it will not be explored further here.

Table 12.3. Estimates for sex-preference transmission effects

	Old generation equation (12.4)	Young generation equation (12.3)
Father's birth cohort		
Before 1920	−1.566***	
	(0.516)	
1920–9	−0.390	−0.769
	(0.514)	(0.688)
After 1940		−0.038
		(0.175)
Born after 1956	0.545**	
	(0.255)	
Previous generation's family-specific Gender effect × gender		0.035*
		(0.020)
Number of elder brothers	0.131	−0.347***
	(0.111)	(0.120)
Number of elder sisters	0.289***	−0.156*
	(0.098)	(0.084)
Number of younger brothers	−0.299***	−0.353**
	(0.098)	(0.139)
Number of younger sisters	−0.247***	−0.292***
	(0.087)	(0.084)
Father's education	0.286***	0.177***
	(0.048)	(0.027)
Mother's education	0.320***	0.233***
	(0.053)	(0.030)
Father's occupation	0.216**	0.026
	(0.085)	(0.028)
Father's ethnicity		
Aborigine	−2.414***	−1.996***
	(0.792)	(0.390)
Hakka	0.625*	0.136
	(0.347)	(0.276)
Mainlander	1.560***	0.428
	(0.581)	(0.358)
Constant	5.698***	10.180***
	(0.617)	(0.360)
Number of observations	3,762	2,054
Number of families	971	750

Notes: Standard errors are in parentheses. *, **, and *** denote 10%, 5%, and 1% significance levels respectively.

12.3.2. *Elimination of Possible Explanations*

The reduced-form model in equation (12.3) alone cannot identify the cause for the observed carry-over effect between generations. In this subsection, we use the concept of contraposition to eliminate some possible explanations for the carry-over effect. The basic idea is simple. We divide the data of the young generation into two sub-samples based on the old generation's (interviewee's) gender and run regression (12.3) separately for the two sub-samples. This division serves two important purposes. First, the division is not related in any way to (1) eased budget constraints, or (2) the change in gender cost, or (3) the change in gender wages. As such, the division should have no impact on the carry-over effect if the effect was caused by the aforementioned explanations. This means that the regression results should be the same for both sub-samples if the carry-over effects were caused by any factor other than parents' gender.

If, however, there is a gender-specific differential treatment in an old-generation family, the psychological imprints on an old-generation boy (the privileged) and an old-generation girl (the deprived) should be different. Intuitively the psychological imprint on the privileged male respondents, who did not suffer the trauma of "losing" support, may not be very strong. The deprived female respondents, who had less education compared with their male siblings, may, on the other hand, be more likely to preserve the habitus imprint of their families and to treat their children in a similar pattern.

From columns 2–4 of Table 12.4 we see that the estimated generational carry-over effects are rather different for the two sub-samples. Regression results always show that children of male respondents have a carry-over effect with a much smaller *t*-statistic than that of the counterpart of female respondents; and the habitus effect is mainly contributed by the female sample. By contraposition, neither the easing of budget constraints, nor a change in gender cost, nor a change in gender wages can fully explain the carry-over effect. This suggests that the psychological imprints are indeed more likely to affect the "deprived" rather than the "privileged" children. This is an interesting result which may deserve more attention and discussion from psychologists. The family-level causes of such a carry-over will be discussed in Section 12.4.

12.4. Some Sensitivity Analysis

To further confirm our results, we consider two alternative sub-samples of the young generation with different cutoff ages. In Table 12.3, we only include young-generation respondents aged older than 25. To test the sensitivity of this cutoff age, we also tried other cutoff thresholds, such as 27 and 29 in columns 5–7 and 8–10 of Table 12.4 respectively. As far as the intergenerational carry-over effect of gender distortion is concerned, the change of age-group thresholds does not have much impact on the

Table 12.4. Estimates for sex-preference transmission effects for young generation (by age groups): OLS with Huber adjustment

	Age ≥ 25			Age ≥ 27			Age ≥ 29		
	Children of all respondents	Children of male respondents	Children of female respondents	Children of all respondents	Children of male respondents	Children of female respondents	Children of all respondents	Children of male respondents	Children of female respondents
Previous generation's family-specific gender effects × gender	0.035* (0.020)	0.031 (0.042)	0.031† (0.024)	0.038* (0.022)	0.025 (0.046)	0.034† (0.025)	0.046* (0.024)	0.024 (0.052)	0.046† (0.028)
Number of elder brothers	−0.344*** (0.120)	−0.400*** (0.155)	−0.258 (0.174)	−0.385*** (0.130)	−0.411** (0.169)	−0.343* (0.187)	−0.412*** (0.146)	−0.400** (0.201)	−0.401* (0.206)
Number of elder sisters	−0.152* (0.084)	−0.250** (0.120)	−0.066 (0.117)	−0.163* (0.089)	−0.237* (0.133)	−0.094 (0.120)	−0.169* (0.098)	−0.256* (0.146)	−0.093 (0.135)
Number of younger brothers	−0.348** (0.139)	−0.272* (0.155)	−0.385* (0.208)	−0.378** (0.151)	−0.269 (0.168)	−0.447** (0.228)	−0.397** (0.169)	−0.296 (0.190)	−0.462* (0.258)
Number of younger sisters	−0.292*** (0.084)	−0.366*** (0.108)	−0.200 (0.132)	−0.349*** (0.088)	−0.380*** (0.116)	−0.302** (0.135)	−0.377*** (0.092)	−0.415*** (0.120)	−0.321** (0.144)
Father's education	0.177*** (0.027)	0.204*** (0.041)	0.159*** (0.037)	0.185*** (0.029)	0.215*** (0.044)	0.167*** (0.039)	0.180*** (0.033)	0.205*** (0.051)	0.168*** (0.045)
Mother's education	0.233*** (0.030)	0.232*** (0.043)	0.232*** (0.042)	0.237*** (0.033)	0.255*** (0.048)	0.223*** (0.046)	0.249*** (0.038)	0.256*** (0.054)	0.241*** (0.053)
Father's occupation	0.027 (0.028)	0.041 (0.044)	0.011 (0.037)	0.041 (0.031)	0.044 (0.049)	0.038 (0.042)	0.054 (0.035)	0.053 (0.055)	0.058 (0.048)
Father's ethnicity Fukienese	1.999*** (0.391)	2.079*** (0.434)	1.904*** (0.593)	1.856*** (0.425)	1.929*** (0.334)	1.733** (0.702)	1.513*** (0.396)	1.673*** (0.277)	1.332* (0.780)
Hakka	2.133*** (0.461)	2.303*** (0.532)	1.957*** (0.690)	2.019*** (0.514)	1.996*** (0.503)	1.977*** (0.820)	1.484*** (0.534)	1.503*** (0.532)	1.445 (0.939)
Mainlander	2.440*** (0.528)	1.629** (0.745)	2.648*** (0.723)	2.389*** (0.573)	1.265** (0.604)	2.625*** (0.835)	2.186*** (0.594)	1.076 (0.660)	2.317** (0.958)
Constant	7.388*** (0.870)	7.852*** (0.634)	7.374*** (1.058)	7.134*** (0.905)	7.969*** (0.667)	7.151*** (1.146)	7.077*** (0.984)	8.090*** (0.593)	7.024*** (1.325)
R^2	0.2806	0.3145	0.2607	0.2912	0.3179	0.2784	0.2869	0.2954	0.2861
Number of observations	2,049	903	1,146	1,727	755	972	1,406	605	801
Number of families	750	328	424	638	277	362	536	237	299

Notes: Standard errors are in parentheses. † denotes significance at one-tailed 10% level. *, **, and *** denote significance at 10%, 5%, and 1% levels respectively.
Father's birth cohort dummies are omitted from the table for brevity.

coefficients and their significance levels. However, as the age threshold becomes higher, we are moving toward older cohorts, and this also shifts the coefficients toward the "old generation." For instance, the coefficient of parental education (either father's education or mother's education) increases as the age of children in question becomes older. This is, of course, consistent with our previous discussion.

An alternative measure of education achievement is the dummy variable "whether the child receives education beyond the mandatory years," with 1 indicating yes and 0 otherwise. For this dependent variable, we can use the same set of explanatory variables to run a probit regression with Huber adjustment, except that in this new regression, the dummy variable for "born after 1956" (the extension of mandatory education from six to nine years is applicable to cohorts born after 1956) is not necessary. The regression results are qualitatively the same, and we shall skip the interpretation.

12.4.1. *The Endogeneity of Sibship Size*

In the analysis in previous sections, we used gender-seniority-specific sibling numbers to control the possible resource-dilution effect on the education opportunity of the respondent. However, as is well known in the literature, both the quantity and the quality of children are endogenously chosen by parents, and hence in equation (12.2) or (12.3), the gender-seniority-specific sibship variables may be correlated with the error term. This problem of endogenous child number has different impacts in different research contexts, and there has not been any consensus in the literature concerning how we should deal with it. Here we follow the approach of Conley and Glauber (2006) to tackle the problem.

To control the impact of sibling numbers on child education, first we follow Conley and Glauber and replace the gender-seniority-specific sibling numbers by a much rougher dummy variable "whether there are more than three children (including the respondent)" in the family in question. It turns out that the coefficients of gender and gender × generation are roughly the same as those in Table 12.1.

Then we apply the method of instrumental variable to take care of the problem of possible endogeneity. The explanatory variables used to estimate the "more-than-three children" variable, again following Conley and Glauber (2006), include two dummies: one is "whether the first-born is female" and the second is "whether the first two children are both female." The regressions applying this instrumental variable approach are not presented here and the coefficients associated with gender and gender × generation are qualitatively the same as before. Furthermore, none of the other estimates shows any substantial discrepancy.

The corresponding micro analysis using "more-than-three-children" as an explanatory variable is also implemented. We find that the across-generation habitus effect is always weak but significant, similar to what we find in Table 12.3. This shows that our previous conclusions are robust with respect to the possible endogeneity of sibling numbers.

12.4.2. The Cause of the Egalitarian Tendency

The weak habitus results shown in Table 12.3 indicate that girls' disadvantage in parental education resource allocation has gradually diminished with time. Our discussion in Section 12.3 also shows that a more plausible explanation for this tendency is the change in parents' subjective gender preferences. Our next question is: what might cause such a change intergenerationally? Below we provide some preliminary answers to this question.

For generations o and y, equation (12.2) can give us two estimate series of $\hat{\gamma}_{oi}$ and $\hat{\gamma}_{yi}$, respectively. The difference $\hat{\gamma}_{yi} - \hat{\gamma}_{oi}$ measures the *intergenerational change* of boys' advantage over girls in lineage i; the larger it is, the weaker is family i's egalitarian tendency. We now regress $\hat{\gamma}_{yi} - \hat{\gamma}_{oi}$ with respect to (1) the difference in fathers' education between young and old generations, (2) the difference in mothers' education between young and old generations, (3) the difference in fathers' occupation status between young and old generations, (4) the old-generation fathers' ethnic background, and (5) the old-generation fathers' birth cohort. The results are listed in Table 12.5. It appears from the table that change in education is the most important factor that explains the changes in parents' egalitarian perception, whereas change in occupation status has an insignificant impact. Relative to the Fukienese, the aborigines are less persistent in sticking to their male preferences.

12.5. Conclusions

The purpose of this chapter is to test whether there is an intergenerational transmission of gender preferences in educational resource allocation among children. We performed our analysis along two lines of enquiry: the first is to see whether society as a whole has any macro change in gender-specific education achievement, and the second is to see whether there is any within-lineage transmission of gender preferences across

Table 12.5. Regression models for $\hat{\gamma}_{yi} - \hat{\gamma}_{oi}$

	Model A	Model B	Model C
Generational difference of father's education	0.233***	0.237***	0.232***
	(0.054)	(0.054)	(0.054)
Generational difference of mother's education	0.180***	0.201***	0.213***
	(0.058)	(0.059)	(0.059)
Generational difference of father's occupation	0.042	0.054	0.046
	(0.056)	(0.056)	(0.056)
Father's ethnicity of the old generation			
Aborigine		−3.578***	−3.801***
		(1.329)	(1.330)
Hakka		0.303	0.450
		(0.620)	(0.621)
Mainlander		−0.903	−0.871
		(1.199)	(1.196)
Father's birth cohort of old generation (>1929 being ref. group)			
Before 1920			−0.309
			(1.138)
1920–9			0.780
			(1.185)
Constant	−0.838**	−0.634*	−0.597
	(0.365)	(0.376)	(1.172)
Number of observations	580	580	580

Notes: $\hat{\gamma}_{yi}$ and $\hat{\gamma}_{oi}$ are estimated from equation (12.2). Standard errors are in parentheses. *, **, and *** denote 10%, 5%, and 1% significance levels respectively.

generations. Data and institutional limitations only allow us to study the case of Taiwan, but not of China.

We set up an empirical model to estimate and test the hypotheses of intergenerational transmission of gender preferences, and use the concept of contraposition to eliminate various explanations for the observed intergenerational carry-over effect. As far as the macro pattern is concerned, we found that although there is a clear tendency of differential treatment against females in the old generation, this tendency is significantly weakened and has nearly vanished in the young generation. Moreover, the supporting effect of senior siblings in the old generation becomes a crowding (resource-dilution) effect in the young generation. However, within each micro lineage, there is a mild habitus effect in gender-specific educational resource allocation in the sense that parents who had the experience of gender-specific differential treatment tend to treat their children in a similar fashion. This habitus effect is stronger for female respondents (who were the deprived group) than for male respondents (who were the privileged group). We show that this habitus effect is robust with respect to various sensitivity analyses. By excluding other possible explanations using the contraposition argument, we assert that the weak habitus effect may be due to the change in parents' gender perceptions, and this change is more likely when the young parents receive more education.

Our analysis can be compared with Fernandez et al. (2004), who studied how a man's attitude toward female labor force participation depends on whether he himself was brought up in a family with a working mother. The context of our intergenerational transmission of attitude is similar. And Fernandez et al. also provided some arguments behind such a transmission. The psychological imprint we mentioned is what Fernandez et al. called the *culture* effect. Table 12.5 in a sense tells us what causes a change in the culture of gender preferences.

Notes

1. Concerning the correspondence between parents' and children's ideas and values, see for instance the discussion in Goodnow (1992). In fact, what was characterized in Fernandez et al. (2004) was also the influence of stereotypical ideas.
2. For the older generation, there are 2,496 observations with fathers born before 1920, 1,088 observations with fathers born in 1920–9, and 178 observations with fathers born after 1929. For the younger generation, there are 57 observations with fathers born before 1929, 732 observations with fathers born during 1930–9, and 1,870 observations with fathers born after 1940.
3. See Chapter 2 for a detailed review of the changes in the educational system of Taiwan.
4. The occupation variable used here is similar to that in Erikson and Goldthorpe (1992), where the authors classify occupations into eleven categories according to the skill level, from higher-grade professionals to unskilled manual and agricultural workers. Readers can find a more detailed explanation in their work.
5. As one can see, 1,364 families could be retrieved from the PSFD data. To estimate the completed education achievement of children in Table 12.3, we delete lineages which have no child aged older than 25 (we also try cases with 27 and 29 the critical ages). This additional restriction limits the number of analyzed families to 971. To obtain column 3 of Table 12.3, we only keep lineages which have children of *both* sexes in order to do the gender-specific differential analysis. The lineage size then becomes 750. Notice that equation (12.2) involves sibling data, hence the number of actual individuals' *observations* used in the regression is much larger than the number of families.

13

Concluding Remarks

In the previous chapters we have studied various aspects of the Chinese family. These aspects may look dispersed and disjointed, but in this concluding chapter we would like to list the topics we have discussed, and summarize our analysis in a systematic way.

13.1. Listing Chinese Family Features

Although the characteristics of Chinese families are revealed in several different dimensions, we believe that they can be understood under two unique and well-established concepts, namely the parents' desire to sustain lineage prosperity and their emphasis on child education. We cannot pinpoint the exact time when lineage preservation and expansion became a doctrine popular with most families, but in the literature scholars such as Cole and Wolf (1974) and Freedman (1966) have all emphasized the importance of this doctrine. With lineage prosperity as a main, if not the sole, purpose of Chinese families in ancient time, there did not exist much room for individualism. Although such emphasis on lineage prosperity was an old doctrine, indirectly it still dominates many dimensions of family behavior today.

With individualism suppressed, most activities in the Chinese family are of course joint rather than individual decisions. Starting from the initial stage of family formation, we noted that traditional Chinese marriages were mostly arranged, or at least subject to approval, by parents. This custom has certainly changed or has even been prohibited by law in recent years, but even today, a majority of Chinese still claim that their marriages were *jointly* determined by themselves and their parents. This indicates that the parental influence on marriage really has not disappeared; the most we can say is that parents are not as dominant as before in the matter of their children's marriage.

With individualism discouraged, Chinese children are expected to respect their parents' opinion to a greater extent than their Western counterparts. Other than this, the assortative mating in class, education, and ethnicity in Chinese marriages is not very different from that in the West. This is so mainly because the objective of lineage prosperity itself also implies that the lineage with a strong background should look for a marriage counterpart with similar background.

The lack of individualism also suggests that Chinese children are more dutiful to their parents. This filial piety finds its expression in the involvement of parents in child marriage as mentioned before, the frequent visits of adult children, and the high proportion of parental co-residence with married children. In particular, the popular co-residence practice has created in Western scholars the general impression of "large" Chinese families. Thus, many earlier studies by Western scholars have concentrated on the *size* of Chinese families. Although this large-family practice has changed much in the past few decades, the transition has been slow and the phenomenon still deserves our attention.

The co-residence of parents with their married children affects not only the size of the family, but also other dimensions. For instance, parents having a traditional concept of lineage preservation may like to push the couple to have more children, or at least to have them earlier. For many mammals, grandparents often have a sophisticated division of labor with their married children (Voland et al. 2005). For human beings, the practice usually consists in the co-residing grandparents' taking care of their grandchildren. However, this practice has gradually disappeared in recent years, when the average fertility rate has maintained a downward trend, and professional babysitting has become more popular. In the twenty-first century, it turns out that the number of children aged 3 or under helps explain the co-residence of grandparents in China, but not in Taiwan, where the economic capacity of families is greater.

What do adult children do if the norm of filial piety is still present whereas public pensions and facilities for old-age support are not prevalent? We found that married couples use their economic capacities, in the form of either education or incomes, to *veto* co-residence with their parents-in-law, but not to welcome co-residence with their own parents.

In a large traditional Chinese family, the husband and the wife are often considered junior members, and most family decisions are in the hands of members with higher seniority, i.e. their parents or grandparents. But as the family size gradually shrinks along with demographic transition, the couple begins to take power, and make most relevant decisions. In this aspect, the Chinese families in Taiwan and China do seem to follow the pattern in Western families, where the power to make the most important family decisions is related to the respective resource holdings of the husband and of the wife. The allocation of housework loads between the couple is also inversely related to their respective resource endowments. It turns out that the family power structure in Taiwan is more like that in Japan, and in China it is closer to what is found in the USA and European countries. We believe that the difference may be explained by the Chinese Communist government's effort in promoting gender equality and the Japanese colonial occupation of Taiwan. In general, husbands are much more "powerful" than wives in Chinese families.

Given the rule of surname succession, the concern for lineage preservation also results in son preferences. The male line used to inherit the family name, while the females were married *out* to other lineages. Although the concept of lineage preservation has been losing currency, ironically the various other customs associated with son preferences do not go away easily. This is a typically long-lasting effect of the influence of culture. For instance, if children grow up in a family in which their mothers do most of the household chores and have minimal participation in making family decisions, it is not unusual for them to have a similar mindset when they grow up and form their own families. The children's generation may not be encumbered by any gender ideology, and they certainly do not care much about lineage preservation. But their behavior is still affected by the gender stereotypes of their childhood. Thus, son preferences do not disappear easily even though the concept of lineage preservation has gone by the wayside.

Although a macro change in the concept of lineage preservation is slow, we do, however, observe micro changes in Chinese families. What then exactly is the mechanism behind the macro–micro interactions? More specifically, what determines the attitude of the young couple, given that they were reared in a traditional environment? We believe that the most important factor is education. This brings us to the second unique concept of Chinese families: the parental emphasis on child education.

It is hard to say why Chinese parents place so much emphasis on their children's education, but according to Ho (1962), the civil-service exams prevalent in imperial China for roughly 600 years before 1905 might be partly responsible. In an ancient China characterized by imperial control and few market activities, taking and passing the civil-service exam to enter officialdom seemed to be the only way for members of the numerically preponderant peasant class to move up the social ladder. These exams used standard test materials, most of which were ancient writings by sages such as Kong Zi (Confucius) and Meng Zi (Mencius). The emperors in ancient times might use these controlled, systematic exams to unify thoughts and to inhibit intellectual fermentation; but these exams did make education the most important means of parental investment in their children.

If traditional-minded Chinese parents have son preferences, and if education is their only perceived means of child investment, they would naturally adopt a gender-specific differential approach in child education. Intuitively, this differential treatment is unlikely to appear when parents' decisions are so constrained (as in an earlier period in China) that they do not have much discretion in resource allocation anyway, or when parents' economic well-being is much improved (as in recent times in Taiwan) so that they do not have to sacrifice any of their children. This therefore sets the stage for our research, and identifies the variables that we expect to have influenced the outcome.

Concerning the allocation of education resources, the patterns of gender preferences in Chinese societies may be fundamentally different from what is studied in the research schemes in the West, where gender neutrality is presumed. In a gender-neutral scenario, there can be at most a resource-dilution effect and a birth-spacing (crowding) effect, whereas in Chinese societies there is also the density–seniority effect, which tends to hurt the education opportunity of senior children who have younger siblings spaced apart. Moreover, the gender of the person being impacted by siblings is itself important. This adds a new dimension to, and therefore enriches, the traditional discussion in the literature.

Researchers in the West used to treat education as a proxy of permanent income; they often study the parent–child transition matrix of education and calculate various intergenerational mobility indexes from such a matrix. In Chinese societies, this exercise can also be done. It turns out that the large geographic area and the turbulent political environment of China in the recent past have made it much more likely for its upper educational classes to move downward. The intergenerational mobility in Chinese societies is further complicated by the widespread practice of *inter vivos* transfers by parents. How are these transfer decisions related to the parental decision on child education? If Chinese parents in general provide less education to their daughters than to boys, will the transfer of their physical resources worsen or improve this discrepancy? What kind of information could the parental decision interaction reveal? This is another rich and unique dimension of the Chinese families we studied.

271

Chinese parents emphasize child education since it can help the upward mobility of children. Because of the common son preference, boys usually receive better education than girls. Thus, education plays the role of preserving the males' advantage in a Chinese society. Ironically, since higher education is also correlated with more egalitarian conceptions, education also plays the role of eliminating the gender gap for the young generation. In the long run, the Chinese traditional emphasis on education may turn out to be the major force hastening the decline of another Chinese tradition—that of male dominance.

13.2. Future Effort

Throughout this book we have, as a rule, tried to maintain a balanced discussion of China and Taiwan, the two most important Chinese societies. There is only one exception. In Chapter 12, we needed three generations of education data to study the transmission of gender preferences. The one-child policy in China has meant that the sibling data of the younger generation carry little meaningful information, thus the relevant analysis has to be confined to Taiwan. For all other topics, our coverage is parallel between China and Taiwan.

Since the PSFD survey in China has only proceeded to the second wave at the time of this writing, some of the topics in this monograph do not readily lend themselves to a panel data analysis. However, in Chapter 6 we made use of the panels starting from first wave to the 2005 survey of Taiwan to analyze the housework share between the couple, in response to changes in labor market characteristics; and in Chapter 10 we used the same panel data to study the dynamics of transfers between parents and children. These are pioneer trials in the application of a panel data analysis to Chinese families. We also expect to use the panel data to study other topics as well in the future, when more waves of panels are available. For instance, parallel analysis of housework allocation and dynamic transfers among family members in China would be equally interesting. We shall wait for the availability of the China panel to accomplish this work, and also to make interesting comparisons between China and Taiwan.

In the West, the altruism studied is often between the couple, or between parents and children. In Chinese families, where ties between members are believed to be stronger, the altruism is also expected to be more various. With family members forming a special social network, one may observe not only active altruism, but also passive *insurance* among members. For instance, if a person belongs to a close-knit network of family members, would he or she be less likely to buy life or health insurance? Or, how good a substitute for social insurance schemes is the family network? In terms of policy, would the Chinese family network render some of the social welfare programs unnecessary? Research along this line also needs more waves of panel data on the economic capacity of individuals, and this is what the PSFD survey has tried to cover in recent years.

In summary, in this monograph we have covered many important topics concerning Chinese families. We related these topics to the existing literature, explored the possible differences and idiosyncrasies of Chinese societies, explained the possible causes of such uniqueness, discussed the theoretical implications, and used survey data to estimate and test related hypotheses. We hope that our effort has produced a supplementary document for readers who are interested in Chinese families, and especially those who appreciate the unique features that differentiate Chinese families from Western ones.

We understand that the Chinese economy is changing at a fast pace as it enters the twenty-first century, and we expect that the behavioral pattern of some family decisions may be different after a decade or two. This expectation of changes, however, does not hinder our research effort now, even if some modifications are needed after several years. Indeed, it is the rich transitional dynamics that make the analysis of social sciences interesting. After a decade, this monograph may document either evidence of unchanged features, or a baseline for comparisons of changes. In either case, we will be glad then that we have made this effort now.

References

Adams, Bert N. (1972) "Birth Order: A Critical Review," *Sociometry* 3: 411–39.

Adams, Jennifer and Emily Hannum (2005) "Children's Social Welfare in China, 1989–1997: Access to Health Insurance and Education," *China Quarterly* 181: 100–21.

Alenezi, Mohammad and Michael L. Walden (2004) "A New Look at Husbands' and Wives' Time Allocation," *Journal of Consumer Affairs* 38: 81–106.

Altonji, Joseph G., Fumio Hayashi, and Laurence J. Kotlikoff (1992) "Is the Extended Family Altruistically Linked? Direct Tests Using Micro Data," *American Economic Review* 82: 1177–98.

—— —— —— (1997) "Parental Altruism and Inter Vivos Transfers: Theory and Evidence," *Journal of Political Economy* 105: 1121–66.

Alvarez, Begona and Daniel Miles (2003) "Gender Effect on Housework Allocation: Evidence from Spanish Two-Earner Couples," *Journal of Population Economics* 16: 227–42.

Anderberg, Dan and Alessandro Balestrino (2003) "Self-Enforcing Intergenerational Transfers and the Provision of Education," *Economica* 70: 55–71.

Andreas, Joel (2004) "Leveling the Little Pagoda: The Impact of College Examinations, and their Elimination, on Rural Education in China," *Comparative Education Review* 48: 1–47.

Angrist, Joshua, Victor Lavy, and Analia Schlosser (2006) "Multiple Experiments for the Causal Link between the Quantity and Quality of Children," MIT Department of Economics Working Paper No. 06–26.

Baker, Hugh D. R. (1979) *Chinese Family and Kinship*. New York: Columbia University Press.

Bauer, John (1992) "Industrial Restructuring in the NIEs: Prospects and Challenges," *Asian Survey* 32: 1012–25.

—— Wang Feng, Nancy E. Riley, and Zhao Xiaohua (1992) "Gender Inequality in Urban China: Education and Employment," *Modern China* 18: 333–70.

Becker, Gary S. (1965) "A Theory of the Allocation of Time," *Economic Journal* 75: 493–517.

—— (1974) "A Theory of Social Interactions," *Journal of Political Economy* 82: 1063–93.

—— (1985) "Human Capital, Effort, and the Sexual Division of Labor," *Journal of Labor Economics* 3: S33–58.

Becker, Gary S. (1991) *A Treatise on the Family*. Cambridge, Mass.: Harvard University Press.

—— and H. Gregg Lewis (1973) "On the Interaction between the Quantity and Quality of Children," *Journal of Political Economy* 81: S279–88.

—— and Kevin M. Murphy (1988) "The Family and the State," *Journal of Law and Economics* 31: 1–18.

Behrman, Jere R. (1988) "Intrahousehold Allocation of Nutrients in Rural India: Are Boys Favored? Do Parents Exhibit Inequality Aversion?" *Oxford Economic Papers* 40: 32–54.

—— (1992) "Intrahousehold Allocation of Nutrients and Gender Effects: A Survey of Structural and Reduced-Form Estimates," in *Nutrition and Poverty*, ed. Siddiq Osmani. World Institute for Development Economics Research (WIDER) Series on Studies in Development Economics. Oxford: Clarendon Press.

—— and Anil B. Deolalikar (1995) "Are There Differential Returns to Schooling by Gender? The Case of Indonesian Labor Markets," *Oxford Bulletin of Economics and Statistics* 57: 97–117.

—— and Mark Rosenzweig (2002) "Does Increasing Women's Schooling Raise the Schooling of the Next Generation?" *The American Economic Review* 92: 323–34.

—— and Paul Taubman (1985) "Intergenerational Earning Mobility in the United States: Some Estimates and a Test of Becker's Intergenerational Endowment Model," *Review of Economics and Statistics* 67: 144–51.

—— Robert Pollak, and Paul Taubman (1982) "Parental Preferences and Provision for Progeny," *Journal of Political Economy* 90: 52–73.

—— —— —— (1986) "Do Parents Favor Boys?" *International Economic Review* 27: 33–54.

—— —— —— (1989) "Family Resources, Family Size, and Access to Financing for College Education," *Journal of Political Economy* 97: 398–419.

—— Nancy Birdsall, and Miguel Szekely (2000) "Intergenerational Mobility in Latin America: Deeper Markets and Better Schools Make a Difference," in *New Markets, New Opportunities? Economic and Social Mobility in a Changing World*, ed. Nancy Birdsall and Carol Graham. Washington, DC: Carnegie Endowment for International Peace.

Bergstrom, Theodore C. (1989) "A Fresh Look at the Rotten-Kid Theorem—and Other Household Mysteries," *Journal of Political Economy* 97: 1138–59.

—— (1995) "On the Evolution of Altruistic Ethical Rules for Siblings," *American Economic Review* 85: 58–81.

—— and Mark Bagnoli (1993) "Courtship as a Waiting Game," *Journal of Political Economy* 101: 185–202.

Bernheim, B. Douglas, Andrei Shleifer, and Lawrence H. Summers (1985) "The Strategic Bequest Motive," *Journal of Political Economy* 93: 1045–76.

Bian, Yanijie, Ronald Breiger, Deborah Davis, and Joseph Galaskiewicz (2005) "Occupation, Class, and Social Networks in Urban China," *Social Forces* 83: 1443–68.

References

Bianchi, Suzanne M., Melissa A. Milkie, Liana C. Sayer, and John P. Robinson (2000) "Is Anyone Doing the Housework? Trends in the Gender Division of Household Labor," *Social Forces* 79: 191–228.

Binder, Melissa and Christopher Woodruff (2002) "Inequality and Intergenerational Mobility in Schooling: The Case of Mexico," *Economic Development and Cultural Change* 50: 249–67.

Bittman, Michael, Paula England, and Nancy Folbre (2003) "When Does Gender Trump Money? Bargaining and Time in Household Work," *American Journal of Sociology* 109: 186–214.

Blake, Judith (1981) "Family Size and the Quality of Children," *Demography* 18: 421–42.

Blood, Robert F. and Donald M. Wolfe (1960) *Husbands and Wives*. Glencoe, Ill.: Free Press.

Bott, Elizabeth (1968) *Family and Social Network: Roles, Norms and External Relationships in Ordinary Urban Families*. London: Tavistock Publication.

Brines, Julie (1994) "Economic Dependence, Gender, and the Division of Labor at Home," *American Journal of Sociology* 100: 652–88.

Brinton, Mary C., Yean-Ju Lee, and William L. Parish (1995) "Married Women's Employment in Rapidly Industrializing Societies: Examples East Asia," *American Journal of Sociology* 100: 1099–130.

Broman, Sarah H., Paul L. Nichols, and Wallace A. Kennedy (1975) *Preschool IQ: Prenatal and Early Development Correlates*. Mahwah, NJ: Erlbaum.

Burdett, Kenneth and Melvyn Coles (1999) "Long-Term Partnership Formation: Marriage and Employment," *Economic Journal* 109: F307–34.

Butcher, Kristin F. and Anne Case (1994) "The Effect of Sibling Sex Composition on Women's Education and Earnings," *Quarterly Journal of Economics* 109: 531–63.

Cabrillo, Francisco (1999) *The Economics of the Family and Family Policy*. Cheltenham: Edward Elgar.

Card, David (1999) "The Causal Effect of Child Education on Earnings," in *Handbook of Labor Economics*, ed. Orley Ashenfelter and David Card. Amsterdam: North Holland.

Checchi, Daniele and Valentino Dardanoni (2002) "Mobility Comparisons: Does Using Different Measures Matter?" Working Paper, State University of Milan.

—— Andrea Ichino, and Aldo Rustichini (1999) "More Equal But Less Mobile? Education Financing and Intergenerational Mobility in Italy and in the US," *Journal of Public Economics* 74: 351–93.

Chen, Chao-nan (1996) "Living Arrangements and Economic Support for the Elderly in Taiwan," *Journal of Population Studies* 17: 59–81 (in Chinese).

Chiappori, Pierre A. (1992) "Collective Labor Supply and Welfare," *Journal of Political Economy* 100: 437–67.

Choo, E. and A. Siow (2006a) "Who Marries Whom and Why?" *Journal of Political Economy*, 114: 175–201.

—— —— (2006b) "Estimating a Marriage Matching Model with Spillover Effects," *Demography* 43: 463–90.

Chu, C. Y. Cyrus (1991) "Primogeniture," *Journal of Political Economy* 99: 78–99.

—— and Ronald Demos Lee (eds.) (2000) *Population and Economic Change in East Asia*, a special supplement to *Population and Development Review* 26s.

—— and Terrance Tai (1996) *Deregulating the Education*. Taipei: Far Stream (in Chinese).

—— and Ruoh-rong Yu (1998) "Individual Sex Preferences and the Population Sex Ratio of Newborns," *Journal of Theoretical Biology* 194: 383–90.

—— Yu Xie, and Ruoh-rong Yu (2007) "Effects of Sibship Structure Revisited: Evidence from Intra-family Resource Transfer in Taiwan," *Sociology of Education* 80: 91–113.

Cicirelli, Victor G. (1976) "Sibling Structure and Intellectual Ability," *Development Psychology* 12: 69–70.

Cigno, Alessandro (1991) *The Economics of the Family*. Oxford: Clarendon Press.

Coale, Ansley (1989) "Marriage and Childbearing in China since 1940," *Social Forces* 67: 833–50.

Cohen, M. L. (1976) *House United, House Divided: The Chinese Family in Taiwan*. New York: Columbia University Press.

Cole, John W. and Eric R. Wolf (1974) *The Hidden Frontier: Ecology and Ethnicity in an Alpine Valley*. New York: Academic Press.

Coltrane, Scott (2000) "Research on Household Labor: Modeling and Measuring the Social Embeddedness of Routine Family Work," *Journal of Marriage and Family* 62: 1208–33.

Conley, D. (2000) "Sibship Sex Composition: Effects on Educational Attainment," *Social Science Research* 29: 441–57.

—— and Rebecca Glauber (2006) "Parental Educational Investment and Children's Academic Risk: Estimates of the Impact of Sibship Size and Birth Order from Exogenous Variation in Fertility," *Journal of Human Resources* 41: 722–37.

Corak, Miles (2001) "Are the Kids All Right? Intergenerational Mobility and Child Well-Being in Canada," in *The Review of Economic Performance and Social Progress*, Keith G. Banting, Andrew Gharpe and France St-Hilaire (eds.) Centre for the Study of Living Standards.

Cornman, Jennifer C., Jieming Chen, and Albert I. Hermalin (2003) "Patterns of Intergenerational Support in Urban China and Urban Taiwan," in *China's Revolutions and Intergenerational Relations*, ed. Martin K. Whyte. Ann Arbor: Center for Chinese Studies, University of Michigan: 277–301.

Cox, Donald (1987) "Motives for Private Income Transfers," *Journal of Political Economy* 95: 1045–76.

—— (1990) "Intergenerational Transfers and Liquidity Constraints," *Quarterly Journal of Economics* 105: 187–217.

—— (2007) "Biological Bases and the Economics of the Family," *Journal of Economics Perspectives* 21: 91–108.

—— and Mark Rank (1992) "Inter-Vivos Transfers and Intergenerational Exchange," *Review of Economics and Statistics* 74: 305–14.

—— and Oded Stark (1993) "Intergenerational Transfers and the Demonstration Effect," Working Paper.

References

Cox, Ronald, Bruce E. Hansen, and Emmanuel Jimenez (2004) "How Responsive Are Private Transfers to Income: Evidence from a Laissez-Faire Economy," *Journal of Public Economics* 88: 2193–219.

Dahan, Momi and Alejandro Gaviria (2001) "Sibling Correlations and Intergenerational Mobility in Latin America," *Economic Development and Cultural Change* 49: 537–54.

Dalmia, Sonia and Pareena Lawrence (2001) "An Empirical Analysis of Assortative Mating in India and the U.S." *International Advances in Economic Research* 7: 443–58.

Davies, James and Junsen Zhang (1995) "Gender Bias, Investment in Children and Bequests," *International Economic Review* 36: 795–818.

Davis, Deborah (1993) "Urban Households: Supplicants to a Socialist State," in *Chinese Families in the Post-Mao Era*, ed. Deborah Davis and Stevan Harrell. Berkeley and Los Angeles: University of California Press.

—— and Stevan Harrell (eds.) (1993) *Chinese Families in the Post-Mao Era*. Berkeley and Los Angeles: University of California Press.

Davis, Kingsley (1955) "Institutional Patterns Favoring High Fertility in Underdeveloped Areas," *Eugenics Quarterly* 2: 33–9.

Dawkins, Richard (1989) *The Selfish Gene*. New York: Oxford University Press.

Dearden, Lorraine (1999) "The Effects of Families and Ability on Men's Education and Earnings in Britain," *Labour Economics* 6: 551–67.

Di Pietro, Giorgio and Peter Urwin (2003) "Intergenerational Mobility and Occupational Status in Italy," *Applied Economics Letters* 10: 793–7.

Downey, Douglas B. (1995) "When Bigger is Not Better: Family Size, Parental Resources, and Children's Educational Performance," *American Sociological Review* 60: 746–61.

Dwyer, Daisy and Judith Bruce (1988) *A Home Divided: Women and Income in the Third World*. Stanford, Calif.: Stanford University Press.

Ebenstein, Avraham Y. (2007) "Sex Preference, Sex Selection, and Women's Labor Supply." University of California, Berkeley, Ph.D. thesis.

Engle, John W. (1984) "Marriage in the People's Republic of China: Analysis of a New Law," *Journal of Marriage and the Family* 46: 955–61.

Engle, Patrice L. (1993) "Influences of Mothers' and Fathers' Income on Children's Nutritional Status in Guatemala," *Social Science and Medicine* 37: 1303–12.

Erikson, Robert and John H. Goldthorpe (1992) *The Constant Flux: A Study of Class Mobility in Industrial Societies*. Oxford: Clarendon Press.

Ermisch, John F. (2003) *An Economic Analysis of the Family*. Princeton: Princeton University Press.

—— and Marco Francesconi (2001) "Family Matters: Impacts of Family Background on Educational Attainments," *Economica* 68: 137–56.

Estudillo, Jonna P., Agnes R. Quisumbing, and Keijiro Otsuka (2001) "Gender Differences in Land Inheritance and Schooling Investments in the Rural Philippines," *Land Economics* 77: 130–43.

278

Fan, C. Cindy and Youqin Huang (1998) "Waves of Rural Brides: Female Marriage Migration in China," *Annals of the Association of American Geographers* 88: 227–51.

Fei, Xiaotong (1992) *From the Soil: The Foundations of Chinese Society*, trans. Gary Hamilton and Wang Zheng. Berkeley and Los Angeles: University of California Press.

Feldstein, Martin (1998) *Social Security Pension Reform in China*. NBER Working Paper No. 6794.

Fernandez, Raquel and Alessandra Fogli (2005) "Culture: An Empirical Investigation of Beliefs, Work, and Fertility," NBER Working Paper No. 11268.

—— —— and Claudia Olivetti (2004) "Mothers and Sons: Preference Formation and Female Labor Force Dynamics," *Quarterly Journal of Economics* 119: 1249–99.

Formby, John P., W. James Smith, and Buhong Zheng (2004) "Mobility Measurement, Transition Matrices and Statistical Inference," *Journal of Econometrics* 120: 181–205.

Freedman, Maurice (1966) *Chinese Lineage and Society: Fukien and Kwantung*. London: Athlone.

—— (1970) *Chinese Family and Marriage in Singapore*. New York: Johnson Reprint Corporation. 1st pub. 1957.

Freedman, Ronald, Ming-cheng Chang, and Te-hsiung Sun (1982) "Household Composition, Extended Kinship and Reproduction in Taiwan: 1973–1980," *Population Studies* 36: 395–411.

—— —— —— and Maxine Weinstein (1994) "The Fertility Transition in Taiwan," in *Social Change and the Family in Taiwan*, ed. Arland Thornton and Hui-sheng Lin. Chicago: University of Chicago Press: 264–304.

Freeman, Richard, Arland Thornton, and L.-S. Yang (1994) "Determinants of Coresidence in Extended Households," in *Social Changes and the Family in Taiwan*, ed. Arland Thornton and Hui-sheng Lin. Chicago: University of Chicago Press.

Friedman, Milton (1982) *Capitalism and Freedom*. Chicago: University of Chicago Press.

Gailbraith, Richard C. (1982) "Sibling Spacing and Intelligence Development: A Closer Look at the Confluence Model," *Development Psychology* 18: 151–73.

Gallin, Bernard (1966) *Hsin Hsing, Taiwan: A Chinese Village in Change*. Berkeley and Los Angeles: University of California Press.

Gershuny, Jonathan and John P. Robinson (1988) "Historical Changes in the Household Division of Labor," *Demography* 25: 537–52.

Ginther, Donna K. and Robert A. Pollak (2004) "Family Structure and Children's Outcomes: Blended Families, Stylized Facts, and Descriptive Regressions," *Demography* 41: 671–96.

Goode, William (1963) *World Revolution and Family Patterns*. New York: Free Press.

—— —— —— (1982) *The Family*. Englewood Cliffs, NJ: Prentice-Hall.

Goodnow, Jacqueline J. (1992) "Parent's Idea, Children's Idea: Correspondence and Divergence," in *Parental Belief Systems: The Psychological Consequences for Children*, ed. Irving E. Sigel, Ann V. McGillicuddy-DeLisi, and Jacqueline J. Goodnow. Hillsdale, NJ: Lawrence Erlbaum Associates.

Greene, William H. (2003) *Econometric Analysis*, 4th edn. New York: Prentice Hall.

Greenhalgh, Susan (1984) "Networks and their Nodes: Urban Society on Taiwan," *China Quarterly* 99: 529–52.

—— (1985) "Sexual Stratification: The Other Side of 'Growth with Equity' in East Asia," *Population and Development Review* 11: 265–314.

—— (1994) "Controlling Births and Bodies in Village China," *American Ethnologist* 21: 3–30.

Greenstein, Theodore N. (2000) "Economic Dependence, Gender, and the Division of Labor in the Home: A Replication and Extension," *Journal of Marriage and the Family* 62: 322–35.

Griliches, Zvi (1979) "Sibling Models and Data in Economics: Beginning of a Survey," *Journal of Political Economy* 87: S37–64.

Gronau, Reuben (1977) "Leisure, Home Production, and Work: The Theory of the Allocation of Time Revisited," *Journal of Political Economy* 85: 1099–124.

—— (1980) "Home Production: A Forgotten Industry," *Review of Economics and Statistics* 62: 408–16.

Guo, Zhugang, Erli Zhang, Baochang Gu, and Feng Wang (2003) "The Diversity of Chinese Fertility Policies: A Perspective of Policy Fertility Rate," *Population Research* 5: 1–27 (in Chinese).

Gupta, Sanjiv (1999) "The Effects of Transitions in Marital Status on Men's Performance of Housework," *Journal of Marriage and the Family* 61: 700–11.

Ha, Jung-Hwa, Deborah Carr, Rebecca L. Utz, and Randolph Nesse (2006) "Older Adults' Perceptions of Intergenerational Support after Widowhood," *Journal of Family Issues* 27: 3–30.

Hannum, Emily (1999) "Political Change and the Urban–Rural Gap in Basic Education in China, 1949–1990," *Comparative Education Review* 43: 193–211.

—— (2003) "Poverty and Basic Education in Rural China: Villages, Households, and Girls' and Boys' Enrollment," *Comparative Education Review* 47: 141–59.

—— (2005) "Market Transition, Educational Disparity, and Family Strategies in Rural China: New Evidence on Gender Stratification and Development," *Demography* 42: 275–99.

Hauser, Robert M. and Hsiang-hui Kuo (1998) "Does the Gender Composition of Sibships Affect Women's Education Attainment?" *Journal of Human Resources* 33: 644–57.

Hayashi, Fumio, Joseph Altonji, and Laurence Kotlikoff (1996) "Risk-Sharing between and within Families," *Econometrica* 64: 261–94.

Heckman, James (1974) "Shadow Prices, Market Wages, and Labor Supply," *Econometrica* 42: 679–94.

—— (1978) "Dummy Endogenous Variables in a Simultaneous Equation System," *Econometrica* 46: 931–59.

—— (1997) "Instrumental Variables: A Study of Implicit Behavioral Assumptions Used in Making Program Evaluations," *Journal of Human Resources* 32: 441–62.

Hermalin, Albert I. and Li-shou Yang (2004) "Levels of Support from Children in Taiwan: Expectations versus Reality, 1965–99," *Population and Development Review* 30: 417–48.

—— Paul K.-C. Liu, and Ronald Freedman (1994) "The Social and Economic Transformation of Taiwan," in *Social Change and the Family in Taiwan*, ed. Arland Thornton and Hui-sheng Lin. Chicago: University of Chicago Press.

—— Mary B. Ofstedal, and Shiauping R. Shih (2003) "Patterns of Intergenerational Support in Urban China and Urban Taiwan," in *China's Revolutions and Intergenerational Relations*, ed. Martin K. Whyte. Ann Arbor: Center for Chinese Studies, University of Michigan: 255–76.

Hersch, Joni (1991) "The Impact of Non-Market Work on Market Wages," *American Economic Review* 81: 157–60.

—— and Leslie S. Stratton (1994) "Housework, Wages, and the Division of Housework Time for Employed Spouses," *American Economic Review* 84: 120–5.

Heyneman, Stephen P. and William A. Loxley (1983) "The Effect of Primary School Quality on Academic Achievement across Twenty-Nine High- and Low-Income Countries," *American Journal of Sociology* 88: 1162–94.

Ho, Ping-ti (1962) *The Ladder of Success in Imperial China: Aspects of Social Mobility, 1368–1911*. New York: Columbia University Press.

Hotz, V. Joseph, Jacob A. Klerman, and Robert J. Willis (1997) "The Economics of Fertility in Developed Countries," in *Handbook of Family and Population Economics* vol. ia, ed. Mark R. Rosenzweig and Oded Stark. Amsterdam: North Holland: 275–347.

Hsieh, Jih-chang and Ying-chang Chuang (eds.) (1985) *The Chinese Family and its Ritual Behavior*. Taipei: Institute of Ethnology, Academia Sinica.

Hu, Sheng-cheng, Kuo-mei Chen, and Lii-tarn Chen (2000) "Demographic Transition and Social Security in Taiwan," *Population and Development Review* 26: 117–38.

Huber, Peter J. (1967) "The Behavior of Maximum Likelihood Estimates under Nonstandard Conditions," *Proceedings of the Fifth Berkeley Symposium on Mathematical Statistics and Probability* 1: 221–33.

Jao, Jui-Chang and Matthew McKeever (2006) "Ethnic Inequalities and Educational Attainment in Taiwan," *Sociology of Education* 79: 131–52.

Jenkins, Stephen and Nigel C. O'Leary (1995) "Modeling Domestic Work Time," *Journal of Population Economics* 8: 265–79.

Juster, F. Thomas and Frank P. Stafford (1991) "The Allocation of Time: Empirical Findings, Behavioral Models, and Problems of Measurement," *Journal of Economic Literature* 29: 471–522.

Kalmijn, Matthijs (1991a) "Shifting Boundaries: Trends in Religious and Educational Homogamy," *American Sociological Review* 56: 786–800.

—— (1991b) "Status Homogamy in the United States," *American Journal of Sociology* 97: 496–523.

Kanbur, Ravi and Xiabo Zhang (2001) "Fifty Years of Regional Inequality in China: A Journey through Evolution, Reform and Openness," CEPR Working Paper, No. 2887.

References

Kandel, Eugene and Edward P. Lazear (1992) "Peer Pressure and Partnership," *Journal of Political Economy* 100: 801–17.

Kao, Grace and Jennifer S. Thompson (2003) "Racial and Ethnic Stratification in Educational Achievement and Attainment," *Annual Review of Sociology* 29: 417–42.

Kochar, Anjini (2000) "Parental Benefits from Intergenerational Coresidence: Empirical Evidence from Rural Pakistan," *Journal of Political Economy* 108: 1184–209.

Konrad, Kai A., Harald Künemund, Kjell Erik Lommerud, and Julio R. Robledo (2002) "Geography of the Family," *American Economic Review* 92: 981–98.

Koopmans, Tjalling C. and Martin J. Beckmann (1957) "Assignment Problems and the Location of Economic Activities," *Econometrica* 25: 53–76.

Kotlikoff, Lawrence J. and Lawrence H. Summers (1981) "The Role of Intergenerational Transfers in Aggregate Capital Accumulation," *Journal of Political Economy* 89: 706–32.

Kroska, Amy (2004) "Divisions of Domestic Work: Revising and Expanding the Theoretical Explanations," *Journal of Family Issues* 25: 900–32.

Kuo, Hsiang-Hui D. and Robert M. Hauser (1997) "How Does Size of Sibship Matter? Family Configuration and Family Effect on Education Attainment," *Social Science Research* 26: 69–94.

Kusago, Takayoshi and Bradford L. Barham (2001) "Preference Heterogeneity, Power, and Intrahousehold Decision-Making in Rural Malaysia," *World Development* 29: 1237–56.

Laitner, John (1997) "Intergenerational and Intrahousehold Economic Links," in *Handbook of Population and Family Economics* vol. ia, ed. Mark R. Rosenzweig and Oded Stark. Amsterdam: North-Holland.

Lang, Olga (1946) *Chinese Family and Society.* New Haven: Yale University Press.

Lavely, William and Xinhua Ren (1992) "Patrilocality and Early Marital Co-residence in Rural China, 1955–85," *China Quarterly* 130: 378–91.

Lee, Kuo-Jing and Bing-Jiou Wang (eds.) (2000) *Educational System History of China*, vol. viii. Jinan Nan: Shangdong Publisher (in Chinese).

Lee, Yuan-ju, William L. Parish, and Robert Willis (1994) "Sons, Daughters and Intergenerational Support in Taiwan," *American Journal of Sociology* 99: 1010–41.

Leung, Joe C. B. (1997) "Family Support for the Elderly in China: Issues and Challenges," *Journal of Aging and Social Policy* 9: 87–101.

Levy, Marion (1949) *The Family Revolution in Modern China.* Cambridge, Mass.: Harvard University Press.

Lewin, Keith M., Angela W. Little, Hui Xu, and Ji-wei Zheng (1994) *Educational Innovation in China: Tracing the Impact of the 1985 Reforms.* Essex: Long Group Limited.

Light, Audrey and Kathleen McGarry (2004) "Why Parents Play Favorites: Explanations for Unequal Bequests," *American Economic Review* 94: 1669–81.

Lillard, Lee A. and Robert J. Willis (1994) "Intergenerational Educational Mobility: Effects of Family and State in Malaysia," *Journal of Human Resources* 29: 1126–66.

——— ——— (1997) "Motives for Intergenerational Transfers: Evidence from Malaysia," *Demography* 34: 115–34.

Lin, Chen-wei (2002) "The Policymaking Process for the Social Security System in Taiwan: The National Health Insurance and National Pension Program," *Developing Economies* 40: 327–58.

Lin, Yu-shuang, Yi-wen Liu, and Hui-sheng Lin (2002) "The Transition of Fertility Attitude and Practice in Taiwan," Working Paper (in Chinese).

Logan, John R. and Fuqin Bian (1999) "Family Values and Co-residence with Married Children in Urban China," *Social Forces* 77: 1253–82.

——— (2004) "Intergenerational Family Relations in the United States and China," in *International Relations across Time and Place: Annual Review of Gerontology and Geriatrics*, 24, ed. Merril Silverstein. New York: Springer Publishing Company.

—— —— and Yanjie Bian (1998) "Tradition and Change in the Urban Chinese Family: The Case of Living Arrangement," *Social Forces* 76: 851–82.

Lundberg, Shelly and Robert A. Pollak (1993) "Separate Spheres Bargaining and the Marriage Market," *Journal of Political Economy* 101: 988–1010.

—— —— (1996) "Bargaining and Distribution in Marriage." *Journal of Economic Perspectives* 10: 139–58.

—— —— (2007) "The American Family and Family Economics," *Journal of Economics Perspectives* 21: 3–26.

—— —— and Terence J. Wales (1997) "Do Husbands and Wives Pool their Resources?" *Journal of Human Resources*, 32: 463–80.

McElroy, Marjorie (1990) "The Empirical Content of Nash-Bargained Household Behavior," *Journal of Human Resources* 25: 559–83.

—— and Mary J. Horney (1981) "Nash-Bargained Household Decisions: Toward a Generalization of the Theory of Demand," *International Economic Review* 22: 333–49.

McGarry, Kathleen (2008) "Inheritance and Bequests," in *The New Palgrave Dictionary of Economics*, 2nd edn., Steven Durlauf and Lawrence E. Blume (eds.) New York: Macmillan.

Manser, Marilyn and Murray Brown (1980) "Marriage and Household Decision-Making: A Bargaining Analysis," *International Economics Review* 21: 31–43.

Mare, Robert D. (1991) "Five Decades of Educational Assortative Mating," *American Sociological Review* 56: 15–32.

Mauss, Marcel (1954) *The Gift: Forms and Functions of Exchange in Archaic Societies.* London: Cohen Press.

Mayer, Susan E. and Leonard M. Lopoo (2005) "Has the Intergenerational Transmission of Economic Status Changed?" *Journal of Human Resources* 40: 169–85.

Mitchell, Jean M. and J. S. Butler (1986) "Arthritis and the Earnings of Men: An Analysis Incorporating Selection Bias," *Journal of Health Economics* 5: 81–98.

Molm, Linda and Karen Cook (1995) "Social Exchange and Exchange Networks," in *Sociological Perspectives on Social Psychology*, ed. Karen Cook, Gary Fine, and James House. Needham Heights, Mass.: Allyn & Bacon.

Mueller, Eva (1984) "Income, Aspirations, and Fertility in Rural Areas of Less Developed Countries," in *Rural Development and Human Fertility*, ed. Wayne A. Schutjer and C. Shannon Stokes. New York: Macmillan Publishing Company.

References

Newey, Whitney and Kenneth West (1987) "A Simple Positive Semi-Definite, Heteroskedastic and Autocorrelation Consistent Covariance Matrix," *Econometrica* 55: 703–8.

Nuttall, Ena Vazquez, Ronald L. Nuttall, Denise Polit, and Joan B. Hunter (1976) "The Effects of Family Size, Birth Order, Sibling Separation, and Crowding on the Academic Achievement of Boys and Girls," *American Educational Research Journal* 54: 389–412.

Pahl, Jan (1990) "Household Spending, Personal Spending and the Control of Money in Marriage," *Sociology* 24: 119–38.

Parish, William L. and Robert J. Willis (1993) "Daughters, Education, and Family Budgets," *Journal of Human Resources* 28: 863–98.

Perozek, Maria G. (1998) "A Reexamination of the Strategic Bequest Motive," *Journal of Political Economy* 106: 423–45.

Phipps, Shelley A. and Peter S. Burton (1998) "What's Mine is Yours? The Influence of Male and Female Income on Patterns of Household Expenditure," *Economica* 65: 599–613.

Pimentel, Ellen Efron and Jinyun Liu (2004) "Exploring Nonnormative Co-residence in Urban China: Living with Wives' Parents," *Journal of Marriage and Family* 66: 821–36.

Powell, Brian and Lala Carr Steelman (1990) "Beyond Sibship Size: Sibling Density, Sex Composition and Education Outcomes," *Social Forces* 69: 181–206.

—— —— (1993) "The Educational Benefits of Being Spaced Out: Sibship Density and Educational Progress," *American Sociological Review* 58: 367–81.

Powers, D. A. and Yu Xie (2000) *Statistical Methods for Categorical Data Analysis*. San Diego: Academic Press.

Qian, Zhenchao (1997) "Breaking the Racial Barriers: Variations in Interracial Marriage between 1980 and 1990," *Demography* 34: 263–76.

—— (1998) "Changes in Assortative Mating: The Impact of Age and Education, 1970–1990," *Demography* 35: 279–92.

—— and Daniel T. Lichter (2001) "Measuring Marital Assimilation: Intermarriage among Natives and Immigrants," *Social Science Research* 30: 289–312.

Quan, Zhang Xing (1991) "Urbanisation in China," *Urban Studies* 28: 41–51.

Quisumbing, Agnes R. and John A. Maluccio (2003) "Resources at Marriage and Intrahousehold Allocation: Evidence from Bangladesh, Ethiopia, Indonesia, and South Africa," *Oxford Bulletin of Economics and Statistics* 65: 283–327.

Raymo, James M. and Yu Xie (2000) "Temporal and Regional Variation in the Strength of Educational Homogamy," *American Sociological Review* 65: 773–81.

Razin, Assaf and Efraim Sadka (1995) *Population Economics*. Cambridge, Mass.: MIT Press.

Riley, Nancy E. (1994) "Interwoven Lives: Parents, Marriage and Guanxi in China," *Journal of Marriage and the Family* 56: 791–803.

Rivers, Douglas and Quang H. Vuong (1988) "Limited Information Estimators and Exogeneity Tests for Simultaneous Probit Models," *Journal of Econometrics* 39: 347–66.

Rodman, Hyman (1967) "Marital Power in France, Greece, Yugoslavia and the United States: A Cross-National Discussion," *Journal of Marriage and the Family* 29: 320–4.

Rosenberg, Morris (1965) *Society and the Adolescent Self-Image*. Princeton: Princeton University Press.

Rosenzweig, Mark R. and Kenneth I. Wolpin (1993) "Intergenerational Support and the Life-Cycle Incomes of Young Men and their Parents: Human Capital Investments, Coresidence, and Intergenerational Financial Transfers," *Journal of Labor Economics* 11: 84–112.

Ross, Catherine E. (1987) "The Division of Labor at Home," *Social Forces* 65: 816–33.

Samuelson, Paul A. (1948) "Consumption Theory in Terms of Revealed Preferences," *Econometrica* 15: 243–53.

Sanbonmatsu, Lisa, Jeffrey R. Kling, Greg J. Duncan, and Jeanne Brook-Gunn (2006) "Neighborhoods and Academic Achievement: Results from the Moving to Opportunity Experiment," *Journal of Human Resource* 41: 649–91.

Saso, Michael (1999) *Velvet Bonds: The Chinese Family*. Honolulu: University of Hawaii Press.

Schmeer, Kammi K. (2005) "Married Women's Resource Position and Household Food Expenditures in Cebu, Philippines," *Journal of Marriage and Family* 67: 399–409.

Schoeni, Robert F. (1998) "Reassessing the Decline in Parent–Child Old-Age Co-residence during the Twentieth Century," *Demography* 35: 307–13.

Schultz, T. Paul (1997) "Demand for Children in Low Income Countries," in *Handbook of Family and Population Economics* vol. ia, ed. Mark R. Rosenzweig and Oded Stark. Amsterdam: North Holland: 349–432.

Schwartz, Christine R. and Robert D. Mare (2005) "Trends in Educational Assortative Marriage from 1940 to 2003," *Demography* 42: 621–46.

Scott, Mandy and Hak-khiam Tiun (2007) "Mandarin-Only to Mandarin-Plus: Taiwan," *Language Policy* 6: 53–72.

Selden, Mark (1993) "Family Strategies and Structure in Rural North China," in *Chinese Families in the Post-Mao Era*, ed. Deborah Davis and Stevan Harrell. Berkeley and Los Angeles: University of California Press.

Shelton, Beth A. and Daphne John (1996) "The Division of Household Labor," *Annual Review of Sociology* 22: 299–322.

Sheng, Xuewen and Barbara H. Settles (2006) "Intergenerational Relationships and Elderly Care in China: A Global Perspective," *Current Sociology* 54: 293–313.

Solberg, Eric J. and David C. Wong (1992) "Family Time Use: Leisure, Home Production, Market Work, and Work Related Travel," *Journal of Human Resources* 27: 485–510.

Sousa-Poza, Alfonso, Hans Schmid, and Rolf Widmer (2001) "The Allocation and Value of Time Assigned to Housework and Child-Care: An Analysis of Switzerland," *Journal of Population Economics* 14: 599–618.

Steelman, Lala Carr, Brian Powell, Regina Werum, and Scott Carter (2002) "Reconsidering the Effects of Sibling Configuration: Recent Advances and Challenges," *Annual Review of Sociology* 28: 243–69.

References

Stevenson, Betsey and Justin Wolfers (2007) "Marriage and Divorce: Changes and their Driving Forces," *Journal of Economic Perspectives* 21: 27–52.

Sung, Lung-sheng (1974) "Inheritance and Kinship in North Taiwan." Ph.D. dissertation, Department of Anthropology, Stanford University.

Thomas, Duncan (1990) "Intra-household Resource Allocation: An Inferential Approach," *Journal of Human Resources* 25: 635–64.

—— (1996) "Education across Generations in South Africa," *American Economic Review Papers and Proceedings* 86: 330–4.

Thornton, Arland (2005) *Reading History Sideways*. Chicago: University of Chicago Press.

—— and Thomas E. Fricke (1987) "Social Change and the Family: Comparative Perspectives from the West, China and South Asia," *Sociological Forum* 2: 749–79.

—— and Hui-Sheng Lin (1994) *Social Change and the Family in Taiwan*. Chicago: University of Chicago Press.

—— Duane F. Alwin, and Donald Camburn (1983) "Causes and Consequences of Sex-Role Attitudes and Attitude Change," *American Sociological Review* 48: 211–27.

Tien, H. Yuan (1983) "Age at Marriage in the People's Republic of China," *China Quarterly* 93: 90–107.

Townsend, R. M. (1994) "Risk and Insurance in Village India," *Econometrica* 62 (3): 539–91.

Treas, Judith and Jieming Chen (2000) "Living Arrangements, Income Pooling and the Life Course in Urban Chinese Families," *Research on Aging* 22: 238–62.

Tsai, I-ju, C. Y. Cyrus Chu, and Ching-fan Chung (2000) "Demographic Transition and Household Saving in Taiwan," *Population and Development Review* 26: S174–93.

Tsai, Shu-ling (1994) "The Pattern of Marriages in Taiwan," *ISSP Essays on Humanities and Social Sciences* 6: 335–71 (in Chinese).

Tsay, Wen-jen (2006) "The Educational Attainment of Second-Generation Mainland Chinese Immigrants in Taiwan," *Journal of Population Economics* 19: 749–67.

—— and C. Y. Cyrus Chu (2005) "The Pattern of Birth Spacing During Taiwan's Demographic Transition," *Journal of Population Economics* 18: 323–36.

Tsui, Ming (1989) "Changes in Chinese Urban Family Structure," *Journal of Marriage and the Family* 51: 737–47.

—— and Lynne Rich (2002) "The Only Child and Education Opportunity for Girls in Urban China," *Gender and Sociology* 16: 74–92.

Unger, Jonathan (1993) "Urban Families in the Eighties: An Analysis of Chinese Surveys," in *Chinese Families in the Post-Mao Era*, ed. Deborah Davis and Stevan Harrell. Berkeley and Los Angeles: University of California Press.

Vella, Francis (1993) "A Simple Estimator for Simultaneous Models with Censored Endogenous Regressors," *International Economic Review* 34: 441–57.

Voland, Eckart, Athanasios Chasiotis, and Wulf Schienfenhovel (eds.) (2005) *Grandmotherhood*. New Brunswick, NJ: Rutgers University Press.

Wang, Dewen (2006) "China's Urban and Rural Old Age Security System: Challenges and Options," *China & World Economy* 14: 102–16.

Warner, Rebecca L., Gary R. Lee, and Janet Lee (1986) "Social Organization, Spousal Resources, and Marital Power: A Cross-cultural Study," *Journal of Marriage and the Family* 48: 121–8.

Weinstein, Maxine, Te-hsiung Sun, Ming-cheng Chang, and Ronald Freedman (1994) "Co-residence and Other Ties Linking Couples with their Parents," in *Social Change and the Family in Taiwan*, ed. Arland Thornton and Hui-sheng Lin. Chicago: University of Chicago Press.

Wellman, Barry (1990) "The Place of Kinfolk in Personal Community Networks," *Marriage and Family Review* 15: 195–228.

White, Halbert (1980) "A Heteroskedasticity-Consistent Covariance Matrix Estimator and a Direct Test for Heteroskedasticty," *Econometrica* 48: 827–38.

Whyte, Martin K. (2003) "China's Revolutions and Intergenerational Relations," in *China's Revolutions and Intergenerational Relations*, ed. Martin K. Whyte. Ann Arbor: Center for Chinese Studies, University of Michigan.

—— Albert I. Hermalin, and Mary B. Ofstedal (2003) "Intergenerational Relations in Two Chinese Societies," in *China's Revolutions and Intergenerational Relations*, ed. Martin K. Whyte. Ann Arbor: Center for Chinese Studies, University of Michigan: 225–54.

Wilson, R. (1968) "The Theory of Syndicates," *Econometrica* 36 (1): 119–32.

Wolf, Arthur (1985) "Chinese Family Size: A Myth Revisited," in *The Chinese Family and its Ritual Behavior*, ed. Jih-chang Hsieh and Ying-chang Chuang. Taipei: Institute of Ethnology, Academia Sinica.

Wolf, Margery (1984) "Marriage, Family, and the State in Contemporary China," *Pacific Affairs* 57: 213–36.

—— (1985) *Revolution Postponed: Women in Contemporary China*. Stanford, Calif.: Stanford University Press.

Wong, Raymond Sin-Kwok and Hsien-Hen Lu (1999) "Assortative Mating in Taiwan: Cohorts' Trends in Educational and Ethnic Intermarriages," UC Santa Barbara, mimeo.

Xu, Xiaohe and Shu-chuan Lai (2002) "Resources, Gender Ideologies, and Marital Power: The Case of Taiwan," *Journal of Family Issues* 23: 209–45.

Yang, Ching-li, Da-chung Lee, and Kuan-jeng Chen (2004) "Changes in the Marriage Rates and the Patterns of Assortative Mating in Taiwan," paper presented at the Population Association of Taiwan.

Yang, Qingkun (1965) *Chinese Communist Society: The Family and the Village*. Cambridge, Mass.: MIT Press.

Yi, Chin-chun and Ray-may Hsung (1994) "Network and Marriage Connections in the Process of Mate-Searching," *ISSP Essays on Humanities and Social Sciences* 6: 135–77.

Zabel, Jeffrey E. (1998) "An Analysis of Attrition in the Panel Study of Income Dynamics and the Survey of Income and Program Participation with an Application to a Model of Labor Market Behavior," *Journal of Human Resources* 43: 479–506.

Zajonc, Robert B. (1976) "Family Configuration and Intelligence," *Science* 192: 227–35.

—— and Gregory B. Markus (1975) "Birth Order and Intellectual Development," *Psychological Review* 82: 74–88.

Zang, Xiaowei (1993) "Household Structure and Marriage in Urban China: 1900–1982," *Journal of Comparative Family Studies* 25: 35–44.

Zeng, Yi (1989) "Is the Chinese Family Planning Program 'Tightening Up'?" *Population and Development Review* 15: 333–7.

—— (2001) "A Demographic Analysis of Family Households in China, 1982–1995," *Journal of Comparative Family Studies* 33: 17–34.

—— and Deming Wang (1993) "An Event History Analysis of Remarriage in China," selected paper for publication in IUSSP 22nd General Conference volumes, Liège: IUSSP.

—— and Deqing Wu (2000) "A Regional Analysis of Divorce in China since 1980," *Demography* 37: 215–19.

—— and Zhenglian Wang (2003) "Dynamics of Family and Elderly Living Arrangement in China: New Lessons Learned from the 2000 Census," *China Review* 3: 95–119.

Zhang, Junsen and William Chan (1999) "Dowry and Wife's Welfare: A Theoretical and Empirical Analysis," *Journal of Political Economy* 107: 786–808.

Zhang, Weiguo (2000) "Dynamics of Marriage Change in Chinese Rural Society in Transition: A Study of a Northern Chinese Village," *Population Studies* 54: 57–69.

Zimmer, Zachary and Julia Kwong (2003) "Family Size and Support of Older Adults in Urban and Rural China: Current Effects and Future Implications," *Demography* 40: 23–44.

Zuo, Jiping and Yanjie Bian (2001) "Gendered Resources, Division of Housework, and Perceived Fairness: A Case in Urban China," *Journal of Marriage and Family* 63: 1122–33.

Index